SOCIAL NETWORK ANALYSIS IN SECOND LANGUAGE RESEARCH

This text is the first holistic research overview and practical methodological guide for social network analysis in second language acquisition, examining how to study learner social networks and how to use network data to predict patterns of language learner behavior and identity.

Authors Kristen Kennedy Terry and Robert Bayley lay out the history of social network analysis in sociolinguistics, discuss the state of the art in empirical findings in applications to language acquisition, offer how-to guidance and best practices for planning, conducting, and understanding this research, and authoritatively set the agenda for future work.

With a variety of helpful features like case studies, suggested research projects, discussion questions, and recommended further reading, this book will be an invaluable resource for students and researchers in second language acquisition, sociolinguistics, education, and beyond.

Kristen Kennedy Terry is an Assistant Professor of French and Applied Linguistics at Sam Houston State University in Huntsville, Texas. She has published her research on social networks and study abroad in *Studies in Second Language Acquisition*, *The Modern Language Journal*, *The Routledge Handbook of Second Language Acquisition and Sociolinguistics*, *Variation in Second and Heritage Languages: Crosslinguistic Perspectives*, and the *L2 Journal*.

Robert Bayley is Professor Emeritus of Linguistics at the University of California, Davis. His recent publications include articles in *Language* and *Studies in Second Language Acquisition* as well as the edited books *Variation in Second and Heritage Languages: Crosslinguistic Perspectives* (with D. R. Preston and X. Li, 2022) and *Needed Research on North American Dialects* (with E. Benson, 2023). Professor Bayley was President of the American Dialect Society (ADS) and is a Fellow of the ADS and the Linguistic Society of America.

Second Language Acquisition Research Series

Susan M. Gass and Alison Mackey, Series Editors
Kimberly L. Geeslin†, Associate Editor

The *Second Language Acquisition Research Series* presents and explores issues bearing directly on theory construction and/or research methods in the study of second language acquisition. Its titles (both authored and edited volumes) provide thorough and timely overviews of high-interest topics, and include key discussions of existing research findings and their implications. A special emphasis of the series is reflected in the volumes dealing with specific data collection methods or instruments. Each of these volumes addresses the kinds of research questions for which the method/instrument is best suited, offers extended description of its use, and outlines the problems associated with its use. The volumes in this series will be invaluable to students and scholars alike, and perfect for use in courses on research methodology and in individual research.

Conducting Genre-Based Research in Applied Linguistics
A Methodological Guide
Edited by Matt Kessler and Charlene Polio

The Minority Language as a Second Language
Challenges and Achievements
Edited by Jasone Cenoz and Durk Gorter

Social Network Analysis in Second Language Research
Theory and Methods
Kristen Kennedy Terry and Robert Bayley

For more information about this series, please visit: www.routledge.com/Second-Language-Acquisition-Research-Series/book-series/LEASLARS

SOCIAL NETWORK ANALYSIS IN SECOND LANGUAGE RESEARCH

Theory and Methods

Kristen Kennedy Terry and Robert Bayley

Routledge
Taylor & Francis Group

NEW YORK AND LONDON

Designed cover image: © Getty Images | lolon

First published 2024
by Routledge
605 Third Avenue, New York, NY 10158

and by Routledge
4 Park Square, Milton Park, Abingdon, Oxon, OX14 4RN

Routledge is an imprint of the Taylor & Francis Group, an informa business

Library of Congress Cataloging-in-Publication Data
Names: Kennedy Terry, Kristen, author. | Bayley, Robert, 1943– author.
Title: Social network analysis in second language research :
theory and methods / Kristen Kennedy Terry and Robert Bayley.
Description: New York, NY : Routledge, 2024. |
Series: Second language acquisition research series |
Includes bibliographical references and index. |
Summary: "This text is the first holistic research overview and practical
methodological guide for social network analysis in second language acquisition,
examining how to study learner social networks and how to use network
data to predict language learner behavior and identity" – Provided by publisher.
Identifiers: LCCN 2023036988 (print) | LCCN 2023036989 (ebook) |
ISBN 9781032005034 (hardback) | ISBN 9781032005027 (paperback) |
ISBN 9781003174448 (ebook)
Subjects: LCSH: Second language acquisition. |
Social networks. | Social sciences–Network analysis.
Classification: LCC P118.2 .K46 2024 (print) |
LCC P118.2 (ebook) | DDC 418.0078–dc23/eng/20231010
LC record available at https://lccn.loc.gov/2023036988
LC ebook record available at https://lccn.loc.gov/2023036989

ISBN: 978-1-032-00503-4 (hbk)
ISBN: 978-1-032-00502-7 (pbk)
ISBN: 978-1-003-17444-8 (ebk)

DOI: 10.4324/9781003174448

Typeset in Galliard
by Newgen Publishing UK

This book is dedicated to the memory of
Kimberly L. Geeslin.
A consummate scholar, devoted mentor, and steadfast
friend, she represented the very best our profession
has to offer.

CONTENTS

Tables   *ix*
Figures   *xi*
Acknowledgments   *xiii*

1 Introduction   1

2 Social Network Analysis in First Language Speech
   Communities   8

3 Social Network Analysis in Bi- and Multilingual
   Communities   23

4 Social Network Analysis and Theories of Second
   Language Acquisition   39

5 Applications of Social Network Analysis in Second
   Language Research   56

6 Data Collection for Social Network Analysis in Second
   Language Research   75

7 Measuring and Depicting Social Networks in Second
   Language Research   100

8 Using Social Network Analysis to Examine Linguistic
Outcomes: Inferential Statistics   131

9 Using Social Network Analysis to Examine Linguistic
Outcomes: Network Structure and Composition   155

10 Social Network Analysis: New Tools, Communities,
and Learning Contexts   177

References   *201*
Index   *219*

TABLES

3.1	Networks and codes of *el bloque*	25
3.2	Criteria for peer cultural assignment	32
3.3	Endpoints on the continuum of Norteña and Sureña identity	33
3.4	Use of overt SPPs in Puerto Rican and Mexican-American Spanish	35
3.5	The effect on (z)-devoicing of individual orientation to the Courts: four speakers	36
6.1	Sample of questions from Interview 1	77
6.2	Identified themes—high performers	78
6.3	Follow-up questions by person	85
6.4	Follow-up questions by language	86
6.5	Sample SASIQ questions	87
6.6	Excerpt of conversation between Capucine (C) and Amelia (A) about the word 'friend'	93
6.7	Excerpt of conversation between Irène (I), Jean (J), and Corrine (C)	94
7.1	Network effect calculation for learner S36	104
7.2	Descriptive statistics from SASIQ responses from 29 participants	108
7.3	Final SNSS for SA scores by speaker	116
7.4	Social Network Strength Scale	117
7.5	Measurement of overall engagement in French according to profile portrait	128
8.1	Group results from oral production task	138
8.2	Inferential statistics: oral production task results	139

8.3	Hierarchical regression analysis: Contributors to AEP	142
8.4	Rbrul analysis for /l/ deletion by linguistic factor group	145
8.5	Rbrul analysis for /l/ deletion by extralinguistic factor group	147
8.6	Rbrul analysis for schwa deletion by extralinguistic factor group	149
8.7	Rbrul analysis comparing *Vos* and *Tú* verb forms	150
8.8	*Vos* usage by speaker with proficiency level and SNSS score	152
8.9	Rbrul analysis for *sheísmo/zheísmo* (BAS) usage	153
9.1	Source of assistance with English ranked by results of Mann-Whitney U-test for 2018 results	161
9.2	Rates of use of linguistic variants by profile portrait	163
9.3	Social networks by participant and environment	167
9.4	Desired social identity by participant	167
9.5	Qualitative assessments of European and Quebec French guise speech samples	171
9.6	Tokens and frequency of the retroflex/dental merger by Chinese hosts	174
9.7	Tokens and frequency of the retroflex/dental merger by focal participants	174
10.1	Total words posted on Facebook January–September 2011	185
10.2	Comparison of survey results from Warner-Ault (2020) and Litzler et al. (2018)	197
10.3	Comparison of survey results from Warner-Ault (2020) and Warner-Ault (2022)	199

FIGURES

2.1 Hangout patterns of the Thunderbirds 10
2.2 Use of the variable (r) by youth groups in Harlem 11
2.3 Diagram of a dense and multiplex personal network
structure with first- and second-order zones 13
2.4 Diagram of a weak and uniplex personal network
structure with a first-order zone only 13
6.1 Social Network Strength Scale (SNSS) for SA 89
6.2 Video recording and transcript of free play time 98
7.1 Network density calculation for learner S36 102
7.2 Friendship multiplexity calculation for learner S36 104
7.3 Kent—change in modifier use and network diagram 112
7.4 Camille—change in modifier use and network diagram 113
7.5 Stan's first- and second-order network zones 120
7.6 Concentric circles representation of social networks
during study abroad 121
7.7 Closeness network of Program A in week 8 123
7.8 Clusters in Program B in week 8 123
7.9 Closeness network of Program C in week 5 124
8.1 Learner network composition (L1, L2, Mixed) over nine
months in France 134
8.2 Correlations between lexical complexity and 'Top 5'
contacts in learner networks at time 3 136
8.3 Social network interaction data 137
9.1 Head Start preschool classroom network of practice 157
9.2 Sociocentric network diagrams of L2 Polish learners 160

9.3   Network graphs by composition and structure   169
10.1 Significant network patterns based on ALAAM   182
10.2 Number of posts per month in Portuguese by learner   185
10.3 Average number of Portuguese words per post by learner   186
10.4 Representations of bilingual social networks on Twitter   189
10.5 Comparison of sentences and interactions by Facebook
      and Twitter users   192

ACKNOWLEDGMENTS

We gratefully acknowledge the assistance of our institutions in providing appropriate homes for academic activity.

We thank the series editors, the late Kimberly Geeslin, who proposed this volume, Susan Gass, and Alison Mackey and the external proposal reviewers for their helpful suggestions and comments.

Finally, we thank our families, particularly Mark, Katherine, and Ciara Terry, and Ann Robinson, who have supported all our academic endeavors.

1

INTRODUCTION

Social Network Analysis and Sociolinguistics

In sociolinguistics, social network analysis (SNA) was first applied to the study of sociolinguistic variation in the 1970s by James Milroy and Lesley Milroy, who developed a measure of social network strength to predict how closely speakers in working-class Belfast, Northern Ireland, would conform to local, nonstandard speech norms (Milroy & Milroy, 1978; 1992; L. Milroy, 1980). However, prior to the foundational research by the Milroys, scholars in linguistics and other fields had been using the methods of SNA for quite some time. For example, in his highly influential volume, *Language*, Bloomfield (1933) argued for the role of density of communication, conceived of as a network, in giving rise to linguistic differentiation. Additionally, Labov's (1972a) seminal work on African American English in Harlem made use of 'sociograms' similar to those that can be seen in the work of social scientist J. L. Moreno (1934) to illustrate the relationship between the density of vernacular language use and the density of social network ties.

This chapter first provides a brief discussion of the development of SNA in the social sciences. The chapter also provides an overview of the current volume beginning with early studies of monolingual communities and later focusing on studies of bi- and multilingual communities, both at the macro level of minority language maintenance and the micro level of sociolinguistic variation in situations of language contact and second language acquisition (SLA). The second part of the volume then focuses specifically on the last 20 years of research applying SNA to SLA with an emphasis on the

DOI: 10.4324/9781003174448-1

contributions of 16 model studies that demonstrate the important and innovative ways that scholars have used SNA and related frameworks to better understand the second language (L2) learner, the influence of the L2 learning context and the participants within that context, and the process of L2 development.

Social Network Analysis as a Multidisciplinary Enterprise

Traditional social science research focuses on the attributes of individuals such as gender, ethnicity, social class, and educational level, among others. In contrast, SNA focuses on the relationships between individuals and "the intuitive notion that the patterning of social ties in which actors are embedded has important consequences for those actors" (Freeman, 2004, p. 2). Freeman, a mathematical sociologist and a pioneer in the field of SNA, explains that "Network analysts, then, seek to uncover various kinds of patterns. And they try to determine the conditions under which those patterns arise and to discover their consequences" (ibid.).

A number of accounts of the history and development of SNA are available, including a complete volume by Freeman (2004), *The Development of Social Network Analysis: A Study in the Sociology of Science*, as well as chapters by Freeman (2011), and Zhang (2010), to cite only a few. While accounts of the development of SNA differ in emphasis, all stress the interdisciplinary nature of the enterprise. Indeed, the interdisciplinary development of SNA as a framework can be seen clearly in Freeman (2011), where he summarizes various centers of research in the United States and Europe from 1940 to 1969. These centers engaged in research on social networks in communication, community power, geography, linguistic anthropology, mathematical biology, political science, psychology, and sociology at universities in England, France, the Netherlands, Sweden, and the United States.

Freeman (2011) notes, however, that despite the growing acceptance of SNA that resulted from the research of the centers mentioned above, none of the centers was successful in providing "a generally recognized paradigm for the social network approach to social science research" (p. 27). Rather, according to Freeman (2004), it was not until the 1970s, when Harrison White, who had earned PhDs in physics at MIT and sociology at Princeton, began training graduate students at Harvard, that SNA gained wide-spread acceptance in the social sciences:

> From the beginning, White saw the broad generality of the structural paradigm, and he managed to communicate both that insight and his own enthusiasm to a whole generation of outstanding students. Certainly, the majority of the published work in the field has been produced by

White and his former students. Once this generation started to produce, they published so much important theory and research focused on social networks that social scientists everywhere, regardless of their field, could no longer ignore the idea. By the end of the 1970s, then, social network analysis came to be universally recognized among social scientists.

(Freeman, 2004, p. 127)

Following the work of White and his students, SNA became widely accepted ˹ as a research paradigm, and the field has continued to grow in subsequent decades, with the introduction of new methods including computer simulations and statistical modeling and new topical areas such as social capital analysis (Prell, 2012).[1]

The SNA research paradigm is aptly described by Marin and Wellman (2016) who use California's Silicon Valley to illustrate the difference between SNA and more traditional social science approaches. Citing Fleming et al. (2011), Marin and Wellman (2016) suggest that a conventional approach to understanding a high-innovation region such as Silicon Valley would focus on the high levels of education and expertise present in the local labor market. That is, there are many individuals in the local market with advanced degrees in computer science and other relevant scientific and engineering disciplines, many of whom have considerable experience in technology companies. A social network approach, however, "would draw attention to the ways in which mobility between educational institutions and multiple employers has created connections between organizations" (p. 11) and employ both quantitative and qualitative methods (Nooraie, 2020). Marin and Wellman suggest that the pattern of connections among organizations "in which each organization is tied through its employees to multiple other organizations, allows each to draw on diverse sources of knowledge" (p. 2).

Applications of Social Network Analysis in Sociolinguistics

Freeman (2004) summarizes four main features of SNA in the broader social sciences and these features can be observed in the growing number of studies in language variation and change (LVC) and L2 acquisition since the 1980s that have incorporated the SNA research framework. According to Freeman (2004, p. 3), the four main features of SNA are:

1. Social network analysis is motivated by a structural intuition based on ties linking social actors.
2. It is grounded in systematic empirical data.
3. It draws heavily on graphic imagery.
4. It relies on the use of mathematical and/or computational models.

For example, L. Milroy's (1980) study of language variation in Belfast (discussed in detail in Chapter 2) was based on the intuition that close-knit social networks such as those found in Belfast neighborhoods have a norm-enforcing function which, in the case of working-class neighborhoods, leads to greater preservation of traditional vernacular features (feature 1, Freeman, 2004). Milroy's study was also based on extensive empirical data collected in the speech community (feature 2). Additionally, early studies, such as Labov's (1972a) study of African American English in New York relied heavily on graphic imagery, particularly sociograms, to illustrate the relationships and relative centrality or peripherality of members of different youth groups in the community (feature 3). Further, as shown in our discussion of 16 model studies applying SNA to the SLA context later in this volume, graphic imagery continues to be an essential tool for illustrating the social networks developed by language learners (see, e.g., Bernstein, 2018 and Hasegawa, 2019, discussed in Chapter 9 and Chapter 7, respectively). Finally, sociolinguists and researchers in SLA use mathematical and computational models (feature 4) to examine the contribution of speakers' social network ties to other factors that influence speakers' choices among variants of a sociolinguistic variable, the maintenance of a heritage or immigrant language, or the development of proficiency in a second language. For example, using a specialized application of logistic regression, Kennedy Terry (2017, 2022a, 2022b) found that American students studying in France who had developed ties with local speakers used more vernacular features than their counterparts with fewer and/or weaker local ties. The results of Kennedy Terry (2017, 2022a, 2022b) are echoed by a number of model studies described in this volume using inferential statistical analysis to quantify the important role of social networks with target-language (TL) speakers in L2 acquisition, including Carhill-Poza (2015), Pozzi (2021), McManus (2019), and Serrano et al. (2012).

Some of the features and techniques used in the 16 model studies described in this volume are, of course, not confined to linguistics research incorporating SNA. For example, multivariate analysis of the type that Kennedy Terry (2017, 2022a, 2022b), Pozzi (2021), and Pozzi and Bayley (2021) used in their studies of the acquisition of sociolinguistic competence by American students during study abroad (SA) has long been a basic feature of studies of LVC (Bayley, 2013). The use of nonparametric statistical procedures such as logistic regression is made necessary by the fact that data collected in sociolinguistic interviews are usually unevenly distributed. Moreover, the use of logistic regression in studies of LVC is also necessitated by what Young and Bayley (1996) have termed the "Principle of multiple causes" (p. 253), i.e., the idea that the variation that we observe in actual language use is likely to be the result of not one, but of many different causes. Additionally, studies conducted in other frameworks outside of the SNA paradigm have made good use of graphic displays including sociograms. See, for example, Eckert's (2000) study of language use by Detroit area high school students, which is based on the community of practice framework (Eckert & McConnell-Ginet, 1992; Lave & Wenger, 1991). Finally, variationist sociolinguistic studies, whether they employ SNA or not, rely heavily on empirical data, normally in the form of speech data collected during sociolinguistic interviews with the members of the community under study (Labov, 1984).

Overview of the Current Volume

This volume is intended to provide the reader both with the conceptual background and the necessary methodological tools to carry out research using SNA to examine the relationship between social networks and the development of various aspects of L2 proficiency and use.

Chapter 2 begins with a review of early work, such as Bloomfield (1933) and Labov (1972a), that argued for the influence of density of communication and local social structure in the development of speech communities, as well as a number of key sociolinguistic studies of first language (L1) speech communities that relied on SNA (e.g., Bortoni-Ricardo, 1985; Dodsworth & Benton, 2017, 2019; Edwards, 1992; L. Milroy 1987). Chapter 2 also considers work that challenges the importance of social networks compared to other social categories such as social class and ethnicity in studies of LVC (e.g., Labov & Harris, 1986; Marshall, 2004). The chapter concludes with a discussion of why some of the criticisms of SNA may not apply to the use of SNA in studies of L2 learners.

Chapter 3 focuses on the insights that SNA can provide about language maintenance and shift and language contact in bi- and multilingual communities. As in the previous chapter, the aim is not to review all of the relevant literature—that would require a second volume—but to illustrate the ways in which different types of social networks either impede or facilitate minority language maintenance and help to explain which speakers in contact situations adopt or reject particular features.

Chapter 4 focuses on the relationship between SNA and SLA theory. Specifically, this chapter uses Model Studies 1–16 to examine how SLA theory informs and motivates SNA and how SNA research advances our understanding of the interpersonal and relational aspects of SLA. The chapter first discusses how factors such as acculturation (Schumann, 1978), motivation (Gardner, 1985; Gardner & Lambert, 1959), investment

(Norton Peirce, 1995), and identity (Mendoza-Denton, 2002) influence participation in the TL culture and the development of social networks with TL speakers. The chapter also considers how sociocultural theory (SCT; Vygotsky, 1978) and theories of language socialization (Schieffelin & Ochs, 1986; Watson-Gegeo & Nielsen, 2003) support the application of SNA to SLA. Finally, Chapter 4 examines how SNA aligns with theories of L2 acquisition that emphasize the critical role of input (Krashen, 1985), output (Swain, 1985, 1995; Swain & Lapkin, 1995, 1998), and interaction (Long, 1980, 1996) in the development of L2 proficiency and communicative competence (Hymes, 1972).

In Chapter 5, we introduce readers to Model Studies 1–16, which represent the diverse populations of L2 learners that have been examined through the lens of SNA and related frameworks, such as SA learners and others residing temporarily in the TL environment, immigrant student groups in the TL educational system, and at-home language learners. Model Studies 1–16 also provide a comprehensive overview of the varied foci of L2 research employing SNA, including oral proficiency and fluency, grammatical and sociolinguistic competence, learner stance, identity, and socialization, and academic language proficiency.

Chapter 6 uses Model Studies 1–16 to provide a detailed overview of the methods that have been widely used in L2 research to gather data related to learners' social networks. These data collection methods focus on the following: (1) participant interviews; (2) diaries, journals, and contact logs; (3) surveys and questionnaires; and (4) live recordings and observations. This chapter also focuses on defining key terms in SNA that are used throughout the remaining chapters.

Chapter 7 describes in detail what happens after social network data has been collected from study participants—how researchers use this quantitative and qualitative data to measure and depict learners' social networks with TL speakers and others and how these measurements may be correlated with specific linguistic outcomes. This chapter is divided into three sections: quantitative SNA (including social network metrics and scales), network diagrams, and qualitative assessments of network strength and breadth. As in previous chapters, this chapter uses Model Studies 1–16 and supplemental research to demonstrate the methods described in each section.

Chapter 8 uses Model Studies 1–16, and additional research, to exemplify the current methods of inferential statistical analysis used to investigate the relationship between social networks and L2 acquisition. This chapter focuses on how measures of statistical significance and correlations, logistic regression, and multivariate analysis and mixed-effects models have been used to predict various aspects of L2 development, including lexical complexity, grammatical accuracy, oral proficiency, and sociolinguistic competence, based on levels of participation in social networks with TL and L1 speakers.

Chapter 9 continues the discussion begun in Chapter 8 and presents a variety of other tools, in addition to inferential statistics, that SLA researchers use to investigate the relationship between participation in social networks with TL (and co-national/L1) speakers and L2 development and use. In this second chapter on linguistic data analysis, we focus on research that explores the influence of network structure, including both egocentric (at the level of the individual speaker) and sociocentric (macro-level or whole) network analysis, and network composition, including the role of TL speakers, on specific linguistic and sociolinguistic outcomes among L2 learners.

Finally, Chapter 10 examines how continuing advances in technology, such as sophisticated network diagramming software programs, have facilitated SNA research in both physical and online contexts and how these powerful network mapping tools have allowed researchers to pursue unexplored aspects of the relationships within learners' social networks and on a much larger scale than what was previously possible with manual methods of SNA. This chapter also describes how SNA may be leveraged inside and outside of the language classroom to facilitate interactions between groups of L2 learners, and between L2 learners and TL speakers, using virtual social networking sites, online collaborative tools, and video exchange platforms.

Note

1   A full discussion of the development of SNA and of the many different methods and topics developed and examined by social network analysts is beyond the scope of this volume. Readers who wish to examine those topics may consult Freeman's (2004) history of the development of the field as well as Prell's (2012) overview and the available handbooks including Light and Moody (2020), Furht (2010), and Scott and Carrington (2011/16).

2

SOCIAL NETWORK ANALYSIS IN FIRST LANGUAGE SPEECH COMMUNITIES

Introduction

Much of the recent sociolinguistic work that employs social network analysis (SNA) to understand language variation and change (LVC) has been greatly influenced by the studies of James Milroy and Lesley Milroy (Milroy & Milroy, 1978, 1992; L. Milroy, 1987). However, the role of social networks, viewed as density of communication, has been studied as a factor in LVC long before James and Lesley Milroy began their seminal work in Belfast, Northern Ireland. In addition to discussing the methods and findings of the Belfast studies, this chapter examines a number of early and more recent studies that illustrate the strengths and limitations of SNA in understanding LVC. The chapter also considers critiques of social networks and alternative methods that take into account variation at both micro and macro levels. We focus most directly on studies of LVC in first languages, beginning with Bloomfield (1933). In addition to the important work of the Milroys, we also consider Labov (1972a) on young African Americans in Harlem, Edwards (1992) on the use of local linguistic variants in inner-city Detroit, and Lippi-Green (1989) on dialect maintenance in Grossdorf, Austria. Other studies include Marshall (2004) on dialect maintenance and change in Aberdeenshire, Scotland, and Dodsworth and Benton (2020; Dodsworth, 2019) on dialect change in Raleigh, North Carolina. Finally, we examine the limitations of SNA in explaining large-scale patterns of language change, with a focus on work by Labov (2001; Labov & Harris, 1986) and Marshall (2004).

DOI: 10.4324/9781003174448-2

Early Studies: Bloomfield and Labov

In his highly influential volume, *Language*, Bloomfield discussed the role of density of communication, conceived of as a network, in giving rise to linguistic differentiation. He wrote:

> We believe that differences in density of communication within a speech-community are not only personal and individual, but that the *community* is divided into various systems of sub-groups such that the persons within a sub-group speak much more to each other than to persons outside their sub-group. Viewing the system of arrows as a network, we may say that these sub-groups are separated by *lines of weakness* in this net of oral communication. The lines of weakness and, accordingly, the differences of speech within a speech-community are local—due to mere geographic separation—and non-local, or as we usually say, *social*.
>
> *(1933, p. 47)*

Although Bloomfield does not set forth a measure of communication density in the previous passage nor in the following, the implications for the relationship between communication density and the role of different social factors in either facilitating or impeding linguistic change are clear:

> Within the standard language ... there are differences that obviously depend upon density of communication: different economic classes,—say, the very rich and the so-called "middle class" in its various gradations,—differ in speech. Then there are differences of education, in the way both of family tradition and schooling. These differences are crossed by less important divisions of technical occupation ... Sports and hobbies have at least their own vocabulary.
>
> *(1933, p. 49)*

While Bloomfield described the relationship between social networks and language change, Labov explored the role of social networks much more directly. Although much of Labov's work focuses on the relationship between large scale social categories and language change, a number of his studies carried out in the 1960s and 1970s also considered the important role of other factors in either impeding language change or in fostering the use of vernacular forms. For example, in his seminal work on African American English in New York City's Harlem, Labov (1972a), using sociograms, provides a clear illustration of the relationship between the density of vernacular use and density of network ties.

Figure 2.1 from Labov's Harlem study illustrates the hangout patterns of the Thunderbirds, one of the youth groups that provided the data for Labov's Harlem studies. The sociogram also includes three members of the '1390 Lames', Del, Lesley and Curtis, who did not participate in the Thunderbirds' activities, although they lived in the same general area, and whose participation in the culture of the streets was limited.

To explore connections among group members, study participants were asked "Who are all the cats you hang out with?" (p. 261). In Figure 2.1, the solid lines show mutual naming, while the dashed lines with arrows show someone who is not named. As can be seen, the leaders, Boot and Roger, as well as other central members form a network of mutual naming. Labov notes that three speakers, Billy, Gary, and Robbie, form a younger subgroup, while the three 'Lames', Del, Lesley, and Curtis, are in very peripheral positions.

Although the network ties of the Thunderbirds can be clearly seen in Figure 2.1, the question remains: How do these ties relate to features of language use? Figure 2.2, also from Labov (1972a), provides a convenient illustration. It shows the use of the variable postvocalic (r) in three speech

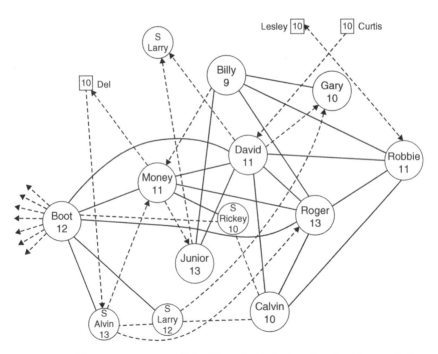

FIGURE 2.1 Hangout patterns of the Thunderbirds (reprinted with permission from Labov 1972a, p. 262)

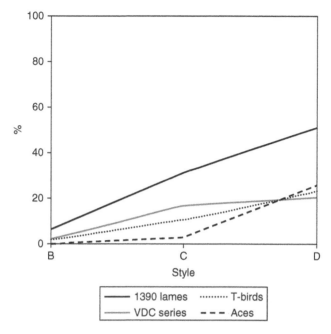

FIGURE 2.2 Use of the variable (r) by youth groups in Harlem (reprinted with permission from Labov 1972a, p. 265)

styles by four groups: the 1390 Lames, the Vacation Day Camp (VDC) boys, the Thunderbirds, and the Aces. In this graph, Style B is the main body of conversation, Style C is reading style, and Style D is based on word lists and minimal pairs. Labov argues that the three styles reflect an increasing amount of attention to speech. Further, as Labov notes, in areas that have been traditionally r-less, the variable (r) is socially stratified, with /r/ more likely to be realized in more formal styles.

As can be seen in Figure 2.2, all groups seldom pronounce postvocalic /r/ in conversation. In fact, postvocalic /r/ is nearly categorically absent in the conversational styles of the VDC speakers, the Thunderbirds, and the Aces. While all four groups produce postvocalic /r/ more often in the styles requiring more attention to speech, only the 1390 Lames show a sharp increase. That is, the speakers who are somewhat isolated from the vernacular street culture and the associated groups exhibit a substantial increase in the use of the more prestigious form when they are paying more attention to speech. While the VDC speakers, the Thunderbirds, and the Aces all hover around 20 percent pronunciation of postvocalic /r/, even in the style requiring most attention to speech, the 1390 Lames pronounce /r/ half of the time in word lists and minimal pairs.

Labov (1972a) found similar results for a number of other variables. For example, the fricative /ð/ in 'this' and 'then' is much more likely to be realized as (dh) in the speech of the Aces and the Thunderbirds than in the speech of the 1390 Lames or the VDC boys. Similarly, the Aces and the Thunderbirds use the informal variant of the ING variable, e.g., working —> workin', almost categorically in conversational style, while the VDC students and the 1390 Lames use the standard variant at rates of 24 and 22 percent, respectively. Labov (1972a) reports similar results for coronal stop deletion, particularly in cases where the consonant cluster forms a past tense ending (p. 264).

All of the speakers included in Labov (1972a) were economically marginalized. However, as illustrated above, they used vernacular variables at very different rates, depending largely on their social networks. The core members of the Aces and the Thunderbirds consistently selected vernacular forms at higher rates than their counterparts who had fewer associations with the street culture.

Elaborating a Social Network Framework

L. Milroy (2002) writes that SNA examines the personal communities that individuals create, communities that "provide a meaningful framework for solving the problems of daily life" (Mitchell, 1986, p. 74). She further notes that personal communities may be represented by a social network diagram representing the ties, or relationships, between the individual (*ego*) and others. The ties that an individual forms with others may be characterized as strong or weak; strong ties may be multiplex, dense, or both. Multiplex ties refer to the multiple ways that one individual may be linked to another (e.g., they are neighbors and co-workers). Dense ties are those that link many of the same people to each other. The following example represents both a dense and multiplex social network: Anne works with Mary, who is also a neighbor; Anne and Mary both work with Liz and Julie, who are sisters; the four women socialize on the weekends. Conversely, weak ties are neither dense nor multiplex—they refer to the type of uniplex relationship that one might have with a local merchant or an acquaintance.

SNA has usually focused on first-order ties that are directly linked to the individual, the egocentric network, as well as second-order ties that are removed from the individual by one person, such as a friend of a friend (L. Milroy, 2002; L. Milroy & Llamas, 2013). The relationships that link first-order ties are also differentiated on the following basis: exchange network ties refer to family and close friend relationships that involve regular contact and the exchange of direct aid, advice, and criticism (Milardo, 1988, pp. 26–36). Interactive ties, on the other hand, exist between the individual and those with whom the person has regular contact, but on whom the individual does not rely for material or symbolic resources. Thus, exchange networks are normally characterized by strong ties (multiplex and/or dense) and interactive networks by weak ties. Additionally, passive ties (Li, 1994) are those contacts within a personal network who may not be physically present in ego's daily life (such as family and friends living in another country), but who provide a critical form of support.

Figures 2.3 and 2.4 depict two personal social networks, one with dense, multiplex, first and second-order ties (Figure 2.3) and the other with weak, uniplex, first-order ties only (Figure 2.4). As shown in Figure 2.3, the first-order ties linked directly to ego represent the first-order zone of the social network, and the second-order ties that are linked to ego through a member of the first-order zone represent the second-order zone of the network.

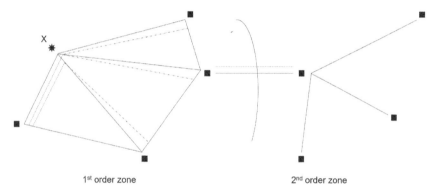

1st order zone   2nd order zone

FIGURE 2.3   Diagram of a dense and multiplex personal network structure with first- and second-order zones (reprinted with permission from L. Milroy & Llamas, 2013, p. 411)

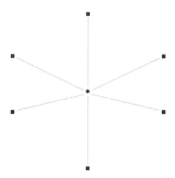

FIGURE 2.4   Diagram of a weak and uniplex personal network structure with a first-order zone only (reprinted with permission from L. Milroy & Llamas, 2013, p. 411)

While the concept of a social network could extend infinitely across an entire society, applications of SNA to language use have focused primarily on the first-order zone of exchange network ties linked directly to ego (L. Milroy, 2002) and on the impact of these first-order network ties on one's linguistic behavior.

In their foundational study on language variation in working-class Belfast, Milroy and Milroy (1978) developed a Network Strength Scale (NSS) to measure the strength of each speaker's social network in order to predict how closely a speaker would conform to local, nonstandard speech norms. As described in L. Milroy (1987), the NSS assigned a score to each speaker based on a set of indicators, each of which contributed 0–1 point to the total strength scale. The indicators focused on neighborhood relationships such as being a member of a territorially based group (e.g., a sports team), having kinship ties with two or more homes in the neighborhood, and working with two or more households from the neighborhood. The NSS provided a means for quantifying the impact of the social network on language use at the level of the individual and facilitated group-level analysis demonstrating that dense and multiplex social networks with members of the immediate community were correlated with increased use of local, nonstandard variants characteristic of the Belfast dialect (Milroy & Milroy, 1978; L. Milroy 1987; 2002).

Many other studies have used network strength scales, with features adapted to the characteristics of particular communities, to examine language variation and either preservation of traditional vernacular features or change to more standard features. Cheshire (1982), for example, in a study of adolescent boys in Reading, England, developed a vernacular culture index (VCI) based on five characteristics: skill in fighting, habitual carrying of weapons, participation in certain minor crimes, certain job preferences, and propensity for swearing. She studied a number of vernacular features and found that youths with the highest VCI used the greatest number of nonstandard forms, such as multiple negation or 'was' with plural subjects (as in 'they was there'), while youths with lower VCI used fewer vernacular forms and more standard forms.

In the United States, Edwards (1992) examined the relationship between social networks and the use of well-documented features of African American English (AAE) in a Detroit, Michigan, neighborhood of slightly more than 18,000 people, 95 percent of whom were African American, and where there was a high incidence of poverty. Like Milroy and Milroy (1978), Edwards included responses to statements about residence of respondents' kin, relatives, and friends, where the respondents worked, and frequency of interactions with neighbors. Edwards also included questions about the strength of the respondents' desire to remain in the neighborhood, their level of disapproval of street culture, and their assessment of the suitability of the neighborhood for raising children. In response to Labov and Harris' (1986) argument that Black and white vernaculars were diverging as a result of decreasing interethnic contact, Edwards also asked for responses to the statement "I do not have white friends with whom I interact frequently".

Edwards (1992) examined the speech of a random sample of 66 neighborhood residents ranging in age from 18 to 66 and older, and equally divided between men and women. The linguistic variables included four AAE phonological variables and one syntactic variable, copula deletion, as well as a sixth variable, the average of the percentage of use of the five individual variables. To measure the degree of speakers' integration into the neighborhood, Edwards developed a VCI scale based on speaker responses to the following ten statements (p. 101), which participants were asked to rate on a scale of 1 to 4:

1. Most of the members of my family live in the neighborhood or with me.
2. Most of my relatives live in the neighborhood or with me.
3. Most of the jobs I have held have been in this neighborhood.
4. Most of my friends live in this neighborhood.
5. I have frequent daily interactions with people in this neighborhood.
6. I would like to remain living in this neighborhood.
7. I do not have white friends with whom I interact frequently.
8. If I move, I would like to move to a neighborhood like this one.
9. The street culture doesn't bother me; people have to survive.
10. This is a good neighborhood to raise kids.

Results of the quantitative analysis showed a strong correlation between scores on the VCI and the use of AAE variants. Speakers who were relatively isolated in the neighborhood or who were favorable to the neighborhood chose the vernacular variants more frequently than their counterparts who regularly had contact with people outside the neighborhood or who had negative attitudes toward the neighborhood. Edwards (1992) concluded that the results demonstrated that "linguistic behavior in socioeconomically homogenous inner-city Black neighborhoods is not necessarily homogeneous" (p. 111) and that significant patterns of variation can be discovered using a sociolinguistic model drawn from social network theory. Finally, Edwards suggested that the study provided evidence that speakers' attitudes influence their linguistic behavior just as much as their objective social characteristics.

While the Milroys (1978), Cheshire (1982), and Edwards (1992) applied SNA to urban communities, Lippi-Green (1989) examined how SNA, along with other more traditional social factors, might contribute to the understanding of patterns of language use in Grossdorf, a small agricultural village in western Austria. Dairy farming was the traditional occupation in the village; however, in the twentieth century, daily transportation to the Rhine Valley became available, leading to a more diversified economic and social structure. Lippi-Green focused on a change in progress from conservative [ɔ] to innovative [a] in German in the following environments, nd, td, ts, tk, mpf, ntl, and ndl.

To examine the extent to which the 42 speakers in the study participated in this ongoing change, Lippi-Green constructed a 16-point scale based on two density measures and two multiplexity measures. Density measures focused on the speaker's active and passive relationships to the core families in the village and the speaker's workplace network (i.e., local, in Grossdorf, or the neighboring village of Egg), whether the speaker had always worked there, and whether the speaker was a farmer or a member of a farming family. Multiplexity measures focused on the nature of the ties between the speaker and co-workers, regardless of where the speaker was employed, as well as voluntary associations, particularly whether the speaker was socially active in Grossdorf or Egg. The scale had 16 features and the highest possible score was 17 for a married speaker and 16 for a single speaker. Lippi-Green outlined the characteristics of an idealized speaker with the highest possible score (pp. 219–220):

1. involved in two strong and active clans ... who interacted with parents and grandparents....
2. who has remained with the Grossdorf clan structure and strengthened his or her involvement by marrying into it.
3. who pursues traditional employment as a small dairy farmer in Grossdorf and has never pursued any other employment. Here ... ties to co-workers ... are extremely multiplex and contact to nonlocal persons is at a minimum.
4. who is socially active in the community.

Overall results of the quantitative analysis showed that age, education, and network integration significantly affected women's use of innovative or conservative forms. However, the results for men were much more complex as a result of considerable within-group internal inconsistency, as well as a small number of tokens for some participants. Lippi-Green noted that the male results highlight the importance of examining not only group patterns of language use, but also of looking at individual patterns of use. The results also showed that for the younger generation, the women produced more innovative forms than the men. Lippi-Green suggested that the younger men may have lagged behind because they associated the ongoing phonological change with women. While the overall results are revealing, consideration of speakers' social networks clarifies their choices between use of conservative [ɔ] and innovative [ɑ]. Lippi-Green noted that the sum of the three network subsections—kinship, workplace, and voluntary association—was the most significant of all the social factors she examined.

In contrast to the previous studies that focused on the role of networks in contributing to the maintenance or change of traditional dialect features, Bortoni-Ricardo (1985) studied the degree to which rural dialect-speaking migrants to Brazlândia, Brazil, a satellite town located near Brasilia, moved away from near categorical use of stigmatized rural forms to variable use of more standard urban forms. To assess network strength, Bortoni-Ricardo developed two indices, an integration index, a measure of the number of ties an individual migrant developed in the urban environment, and an urbanization index, "the degree to which the people with whom the migrant is directly or indirectly related are exposed to the urban influence" (p. 245).

Bortoni-Ricardo's (1985) results showed different trajectories for male and female migrants. For the men, the degree of dialect diffuseness could be accounted for by the extent and characteristics of their relationships in the public sphere. The women in Bortoni-Ricardo's study, however, had very different life experiences. Their activities were primarily confined to the kinship and neighborhood networks. Hence, they were less likely to be exposed to the influence of mainstream culture and less likely to interact with strangers than their male counterparts. Nevertheless, Bortoni-Ricardo found that in the case of some phonological variables, e.g., /l/ vocalization, the women followed a similar path as the men, while in the case of diphthong reduction, they were more likely to produce the standard variant than were the men. In the case of morphosyntactic variables, however, the men led in acquiring the standard form. Thus, even though the women in the study were not directly exposed to standardizing influences in the public sphere, they still participated in change. Bortoni-Ricardo suggested that women's relationships with their grown children are the main influence on their participation in language change.

More recently, Dodsworth (2019) and Dodsworth and Benton (2017, 2020), in their study of the retreat from the Southern Vowel Shift in Raleigh, North Carolina, aimed to overcome some of the limitations of many previous social network studies in sociolinguistics. As Dodsworth (2019) notes, in many studies, social network data are based on speakers' self-reports, which are subject to inaccuracy and concentrate on the egocentric network only. That is, the data are concerned with speakers' first-order networks and reveal little about the overall network structure of the community. Second, Dodsworth argues that the focus of many studies on small dense neighborhood networks, while allowing for in-depth examination of the local community, excludes speakers outside of those dense communities. As a result, it is difficult to understand how the linguistic practices of a particular dense network relate to the overall practices of the community. Dodsworth (2019) also notes that most social network studies select network criteria that apply to the specific community. While this is understandable, it limits the generalizability of results.

Dodsworth and Benton (2020) outlined three major goals designed "to take sociolinguistic network analysis in some new methodological and empirical directions" (Dodsworth 2019, p. 6). First, they represented speakers' positions in the overall network structure of the community rather than relying on self-reported ego data. Second, they sought to use data and methods that could be replicated in different communities, thus facilitating generalizations. Finally, they sought to engage with social network studies in other disciplines.

Dodsworth and Benton (2020) included 189 speakers from three generations. Moreover, to understand the relationship between individual speakers and the overall network structure of the community, they adopted a bipartite network approach where "one class of nodes represents speakers and one class of nodes represents elementary, middle, and high schools" (Dodsworth, 2019, p. 11). They justified the inclusion of schools as 'network nodes or contacts' on the reasonable grounds that most people acquire their dialect in childhood and adolescence and that changes in speakers' vowel systems in later life tend to be much less pronounced than differences from earlier generations. Importantly, the use of schools as a class of nodes does not imply that two speakers who attended the same school interacted with one another. It does suggest, however, that they interacted with many of the same people and were exposed to the same linguistic and cultural environment. Dodsworth (2017) argued that the bipartite approach, which is elaborated in Dodsworth and Benton (2020), allowed for an examination of "the intersecting and changing effects of network, occupation, and sex" (p. 25) and a representation of individuals' positions in the local network structure while avoiding reliance on self-reported data.

Limitations of Social Network Analysis

While a number of sociolinguistic studies have shown correlations between speakers' social networks and patterns of language variation, some scholars have questioned their explanatory power and it is important to acknowledge these criticisms here. For example, Labov's work on African American and white speech has important implications for our understanding of the effect of social networks, particularly the types of features that are subject to their influence, but Labov has also questioned the relative importance of social networks compared to the more traditional social categories of class, gender, and ethnicity that are usually accounted for in sociolinguistic studies. Labov and Harris (1986), for example, documented the relationship between the divergence of Black and white vernaculars and the increasing neighborhood segregation in Philadelphia from 1850 to 1980. As a result of the increase in racially homogeneous neighborhoods, the number of cross-racial interactions was decreasing for both Black and white speakers. Based on the study of a number of variables, Labov and Harris argued that the Philadelphia speech community was becoming two distinct speech communities: one Black and one white. They noted:

> ... long and close interaction can produce linguistic convergence. Members of the same social network usually share a common ideology and common experience, which leads to the same directions of style shifting and the same attitudes towards other dialects. We have traced small linguistic rules and lexical items that are shared by members of primary networks. But on the whole, social networks have little explanatory power for individual differences in linguistic systems. It is the social history of the speakers that must be taken into account: the kinds of social experience they have had in dealing with members of other groups.
>
> *(1986, p. 22)*

Labov (2001) elaborates on the limitations of a view, such as that expressed by LePage and Tabouret-Keller (1985), that social networks provide a better means of understanding the relationship between linguistic behavior and social factors than membership in social, economic, or other groups. Labov emphasizes the advantages of studying groups of speakers, rather than isolated individuals, because such studies allow for the recording of respondents interacting with the people they usually speak with, rather than reconstructing the hypothetical networks of speakers recorded through random sampling of the speech community.

Despite certain advantages, studies that focus on social networks face a number of obstacles, particularly in studies of large urban areas. For example, Labov (2001) noted that most social network studies, including L. Milroy (1987), have been based on fairly small numbers of speakers. While limiting the number of speakers and studying them in greater depth can reveal important local linguistic patterns, it also precludes studies of large-scale changes that are occurring across broad areas, such as the Northern Cities vowel shift or the California (or western) vowel shift.

Moreover, as Labov noted, the particular forms that a speaker uses derive their social meaning from their use in the wider community, not from their use in a small network. For example, Eckert (2000) studied two social groups, the jocks and burnouts, in a Detroit, Michigan, area high school. The jocks' social lives were centered around the school, while the burnouts were oriented toward the urban scene in neighboring Detroit. Eckert reported that the burnouts were more advanced in the newer changes in the Northern Cities Shift than the jocks, a finding that makes sense given their urban orientation. However, the differences in the two groups' vowel pronunciation can only be interpreted because the large-scale changes occurring across the inland northern United States have been documented in other studies (Labov, 2001). That is, as Labov observes, we can find the greatest linguistic significance of social networks where:

1. Previous studies have identified the major linguistic variables of the wider community and traced their patterns of stylistic and social variation. Social class, age, gender, and ethnicity will continue to explain the greater part of the variation.
2. All members of the group share the same social history in terms of residence and dialect contact. When they do not, the effect of these differences in social history must be accounted for by wider studies of the type indicated in (1).

(2001, p. 327)

An example of how social networks interact with other social influences and individual characteristics is found in the work of Marshall (2004). While most sociolinguistic studies, including many of the studies employing social network analysis, like L. Milroy (1987) and Edwards (1992), have been conducted in urban communities, Marshall (2004) studied the Scottish village of Huntly, near Aberdeen, where the traditional rural dialect was receding. Based on the study of a range of phonological, morphological, and lexical variables, Marshall examined whether a speaker's integration into local social networks was a reliable predictor of maintenance of the local dialect or whether other factors, such as age or attitudes towards rural and urban life, had more explanatory power.

In this study, Marshall conducted sociolinguistic interviews with 64 speakers stratified by age and sex. Speakers were divided by age into four groups: 8 to 12, 14 to 17, 25 to 40, and over 60. Participants also responded to questionnaires about their social networks, social class, and attitudes toward urban/rural lifestyles. The social network questionnaire was based on those used by L. Milroy (1980) and Pedersen (1994), while the social class questionnaire focused on the speaker's and their parents' occupations, education, and the newspapers they read.

Marshall's social network questionnaire, like L. Milroy's (1987) index, measured the number and frequency of interactions, multiplexity, and strength of ties. His results showed that age was the best predictor of the extent of use of local dialect features, with younger speakers being less likely than their elders to use local dialect features. This result is to be expected in a context where the local dialect is receding. Marshall also found that a social network score failed to reach statistical significance and that a mental urbanization score, based on the ten following questions, accounted for more of the variation than either social network or social class indices.

1. I notice what people are wearing in Aberdeen, I like to keep up with fashion.
2. I mostly watch TV programmes about urban life and avoid nature/environmental programmes.
3. I would like to follow a career in the city rather than one where I work in the country or a small town around here.
4. I think it is very important to own a PC or at least have access to one at school/work.
5. I would love to move away from this area to the city.
6. When I am in Aberdeen, I feel at home and unstressed by the crowds and traffic.
7. City folk are just as friendly as anyone and are basically the same as country folk.
8. I never eat brose or any traditional meals. I prefer modern/international dishes.
9. A good education, getting on in life, and having all the modern equipment and appliances is more important than quietness and having a good family life.
10. I'd rather spend a day in Aberdeen playing computer games and shopping than spend it walking up Bennachie [a local mountain range] with friends and family.

(2004, p. 112)

The results of the multivariate analysis of Marshall's (2004) Huntly data showed that age had a significant effect on all of the linguistic measures tested. As Marshall noted, since it is known that the traditional dialect is receding, this was expected. The failure of the social network score to achieve significance, however, was unexpected and indicates that other factors, such as a speaker's orientation to newer ways of living, need to be considered in attempts to explain the types of changes that rural communities such as Huntly are undergoing.

Conclusion

As the research discussed in this chapter demonstrates, SNA has made substantial contributions to our understanding of LVC, particularly to the ways that closely knit neighborhood networks such as those studied by L. Milroy (1987) serve to reinforce vernacular norms. At the same time, the analysis of social networks should supplement, but not replace, the examination of other social factors, such as class and gender, especially in large-scale studies of L1-speaking communities. In the next chapter, we turn to research that has effectively applied SNA to bi- and multilingual communities, particularly to communities undergoing shift from a minority and/or immigrant language to the dominant language of the community.

3

SOCIAL NETWORK ANALYSIS IN BI- AND MULTILINGUAL COMMUNITIES

Introduction

Social network analysis (SNA) has proven to be highly productive in studies of language maintenance and shift in bilingual communities (see, e.g., Gal, 1979; W. Li, 1994; W. Li et al., 1992; Zentella, 1997, 2007). Although the patterns of language use and choice are more complex in multilingual than in bilingual communities, SNA has also contributed to our understanding of multilingual communities (see, e.g., Lanza & Svendsen 2007; Matsumoto & Britain, 2009). As well, analysis of speakers' social networks in bilingual communities, including communities undergoing language shift, has provided insights into the particular features of the new language or dialect that speakers choose to adopt (Bayley et al., 2012; Bayley & Holland 2014; Mendoza-Denton 2008; Slomanson & Newman, 2004; Wolfram et al., 2004). This chapter first examines contributions of SNA to bilingual communities undergoing language shift to a dominant language, or in some cases, resisting language shift. It then focuses on the more complex analysis posed by multilingual communities. Finally, it examines several studies of the relationship between speakers' social networks and their adoption, or failure to adopt, features of a particular language variety.

Social Networks and Language Maintenance

In a major study of the shift from Hungarian to German in the bilingual town of Oberwart in eastern Austria, Gal (1979) explored the role of

DOI: 10.4324/9781003174448-3

social networks, among other factors, in predicting speakers' language use. Oberwart was part of Hungary until 1921, when it was given to Austria as part of the post-World War I peace agreements. In the decades following its detachment from Hungary, as Oberwart became a commercial center, the population grew from approximately 600 to more than 5,000. Most of the new settlers were monolingual German speakers from the surrounding region who had been trained in administration or commerce (Gal, 1978), while the original Hungarian-speaking population was predominantly engaged in subsistence agriculture. According to Gal (1978), in the late 1970s, about a third of the population was bilingual. German was the higher status language, particularly for young people, while Hungarian was associated with peasantness.

As would be expected in a community undergoing language shift, in Gal's study, age was strongly correlated with language choice, particularly among women, where the correlation was .93 for a sample of women, compared to .69 for men (Gal, 1978, p. 9). In addition to age and gender, Gal (1979) used a range of criteria to establish speakers' peasant status including type of livestock owned, crops grown, years of schooling, and access to modern plumbing. While she found a strong correlation between peasant status and language choice (.67), the extent to which speakers' social networks consisted of peasants resulted in an even stronger correlation (.78). Gal concluded that a "speaker's social networks can act as powerful constraints on their linguistic presentations of self, and, hence, their language choices" (p. 140).

Li Wei (1994) also used SNA in a major study of language choice among three generations of Chinese migrants and their children in northern England. Not surprisingly, the older generation, who were predominantly Chinese monolinguals or Chinese dominant speakers, had much more extensive Chinese-speaking networks than their younger counterparts. As well, women, particularly women in the "grandparents" generation, tended to have denser Chinese-speaking networks than their male counterparts. As might be expected in a migrant community, the British-born children, who attended English schools, tended to have higher levels of English proficiency than their parents or grandparents and, because they had more opportunities for interactions outside of the Chinese community, their social networks included far fewer Chinese speakers.

Although Li Wei (1994) found that British-born children used a good deal more English than their immigrant parents, social networks proved to have a strong influence on patterns of language use for the British-born generation as well. In a study of the same community, Li Wei et al. (1992) presented an implicational scale illustrating the language choices of 38 children of the immigrant group (including adult children and adolescents) with a variety of interlocutors ranging from grandparents and their generation to

Chinese friends (p. 75). Interestingly, the speakers who reported the most Chinese use were all members of the "True Jesus Church", in which families maintained a close social network with many activities centered around the church. In contrast, the speakers who reported the most use of English were not members of the church.

In another study on language use among bilingual speakers, Zentella (1997) examined the language development of Puerto Rican children living on a single block, *el boque*, in East Harlem in New York City. The study provides a clear description of how the multiple dialects of Spanish and English that predominated in the different social networks on *el bloque* influenced children's language development and later linguistic repertoires. While language choice in communities such as *el bloque* is sometimes characterized as a choice between the dominant language, in this case English, and the migrant language, Zentella showed in fine detail how the choice among different codes is actually far more nuanced than a simple binary choice between Spanish and English. Interactions on *el bloque* included popular Puerto Rican Spanish, standard Puerto Rican Spanish, English-dominant Spanish, Puerto Rican English, African American influenced English, or Hispanicized English, as well as more or less standard New York English. Moreover, speakers normally command a range of different dialects, although, as Zentella showed, particular networks preferred one or another variety (see Table 3.1).

In accounts of several of the young people on *el bloque*, Zentella (1997) showed how their social networks, combined with their home language environments and the schools they attended, conditioned their language choices. For example, one young man, Eddie, spoke both African American Vernacular English (AAVE) and Puerto Rican English (PRE) but no Spanish.

TABLE 3.1 Networks and codes of *el bloque*

Network	Primary code	Other codes
Children	PRE	NSPRS, AAVE
Teens	PRE	NSPRS, AAVE, SE
Young Dudes	AAVE	PRS, NSPRS, SE
Young Mothers	PRE	NSPRS, NSPRS, SE
Mature Females	NSPRS	SPRS, HE
Mature Males	NSPRS	SPRS, HE, SE

Notes: PRE, Puerto Rican English; NSPRS, Nonstandard Puerto Rican Spanish; AAVE, African American Vernacular English; PRS, Puerto Rican Spanish; SE, Standard English; SPRS, Standard Puerto Rican Spanish; HE, Hispanicized English.

Source: Reprinted with permission from Zentella, 1997, p. 48

Eddie was part of a network that spoke predominantly AAVE. Like many Caribbean people, he was of African descent, and commented, "People mostly think I'm Black. When they hear my name they be tryin' to talk to me [in Spanish]" (Zentella, 1997, p. 140). The case of Marta, who also grew up on *el bloque*, presents a stark contrast to Eddie. Marta spent very little time in a bilingual program and, starting in high school, her jobs, boyfriends, and schools were in non-Spanish-speaking neighborhoods. She later married an Anglo chiropractor, after which her contact with *el bloque* was reduced to weekly visits to her parents. Marta developed control of standard English and adopted a language ideology that led her to condemn the frequent code-switching that characterized the language of many residents of her old neighborhood, commenting: "It's like an insult to our language. You can't develop either by mixing them both" (Zentella, 1997, p 148).

The cases of Eddie, Marta, and the other young people on *el bloque* whose lives Zentella recounted in rich detail illustrate the importance of going beyond broad demographic categories such as gender, ethnicity, and social class, and considering not only speakers' individual aspirations but also their opportunities to acquire different languages or language varieties. SNA offers a way to better understand patterns of language use that the factors traditionally used in sociolinguistic studies sometimes fail to explain.

Many other studies in a variety of contexts have shown a strong correlation between speakers' minority language social networks and minority language maintenance. For example, in their study of three generations of Dutch migrants in New Zealand, Hulsen et al. (2002), found that the number of Dutch speakers in a participant's social network was strongly correlated with language maintenance. As in other communities, there was greater use of Dutch among the immigrant generation, many of whom also belonged to Dutch clubs, and overall results indicated a gradual shift to English. However, as in Li Wei's (1994) study, church membership also was positively associated with Dutch maintenance. Many of the participants in Hulsen et al. (2002) belonged to the Dutch Reformed Church, which, the authors noted, consists largely of people of Dutch descent.

Given what we know about minority language maintenance and shift in immigrant communities, it is not surprising that studies have found that the extent of speakers' participation in minority language social networks is associated with language maintenance and the participation in networks in which the language of the new society predominates is associated with language shift. While consistent minority language use in the home is clearly important if the immigrant language is to be acquired by the next generation (Schecter & Bayley, 2002), use of the minority language in a variety of domains is necessary if language shift is to be avoided (Fishman, 1991). For example, Li Wei et al. (1992) noted that in addition to maintaining a strong kinship-based network, children who belonged to the "True Jesus Church" in Newcastle participated in a variety of activities:

> The chief function of the True Jesus Church seems to be that of maintaining Chinese language and culture, and the activities in which the True Jesus families participate each Sunday do not resemble those of the churchgoing population of Britain generally.... They generally eat a meal together and attend one of two relatively short church services: one is conducted entirely in Chinese and one mainly in English.... There are also lessons in Chinese language and culture for the children during the afternoon, and the families meet otherwise to celebrate special occasions like Chinese New Year or Christmas. Thus, they have ample opportunity to maintain their pre-existing network ties ... and to maintain their knowledge of Chinese language and culture.
>
> *(1992, pp. 73–74)*

The kinds of activities in which the children in the families of the True Jesus Church participated thus provided opportunities for members to use different registers of Chinese in a variety of contexts and domains. They are precisely the kinds of activities that we might expect to lead to greater language maintenance.

In sum, participation in a variety of activities in a minority language, which extensive minority language social networks promote, provides the opportunities for acquisition and use in multiple domains that are crucial to language maintenance. This has been demonstrated repeatedly in studies such as Hulsen et al. (2002) and Li Wei (1994), which demonstrate that the extent of a speaker's social network has a significant impact on language maintenance independent of other factors such as immigrant generation or sex.

Multilingual and Multidialectal Communities

SNA has proven to have predictive power for language maintenance in bilingual communities, particularly immigrant communities such as those discussed in the previous section. The relationship between social network and language choice, however, becomes more complicated when multiple languages are involved. Lanza and Svendsen's (2007) study of the language practices of Filipinos in Oslo, Norway, provides a convenient example.

While the Philippines has only two official languages, Filipino and English (a legacy of American colonialism), there are approximately 120 languages spoken in the islands, ten of which are spoken by more than a million people. Thus, among the speakers Lanza and Svendsen studied, there is not a one-to-one relationship between language as ethnicity or national origin, as there is among the Dutch in New Zealand studied by Hulsen et al. (2002), or the Chinese in Newcastle examined by Li Wei (1994), all of whom were from the same region in China.

Lanza and Svendsen's (2007) study included 54 multilingual speakers (17 men and 37 women) of Filipino, English, and Norwegian living in Oslo. Age of arrival in Norway ranged from 9 to 47, and length of stay varied from 1 to 30 years. In this study, participants were asked to list 10 members of their exchange and interactive networks; from the exchange network, a kin index and ethnic index were created. Results demonstrated that for 23 adult participants, the ethnic index (Filipino rather than a regional Filipino designation) was a significant predictor of the use of a Filipino language (either Filipino or another regional language) at home with their children. This trend was not replicated in the children: the parents' social network was not a significant predictor of language choice by the children who primarily spoke Norwegian. At the same time, the authors noted other important factors influencing language choice between parent and child including language ideology, multilingual identities, and religious affiliation. As the authors point out, Filipino multilingualism and the fact that English, a compulsory subject in Norwegian schools, is also widely spoken in the Philippines and thus can be considered a Philippine language, greatly complicates the issue of maintenance of indigenous Philippine languages because contact with the extended Filipino family can be maintained through English.

In contrast to some of the studies discussed in the previous section, the connection between language and ethnicity in Lanza and Svendsen (2007) is much more fluid than that seen in studies such as Li Wei (1994). In fact, Lanza and Svendsen critique what they view as the essentialist notion of identity in earlier social network studies of bilingual communities. Despite the problems that they point out and despite the more complicated relationship between language and ethnicity in communities such as the Filipino community in Norway, Lanza and Svendsen conclude that social network analysis is a valuable tool for studying language maintenance and shift in migrant communities. However, they also suggest that multilingualism provides a much more complicated reality for identity and suggest that more interpretive approaches are needed to study language choice, including language ideology and identity. Finally, as Lanza and Svendsen point out, in the case of the Filipino community in Norway, English may serve similar purposes as an indigenous Filipino language.

In contrast to Lanza and Svendsen who explored social networks and language use by Filipino migrants in the capital of one of Europe's wealthiest countries, Matsumoto and Britain (2009) examined whether SNA can explain the use of former colonial languages in the small island nation of Palau in the Western Pacific (population 20,300 at the time of the study). Palau has been subject to four colonial masters, Spain (1885–1899), Germany (1899–1914), Japan (1914–1945), and the United States (1945 to independence in 1994). Currently three languages are widely spoken or studied: Palauan, the Austronesian indigenous language, English (an official language), and Japanese, which is studied as a school subject.

Matsumoto and Britain (2009) addressed three questions, drawn from earlier research. First, they investigated whether there is a link between speakers' linguistic behavior and former colonial links in their social networks. In the context of Palau, more specifically, they asked whether the extent of Japanese links in speakers' social networks could predict their level of Japanese maintenance. Second, Matsumoto and Britain, drawing on L. Milroy (1987), investigated whether strong ties lead to maintenance of conservative linguistic behavior, i.e., the maintenance of Japanese in the case of Palau, and resistance to innovation, i.e., the shift to English. Finally, Matsumoto and Britain investigated whether social networks have different effects on various subgroups in a community.

Matsumoto and Britain's study included 53 participants divided into three different family types: Palauan, Japanese Palauan, and returnees (Japanese citizens who had been relocated to Japan under American occupation and later returned). Data were collected using a variety of ethnographic observations, interviews, and questionnaires. Overall results showed that SNA provides a useful means of understanding patterns of language use in post-colonial communities. Simply put, the study showed that the more Japanese links speakers had in their social network, the more they maintained Japanese; the fewer Japanese links they maintained, the more they had shifted to the most recent colonial language, English.

In addition to demonstrating the applicability of SNA to post-colonial societies, results from the Palau study also indicated that the functions of strong and weak ties as norm reinforcers and norm diffusers studied in the urban community of Belfast (L. Milroy, 1987) were applicable to a small rural community. Finally, although Matsumoto and Britain found that SNA was useful in examining the extent of Japanese maintenance, they also noted two limitations. First, social networks cannot reconstruct past networks or the process of migration, and second, they "appear to be a less useful variable in cases where the cause of on-going language shift involves indirect institutionalized or authorized language enforcement" (p. 33).

The influence of institutionalized language enforcement is potentially reflected in the results of Zhang (2012), who examined language maintenance among heritage speakers of Chinese residing in Philadelphia, Pennsylvania, and demonstrated that high density social networks with co-ethnic peers could be a 'double-edged sword' for children from lower social classes. In this study, Zhang found that well-educated Standard Mandarin speakers relied on passive ties with family and friends back home and social networks with other ethnic Chinese in the US to maintain their cultural and linguistic ties to mainland China and to acculturate their children into "transnational citizenship and global mobility" (2012, p. 220). On the other hand, the less well-educated and lower income Fujianese speakers lived primarily within the physical boundaries of Chinatown and their children, who often felt marginalized by mainstream society, tended to form close-knit co-ethnic social networks that reinforced the use of English, rather than their heritage language, because of its associations with social and economic mobility.

Social Network as a Constraint on Sociolinguistic Variation in Bilingual Communities

Thus far, this chapter has focused on the influence of social networks on speakers' choices of different linguistic codes. However, as we have seen in several examples in the previous chapter, the nature of speakers' social networks has also been shown to act as a constraint on choices among sociolinguistic variables, including in language contact situations. Several studies will serve as to illustrate the process: Wolfram et al.'s (2004) study of monophthongization of /ai/, a stereotypical feature of Southern English, in Latino English in North Carolina; Slomanson and Newman's (2004) study of the pronunciation of English laterals by diverse groups of New York City Latinx high school students; Mendoza-Denton's (2008) study of Latina gang girls in northern California; Bayley et al.'s study (2012) of subject pronoun expression by Puerto Rican residents of San Antonio, Texas; and Bayley and Holland's (2014) study of /z/-devoicing by young people in a San Antonio public housing project. Although not all of these studies explicitly used SNA, their discussions of social constraints on the choice of sociolinguistic variables make it clear that speakers' social networks play an important role in their patterns of language use.

Wolfram et al. (2004) examined a number of lexical variants as well as monophthongization of /ai/ among Latinos in two communities in North Carolina—the rural community of Siler City, which had experienced a large influx of Latinos in recent years, and the urban center of Raleigh. The researchers found no overall acquisition of Southern features by Latino speakers in either area; however, a number of Latinos did adopt Southern features, including lexical items such as y'all, depending on the groups with which they identified. For example, Wolfram et al. discussed the example of a 13-year-old brother and 11-year-old sister, who had adopted very different speech patterns. The children, whose parents were immigrants from Mexico, had both spent their entire lives in North Carolina. The brother identified strongly with the local, non-Hispanic jock culture, and in a sociolinguistic interview, his speech contained numerous Southern vernacular features. Moreover, two-thirds of the brother's tokens of /ai/ were unglided, indicating his identification with the local vernacular culture. In contrast, his sister, who identified more with mainstream American institutional values, produced only a single unglided token of /ai/ and few other Southern vernacular features.

Wolfram et al. (2004) suggested that the results for these two speakers demonstrate the role of choice in explaining individual patterns of variation. However, given what we know about the norm-enforcing power of adolescent social structure and the pre-adolescent heterosexual marketplace (Eckert, 1988, 2008), we suggest that the dramatic differences in the speech of the brother and sister might well be a consequence of their participation in different single-sex social networks. As Wolfram et al. noted, not all of the boys in their study adopted Southern vernacular features. Moreover, Wolfram et al. also noted that accommodation to Southern regional norms was not widespread among the Latinos in the communities they studied where the dominant pattern of social interaction was ethnically segregated. However, that does not seem to have been the case with the 13-year-old older brother who had adopted Southern vernacular norms.

Slomanson and Newman (2004) examined the production of apical /l/, a Spanish feature that is foreign to New York European American Vernacular English (NYEAVE) and AAVE, in the English used by four distinct subgroups of New York City Latino high school students (pp. 202–203):

- Hip-hop: associated with rap music, graffiti art, and DJ-ing (using two turntables with vinyl records to make music), as well as urban styles;
- Skater/Bicycle Moto-Cross (BMX): associated with performing tricks using skateboards and special small bicycles;
- Geek: associated with intensive computer gaming, technological sophistication, and sometimes hacking.
- Family oriented: The students in this group tended to be Spanish-English balanced bilinguals and maintained strong links to their national heritage community and often wore accessories in national colors.

Table 3.2 on the following page illustrates the criteria Slomanson and Newman used in classifying Latino students into different groups.

While Slomanson and Newman did not have enough data to allow for multivariate analysis, their results are nevertheless suggestive. The results show that the family-oriented students, i.e., those whose interactional networks included many other Spanish speakers, produced far more apical

TABLE 3.2 Criteria for peer cultural assignment

Hip-hop	Skater/BMX	Geek	Family-oriented
Listening to underground hip-hop artists	Participation in skateboarding or in Bicycle Moto-Cross	Profound knowledge of computers, software and hardware	Mention of inter-generational friendships
Profound knowledge of hip-hop forms	Admiration for famous skaters and BMXers	Heavy playing of computer games and related activities	Overt active bilingualism
Attending live performances of rap	Pride in accomplishments in performing tricks	Plans to use computers in future for career	Overt active bilingualism
Expression of attitudes consonant with hip-hop ideologies (e.g., valuing authenticity, realism, self-assertion, and individualism)	Pride in injuries sustained while performing	Work in computer repair in school	Claims of pride in national heritage and family
Wearing of hip-hop associated clothes or accessories (e.g., "urban" brands, baggy pants, du-rags or bandanas)	Wearing of skating "gear"	Refraining from wearing stylish clothes of any kind	Use of accessories representing national heritage (e.g., beads in Colombian national colors, Dominican flag pendants)
Association with other hip-hoppers	Association with other skaters	Association with other geeks	Mix of friends

Source: Reprinted with permission from Slomanson & Newman, 2004, p. 204

/l/ onsets than students in any of the other groups, who interacted more frequently in English than their family-oriented counterparts. Moreover, unlike the members of the family-oriented group, who tended to be balanced bilinguals, members of the other three groups were either English-dominant or spoke English exclusively.

Turning to the West Coast, Mendoza-Denton's (2008) study of Latina gang girls in northern California offers a dramatic illustration of the power of social networks in influencing the use of specific sociolinguistic variables as well as choice of code. Mendoza-Denton studied two distinct groups, Norteñas and Sureñas, who were distinguished not only by their patterns of language use but also in their music preferences and types of dress and even hairstyles and makeup. Table 3.3 shows a summary of these differences.

Among other variables, Mendoza-Denton (2008) examined the Th-pro variable, i.e., the raising of /ɪ/ to /i/ in words such as anything, something, etc., a distinctive feature of Chicanx English. Results of logistic regression showed that Norteñas and Sureñas were almost equally likely to use the raised variant. These two groups were followed closely by the Norteña and Sureña wannabes. As expected, Latina jocks, who adhered to traditional values and whose social lives centered around the school, were least likely to choose the raised variant.

Given that the Norteñas and Sureñas were hostile to one another, often engaging in fights, and differed in their language practices, why did they use a particular Chicanx English variant at nearly the same rate? Mendoza-Denton suggested that raised /ɪ/, rather than indexing traditional Latina values, is an index of Latina identity and that both Norteñas and Sureñas, despite their opposing ideologies and distinct linguistic practices, wished to highlight their Latina identities. In contrast, the Latina jocks, who interacted frequently with Euro-American students, were the least likely to adopt a feature of Chicano English.

In another study demonstrating the influence of social networks in the context of dialect contact, Bayley et al. (2012) compared patterns of overt and null subject pronoun expression (SPP), e.g., *yo/Ø pienso* 'I think', by Mexican-descent speakers and Puerto Ricans in San Antonio, Texas. San Antonio is a majority Latinx city, with most of the Latinx population

TABLE 3.3 Endpoints on the continuum of Norteña and Sureña identity

Name	Norteñas	Sureñas
Color	Red, burgundy	Blue, navy
Language	English	Spanish
Numbers	XIV, 14, 4	XIII, 13, 3
Music	Motown oldies	Banda music
Hairdo	Feathered hair	Vertical ponytail
Makeup	Deep red lipstick	Brown lipstick
Place	Northern Hemisphere	Southern Hemisphere

Source: Reprinted with permission from Mendoza-Denton, 2008, p. 59

originating in northern Mexico. Puerto Ricans, many of whom settled in the city after having spent time at one of the military bases in the area, constitute less than 1 percent of the Latinx population. Nevertheless, despite their rather small numbers, there are a number of Puerto Rican organizations and churches in the city.

The data considered in Bayley et al.'s (2012) study of SPP use by San Antonio Puerto Ricans were collected in 2003 by Latinx graduate students and the results illustrated the importance of considering the details of speaker's social networks and interlocutors when coding sociolinguistic data. In addition to sociolinguistic interviews, speakers completed questionnaires about the people with whom and situations where they spoke Spanish. Additionally, data from nine interviews with San Antonians from Schecter and Bayley's (2002) corpus of Mexican-origin speakers were used for comparison with the Puerto Rican speakers in Bayley et al. (2012). In total, 5,317 tokens were analyzed for a wide range of social and linguistic factors, including 3,919 from the Puerto Rican speakers and 1,398 from the Mexican-origin speakers.

Overall, results of Bayley et al.'s (2012) multivariate analysis were very similar to what other studies have found. SPP variation by both Puerto Rican and Mexican-origin speakers was constrained by the same factor groups including coreference between the overt or null subject and the subject of the preceding tensed verb, as well as person and number, and tense, mood, and aspect. In further analysis, to test the effect of dialect contact, the Puerto Rican speakers were divided into two groups, those whose Spanish-speaking social networks consisted of mostly Mexican Spanish speakers and those whose Spanish-speaking networks primarily or exclusively consisted of other Puerto Ricans. SPP variation was selected because research has shown that Puerto Rican and other Caribbean Spanish speakers tend to choose the overt option at a much higher rate than speakers of Mexican Spanish (Cameron, 1992; Otheguy & Zentella, 2012). The results of this analysis showed that Puerto Ricans with primarily Puerto Rican networks chose the overt option at the same rate as their compatriots in New York or San Juan, while speakers with primarily Mexican Spanish-speaking networks were much closer to the Mexican norm. Table 3.4 illustrates the rates of overt SPP use from a number of different studies.

While Bayley et al.'s (2012) study of Puerto Rican speakers in San Antonio considered only ten speakers and additional research is clearly needed, the results are suggestive of the important role of social networks in variation patterns involving distinctive dialect features, such as the rate of use of overt subject pronouns. First, differences in the rate of overt pronoun use differ from cases of socially stigmatized variables that are widely commented on in Spanish-speaking communities, such as /s/ aspiration and deletion or pleonastic /s/ in 2 sg. preterit, e.g., *dijistes* 'you said', instead of standard

TABLE 3.4 Use of overt SPPs in Puerto Rican and Mexican-American Spanish

Variety	% overt pronoun
Caribbean newcomers in New York City (Otheguy et al., 2007)	36
Caribbean longer-term residents in New York City (Otheguy et al., 2007)	42
San Juan (Cameron, 1992)	45
New York City Puerto Rican (Flores-Ferrán, 2004)	45
San Antonio Puerto Ricans (Puerto Rican network) (Bayley et al., 2012)	45
San Antonio Puerto Ricans (Mexican network) (Bayley et al., 2012)	23
San Antonio Mexican-background speakers (Bayley et al., 2012)	27
Mexican immigrants in New Jersey (Flores-Ferrán, 2007)	24
Los Angeles Mexican immigrant and Chicano adults (Silva-Corvalán, 1994)	28

Source: Reprinted with permission from Bayley et al., 2012, p. 57

dijiste (Zentella, 2007). That is, although excessive use of overt pronouns may violate expectations and norms of usage and nonuse may occasionally result in ambiguity, use or nonuse of an overt pronoun does not make any particular utterance ungrammatical. Second, although some studies of SPPs in Spanish have shown age and gender effects (see e.g., Orozco & Hurtado, 2021; Shin & Otheguy, 2013), these studies have not identified any consistent social constraints, unlike, for example, variable /s/ aspiration and deletion. In addition, all of the Puerto Rican speakers in Bayley et al. (2012) were fully proficient in English and thus presumably subject to the same degree of influence from English grammar. Although the speakers who had converged with the Mexican norm of overt SPP usage regularly used both English and Spanish in their professional lives, their use of at least one Spanish sociolinguistic variable, overt subject pronouns, appears to have been influenced by the dialect of the Spanish speakers with whom they interacted in that language. That is, the Puerto Rican Spanish speakers with primarily Mexican Spanish-speaking social networks used far fewer overt pronouns in Spanish than is typical of speakers examined in other studies of Puerto Rican Spanish.

A further example of the role of social networks and individual aspirations in influencing speakers' choices among linguistic variants can be seen in Bayley and Holland's (2014) study of variation in final /z/ devoicing, e.g., bɔɪz —> bɔɪs, by 13 Latinx adolescents and young adults living in a public housing project in San Antonio, Texas. Frequent devoicing of /z/ is a feature of many varieties of English, including Maori English in New

Zealand (Holmes, 2007), Jewish English in Michigan (Knack, 1991), and English in northwestern Indiana (José, 2010). Syllable and word final devoicing of fricatives is also common in many languages other than English including German, where syllable final devoicing is obligatory, and European Portuguese, Dutch, Polish, and Russian (Jesus & Shadle, 2002; Wetzels & Mascaro, 2001). In Mexican-American speech, /z/ devoicing has sometimes been attributed to interference from Spanish (e.g., Thompson, 1975), where [z] is simply an allophone of /s/ before voiced consonants (Hualde, 2003).

Like the surrounding community, the residents of the housing project, "Buena Vista Courts" (a pseudonym), examined in Bayley and Holland (2014), were overwhelmingly of Mexican origin, although owing to requirements for residence in public housing, all were US citizens or permanent residents. Data for the project were collected in sociolinguistic interviews conducted by Latinx graduate students in 1991–1993. Speakers, all of whom were bilingual to some degree, were allowed to speak in whichever language they wished, and the interviews contain numerous examples of code-switching. During interviews, speakers were asked in detail about the people they socialized with and to name a person whom they admired. Based on the responses to these questions, Bayley and Holland created a binary factor group, social orientation, i.e., whether speakers were oriented toward life in the "Courts" or whether they aspired to escape the very difficult conditions in which they lived. This factor group proved to be statistically significant in a logistic regression analysis, with speakers whose social contacts and aspirations were limited to life in the Courts much more likely to choose the devoiced variant (51.2 percent) than speakers who were outwardly oriented. As the data from four participants shown in Table 3.5 illustrates, the differences could be very dramatic.

Thirteen-year-old Alicia, for example, who demonstrated a high level of final /z/ devoicing (57 percent), had recently returned to San Antonio after having run away to Dallas with her boyfriend, where they were both

TABLE 3.5 The effect on (z)-devoicing of individual orientation to the Courts: four speakers

Speaker	Orientation	% final /z/ devoicing
Alicia	Courts	57.0
Don	Courts	69.8
Bettina	External	25.0
Keith	External	22.8
All speakers		39.1

Source: Adapted from Bayley & Holland, 2014

involved in various illegal activities. She was not attending school when we met her. Similarly, Don was fully immersed in the life of the Courts. During his entire interview, he did not produce a single sentence entirely in either English or Spanish. Rather, every sentence contained at least one word or phrase from the other language.

The speakers who were less oriented toward the life of the Courts, Bettina and Keith, were remarkably different. When asked about a person she admired, Bettina, for example, named her cousin, who had been in a gang, but after being beaten out, had managed to repair his life. At the time, her cousin was an engineering student at a major Texas university. Keith had more contacts outside of the Courts than any of the other speakers in the study. He had recently returned to Buena Vista Courts after having been through basic training in the Army reserve and was attending a local community college. Keith had an Anglo girlfriend whose father was giving him golf lessons on a course in a more prosperous area of town.

The data collected in the Buena Vista Courts and examined in Bayley and Holland (2014), including Spanish data, have been used in other studies (Bayley, 1994, 1997), and overall, speakers with a greater orientation towards the life and culture of the Courts use more vernacular variants.

Conclusion

As demonstrated by the research described in this chapter, SNA has proven to be a useful analytic tool in a variety of bi- and multilingual contexts, at both the macro level of language choice and the micro level of choice among different variants of sociolinguistic variables. This is not to say, however, that social networks can substitute for the other social factors such as class, age, and gender, among others, that influence speakers' choices of linguistic code or between variable forms. Rather, as the examples in this chapter indicate, examination of social networks can explain differences in speakers' choices even when many of the other factors that sociolinguists have long considered influential remain constant. For example, all the children on *el bloque* followed by Zentella (1997) belonged to the same social class. However, as Zentella's research showed, their linguistic choices turned out to be quite different as they grew into young adulthood. Similarly, the brother and sister who participated in the study by Wolfram et al. (2004) grew up in the same household with Mexican immigrant parents and attended the same schools. However, as their adoption of Southern lexical features and rates of use of monophthongal /ai/ indicate, they adopted very different dialects of their second language, owing in part to the different social networks that they participated in (or aspired to participate in).

Additionally, at the macro level of language choice, strong network ties can provide frequent occasions for minority language use as well as pressure to use the minority language. Weak network ties, if extensive, can also provide a variety of contexts for minority language use and opportunities for speakers to be exposed to and use the language in different registers.

The studies examined in this chapter represent only a small selection of studies in bilingual communities that have considered participants' social networks, whether explicitly or implicitly. As the studies discussed in this and the previous chapter have shown, people tend to speak like the people they speak with on a regular basis. Given that basic fact, and given the overall utility of SNA in documenting speakers' most frequent or important interlocutors, we suggest that SNA can provide a valuable tool in understanding the patterns of variation that we observe in both monolingual and bi-/multilingual communities, particularly when individual patterns diverge from what seems to be the community norm. In the following chapters, we turn to a more detailed discussion of the role of SNA in second language acquisition, using a variety of model studies to illustrate the different approaches that researchers have employed.

4

SOCIAL NETWORK ANALYSIS AND THEORIES OF SECOND LANGUAGE ACQUISITION

Introduction

Chapters 2 and 3 demonstrate that social network analysis (SNA) has been effectively used to examine the maintenance of nonstandard dialectal features in various first language (L1) speech communities (Dodsworth & Benton, 2020; Edwards, 1992; Lippi-Green, 1989; Milroy & Milroy, 1978). Additionally, SNA has been widely used to analyze language use in bilingual (Gal, 1979; W. Li, 1994; Zentella, 1997, 2007) and migrant communities (Bayley et al., 2012; Lanza & Svendsen 2007; Matsumoto & Britain, 2009) where language contact, multilingualism, and patterns of language choice based on cultural, social, and political affiliations serve to distinguish different networks of speakers within a wider geographic region.

As mentioned in Chapter 2, some scholars, such as Labov (2001), have questioned the central role of social networks in explaining patterns of language change or the preservation of vernacular norms; however, it is not clear that the same objections apply to the role of social networks in second language acquisition (SLA) research, particularly in study abroad (SA) and other immersion contexts. It is well established, for example, that second language (L2) learners need substantial comprehensible input as well as opportunities for output to fully acquire a second language (Swain, 1995, 2000, 2005). It is also well established, going back to Schumann's (1978) study of Alberto, that L2 learners who lack opportunities to interact with speakers of the target language (TL) make little progress in acquisition. Finally, it is well known that classrooms tend to be relatively formal environments (Tarone & Swain, 1995), and that teachers tend to

DOI: 10.4324/9781003174448-4

use fewer vernacular forms when teaching than other native speakers of the language (X. Li, 2010; Mougeon et al., 2010).

The paucity of vernacular features in classroom input suggests that learners need opportunities to interact informally with TL speakers in a range of contexts if they are to acquire the ability to style shift, as has been shown, for example, in studies of the L2 acquisition of informal variants in Canadian and hexagonal French (e.g., Mougeon et al., 2010; Nagy et al., 2003; Regan et al., 2009). Moreover, the social network strength indices (Milroy & Milroy, 1978) that scholars such as Kennedy (2012) and Kennedy Terry (2017, 2022a, 2022b) and Pozzi and Bayley (2021) have adapted to the L2 learning context provide a means to measure the informal interactions that research has shown are necessary for the acquisition of registers that extend beyond the classroom. This is particularly true in studies of L2 acquisition during SA, where issues of class are far less relevant than in studies of language variation and change (LVC), in part because most students with the resources to participate in such programs are relatively privileged and because students in SA programs are not as deeply embedded in the web of relationships found in L1 communities such as those studied by Labov (2001) and Marshall (2004).

Before turning our attention to the application of SNA to L2 acquisition, it is important to establish a clear relationship between SNA and current theories of SLA. Specifically, this chapter considers how SLA theory informs and motivates SNA and how SNA research advances our understanding of the interpersonal and relational aspects of SLA. To facilitate this examination, we make reference to Model Studies 1–16 in the current chapter, although these studies are not formally presented until Chapter 5. To be clear, this chapter does not seek to provide a comprehensive review of current SLA theory, which would be beyond the scope of a single chapter. Instead, we make specific references to Model Studies 1–16 that form the basis of our analyses in Chapters 5–9 and that provide a useful framework for examining the intersections between SLA theory and applications of SNA and related frameworks.

Understanding L2 Participation in Target-Language Social Networks

Acculturation to the Target Culture

Schumann's (1978) acculturation model provides a convenient starting point for an examination of how SLA theory both informs and motivates the incorporation of SNA in studies of L2 acquisition. Schumann defined acculturation as "the social and psychological integration of the learner with the target-language (TL) group" (p. 29) and distinguished two types of acculturation. In the first type, the learner is sufficiently integrated in the TL group so that TL input becomes intake. In the second type, the learner has the first type of acculturation, but also regards the TL group as a reference group and seeks to acquire their lifestyle and values. Schumann argued that both types of acculturation lead to higher levels of L2 acquisition.

Schumann (1978) further proposed that during the acquisition period, L2 learners pass through various stages of interlanguage that resemble pidgin languages in that they both generally lack morphological inflection and syntactic variety. Schumann drew comparisons between a lack of acculturation in SLA and the process of pidginization that occurs when speakers of different languages come into contact and need to communicate with each other in a limited fashion. Schumann argued that just as pidginization occurs due to lack of acculturation and access to the superstrate language, lack of development in SLA is caused by lack of acculturation.

In one of the earliest applications of SNA to the L2 learning context, Model Study 1 by Lybeck (2002) operationalized Schumann's (1978) acculturation model to predict acquisition patterns in L2 Norwegian pronunciation. Lybeck demonstrated that learners who achieved higher levels of acculturation through their social networks with Norwegians also achieved more target-like pronunciation in L2 Norwegian. In this study, Lybeck combined Schumann's concepts of *social distance* (pertaining to the learner's membership in a different social group that speaks a different language from the target culture) and *psychological distance* (pertaining to the learner's status as an individual separate from other individuals, regardless of the social group) into one measure of *cultural distance* that could be used to assess the levels of acculturation among the learners in her study. Additionally, Lybeck noted that Schumann's acculturation model ignored the role that members of the target culture play in the acculturation process, only "sometimes including the target culture's reactions to the learner group" (2002, p. 175). Lybeck proposed that incorporating the impact of reactions by target culture members to the learner is essential to understanding the acculturation process. For example, she noted the Norwegian tendency to associate "sameness" with equality, as well as the avoidance of contact with people who are different from the target culture, and argued that these qualities would undoubtedly render acculturation by L1 English speakers into Norwegian culture more difficult.

Finally, Lybeck (2002) explained that one primary drawback of Schumann's (1978) acculturation model is the lack of a tool that can be used to quantitatively measure acculturation and correlate it with L2 acquisition. Lybeck thus incorporated social network theory (L. Milroy, 1987) into the acculturation model in order to fill this gap and to differentiate learners who are able to create and maintain exchange-based networks with L1 Norwegian speakers from those who maintain only interactive ties with L1 Norwegian speakers (see Chapter 2 for an explanation of various types of network ties). Lybeck argued that differentiation based on the type of network ties is especially important to the acculturation process in L2 Norwegian because Norwegian culture is characterized by "encouraging long-term group memberships and reducing the space for the entrance of outsiders, particularly foreigners" (2002, p. 177). Lybeck thus hypothesized that only those learners who could forge exchange-based ties within Norwegian society would achieve high levels of acculturation and high levels of target-like linguistic performance.

Motivation and Investment in the Target Language

Embedded in Schumann's (1978) acculturation model are a number of social and psychological (i.e., affective) factors that are likely to influence a learner's level of acculturation in the TL culture. For example, Schumann argued that social dominance patterns may determine acculturation whereby a politically and economically dominant group, such as French speakers residing in Tunisia, will tend not to learn the TL. Similarly, a socially dominated group with great social distance from the TL group, such as Native Americans in the United States, will also tend not to learn the TL. Schumann further argued that contact between equal groups usually facilitates acculturation, as does assimilation by the learner group to the TL lifestyle and the sharing of public facilities such as schools and churches (referred to as *low enclosure*). Other social factors include the *cohesiveness* of the learner group, the *congruence* between the two groups, the *attitudes* of the groups toward each other, and the *intended length of residence* of the learner group. Many of the social factors that form part of Schumann's acculturation model are key contributors to the patterns of language variation and social network formation in the L1 and multilingual language communities described in Chapters 2 and 3. Additionally, a small number of the Model Studies described in Chapters 5–9 examine entire groups of L2 learners (e.g., Carhill-Poza, 2015; Hasegawa, 2019; Wiklund, 2002) where social factors operating at a group-level are likely to impact the level of acculturation to the TL culture and, consequently, the types of social networks that learners create and maintain in the TL environment.

The majority of the Model Studies described in Chapters 5–9 focus on L2 learners in a SA context, where the learners arrive as a group, but generally form social networks with TL speakers through their individual experiences. In the case of adult learners during SA, the affective factors described in Schumann's (1978) acculturation model, such as *language shock* and *culture shock*, *motivation*, and *ego-permeability*, contribute to the creation of psychological distance between the learner and the TL group and are relevant to much of the research featured in Chapters 5–9. For example, in discussing language shock, Schumann explained that while an adult learner may wish to speak the new language, they may also fear being ridiculed, but the child learner generally does not share this fear. Similarly, while an adult learner worries whether their language accurately reflects their ideas, the child does not and is willing to take risks and even form new words. While the adult takes pride in their native language, and may not receive similar gratification in the L2, the child learner does not. Additionally, Schumann described culture shock as the disorientation and anxiety related to navigating a new culture which may result in the learner being unable to focus on learning the new language. Schumann further explained that lower ego-permeability (Guiora et al., 1972) leads to higher levels of language learning, where the language ego refers to a learner's understanding of the boundaries of their language ability.

Motivation is another affective factor that has been the subject of much research in SLA, including Schumann (1978), and supports the application of SNA to SLA. For example, Model Study 2 by Isabelli-García (2006) explored how motivation, attitude, and investment impacted the social networks that four L2 Spanish learners created with TL speakers during SA in Argentina and hypothesized that dense networks with other L1 English speakers would prevent L2 acquisition and networks with TL speakers would facilitate L2 acquisition. Specifically, Isabelli-García's (2006) study incorporated theories of motivational orientation toward L2 acquisition, such as whether the learner possesses *extrinsic* or *intrinsic* motivation (Dörnyei, 2001), where intrinsic motivation relates to a learner's curiosity and excitement about the TL and the TL culture and extrinsic motivation relates to the pursuit of external rewards or the avoidance of a negative consequence. Isabelli-García further explained that *instrumental* motivation (Gardner & Lambert, 1959; Gardner & MacIntyre, 1991), such as the pursuit of learning in order to achieve a professional goal, or *integrative* motivation (Gardner, 1985; Gardner & Lambert, 1959), relating to a learner's desire to align with and join the TL group, can have a strong influence over the learner's efforts to create and maintain social networks with TL speakers during SA. The qualitative and social network data from Isabelli-García's study demonstrated a link between the learner's success in integrating into social networks and their ongoing motivation to learn the TL which supports the assertion that "there is a conduit between motivation and language acquisition in the SA context, which is interaction in social networks" (Isabelli-García, 2006, p. 255).

In addition to theories of motivational orientation, Model Study 2 by Isabelli-García (2006) incorporated Norton Peirce's (1995) concept of 'investment' to describe how language learners are motivated, or not motivated, to invest time and energy into learning the TL because they seek the social and material benefits associated with speaking the TL. According to Norton Peirce's theory of investment, L2 learners create and maintain a social identity in the L2 because this identity facilitates their full participation in the TL culture and community. Norton Peirce argued that because of the artificial separation between the individual and the social factors contributing to SLA, researchers have not yet "developed a comprehensive theory of social identity that integrates the language learner and the language learning context" (1995, p. 12) and most importantly, researchers have not adequately considered how relations of power affect interactions between L2 and TL speakers. Norton Peirce argued that access to the TL has always been considered available to any learner who is motivated enough to seek it out; however, this concept of motivation in language learning does not consider that in situations of inequitable power relations between L2 learners and TL speakers, L2 learners may have difficulty gaining access to TL interactions and the "powerful social networks that offer the learner the opportunity to speak (Heller, 1987)" (Norton Peirce, 1995, p. 13).

Norton Peirce's (1995) theory of investment in L2 learning draws heavily on the work of Weedon (1987) who argued that identity is subjective and is constructed through the social world, specifically through the power relations that determine the opportunities available to the individual in life. Norton Peirce contrasted motivation, which is controlled by the individual, with investment, a concept that captures the relationship of the learner to the social world and considers how the learner forms her identity by investing herself in the TL. Norton Peirce based her theory of investment on the work of Bourdieu (1977) who maintained that language is a form of 'cultural capital' and that some cultural capital is more valuable in certain social settings. Norton Peirce's theory of investment views the learner as investing in the TL with the expectation of attaining symbolic and material resources which will "in turn increase their cultural capital" (1995, p. 17).

L2 Social Identity

Central to Schumann's (1978) acculturation model, Gardner and Lambert's (1959) theory of integrative motivational orientation, and Norton Peirce's (1995) concept of investment, is the idea that language learners construct an L2 social identity through their ongoing use of the L2, and that this identity is not constructed individually, but is co-constructed with the TL speakers with whom they interact. It is precisely at this point that social network analysis and theories of acculturation, motivation, and investment intersect: the co-construction of L2 identity.

Mendoza-Denton (2002) described identity as "the individual's relationship with larger social constructs, in so far as this negotiation is signaled through language and other semiotic means" (2002, p. 475) and explained that early studies in LVC (e.g., Labov, 1966, 1972a) stratified speakers based on pre-defined socio-demographic categories such as age, gender, social class, and ethnicity. These types of predefined categories, or speaker identities, allowed the researcher to cover a large number of participants via random sampling with a view to illuminating the systematicity and statistical representativeness of variation. Mendoza-Denton (2002) explained that later variationist studies focused on 'practice-based identity' or the identity or identities that speakers create through the joint participation in particular activities. For example, the 'acts of identity' framework established by LePage and Tabouret-Keller (1985) argued that "individual users of language strategically deploy linguistic resources to affiliate themselves with groups with which they want to be identified, or to distinguish themselves from groups with which they do not want to be identified" (2002, p. 487). Mendoza-Denton (2002) further explained that the ability to affiliate oneself with a particular group is predicated upon the speaker's ability to: (1) identify the group; (2) gain access to the group and analyze its behavior; (3) be strongly motivated to join the group (which may be reinforced or reversed by feedback from the group); and (4) modify one's behavior.

Mendoza-Denton (2002) argued that through the 'acts of identity' framework, researchers are able to understand 'practice-shaping' processes that engender linguistic consequences and that allow for comparison of such processes across various settings. In this way, the 'acts of identity' framework may be applied to the study of L2 acquisition through SNA. Similar to the construction of identity by L1 speakers, L2 speakers wishing to affiliate themselves with the TL group must gain access to the group, analyze TL behavior, be motivated to join the TL group, and be able to modify their behavior to align with that of TL speakers. In their interactions with the TL speakers in their social networks, L2 learners engage in 'practice-shaping processes', the linguistic consequences of which may be L2 acquisition and target-like speech. A number of the Model Studies described in Chapters 5–9 incorporate theories of L2 social identity construction through their social networks with TL speakers, including Model Study 3 (LANGSNAP project; Mitchell et al., 2017), Model Study 8 (C. Li et al., 2021), Model Study 10 (Diao, 2017), and Model Study 15 (Kurata, 2010, 2021).

Social Networks and the Co-construction of L2 Development

Sociocultural Theory and Social Network Analysis in SLA

Sociocultural theory (SCT; Vygotsky, 1978) supports the application of SNA to SLA where L2 acquisition develops through social interactions with TL speakers who form a supportive network around the learner and provide the necessary 'scaffolding' (Wood et al., 1976) for learning. Lantolf (2000) explained that a sociocultural approach to language acquisition posits that human language serves as a symbolic tool, among others, that is used to "mediate and regulate our relationships with others and with ourselves" (p. 80). Like other symbolic tools such as numbering systems, music, and art, the Vygotskian or 'neoVygotskian' perspective assumes that language mediates human mental activity by providing a mechanism for humans to evaluate the surrounding environment, organize information, formulate plans, and solve problems (Mitchell et al., 2019, p. 287). Additionally, drawing on the work of Mercer and Howe (2012), Mitchell et al. (2019) explained that SCT assumes that the overall learning process is also mediated by symbolic tools and semiotic systems, such as language, and that learning relies on social interaction and "shared processes such as joint problem-solving and discussion, with experts, mentors, and peers" (p. 288).

In SCT, social interactions and shared processes are viewed as being central to a child's cultural development, or learning, which Vygotsky believed developed initially at a social level and later at an individual level, or "first between people (interpsychological) and then inside the child (intrapsychological)" (Vygotsky, 1978, p. 57). The internalization of learning thus relies on the child having access to the cultural artifacts of their community through ongoing social interactions with the more experienced members of this community (e.g., parents, caregivers, teachers). SCT posits that learning is not simply transmitted from expert to novice (i.e., parent to child), but is instead 'co-constructed' during their social interactions. The most favorable conditions for such learning to occur is in the Zone of Proximal Development (ZPD, Vygotsky, 1978, p. 85), which represents the gap between what the child can do or understand independently and what they can do or understand with the guidance of a more experienced adult or peer.

In L2 acquisition, social networks with TL speakers provide a dynamic ZPD to learners, especially when these TL speakers are willing and able to adapt their language to meet the needs of the learner. That is, in ongoing relationships between L2 learners and TL speakers, the ZPD can be thought of as constantly adjusting and expanding as the learner moves from needing more to less assistance, or scaffolding, in the L2. The flexibility that exists within social networks thus differs greatly from the interactions that a learner might have with a casual acquaintance or in an isolated service encounter where the learner is not operating in the ZPD often because of a mismatch between their current abilities and the TL speaker's language. Moreover, the TL speakers in the learner's network who serve as experts in the collaborative L2 development process can provide feedback that is sensitive to the learner's evolving ZPD because of their ongoing relationship with the learner and their knowledge of the learner's abilities. Through this tailored scaffolding, learners are more likely to engage in "microgenesis" (Lantolf & Thorne, 2006, p. 52), which represents the internalization of co-constructed, locally relevant, cultural and linguistic knowledge of the type that is not often available in the language classroom. Finally, social networks have the potential to provide a constantly changing array of cultural artifacts for mediation through the L2 (e.g., varied speech contexts, interlocutors, conversation topics), which allows for continual and dynamic L2 development.

Many of the Model Studies described in Chapters 5–9 draw on SCT, either implicitly or explicitly, to motivate the application of SNA to the L2 context. For example, Model Study 12 by Carhill-Poza (2015) used SCT to support the application of an 'ecological perspective' to L2 development in a secondary-school setting where peer groups, among others, are seen as direct and important influences on language learning opportunities and outcomes. Similarly. Model Study 13 by Wiklund (2002) incorporated interactions with TL speakers, as well as interactions with the learner's own ethnic group and other ethnic groups, into the overall calculation of social network density to understand the impact of network composition on L2 verbal sophistication among Swedish secondary-school students. Wiklund's social network assessment also incorporated 'nuancing' for participation in different activities such as religion, sports, and artistic activities in order to reflect how participation in varied language learning contexts might influence opportunities for L2 use and development.

Additionally, studies such as Dewey et al. (2012), Kennedy Terry (2017, 2022a, 2022b), Pozzi (2021) and Pozzi and Bayley (2021), Model Studies 4, 6, and 7, respectively, used quantitative measurements to assess the strength and breadth of learners' social networks with TL speakers (i.e., network density, multiplexity, intensity, and frequency) and hypothesized that social networks with TL speakers would be the locus of valuable knowledge co-construction. The results of Model Studies 4, 6, and 7 support this hypothesis. Moreover, research that specifically incorporates measures of density among the TL speakers within the network (e.g., Model Study 6 by Kennedy Terry, 2017, 2022a, 2022b) or interactions through second-order network ties (e.g., Model Study 2 by Isabelli-García,

2006) also implicitly incorporate the concept of the learner's evolving ZPD into their research. In these studies, it was hypothesized that learners who interacted with multiple TL speakers at the same time, or who had second-order network ties with TL speakers, would develop the additional skills needed to participate in group TL interactions, which can be viewed as an expansion of the learner's ZPD. It is also in these social interactions with multiple TL speakers that learners would be expected to encounter more informal and situationally-specific linguistic forms.

Language Socialization and Communities of Practice

Language socialization theory in L1 acquisition draws heavily on the ethnographic research of Ochs (1988), Schieffelin (1990), and Heath (1982, 1983) whose research demonstrates that language and culture are acquired simultaneously throughout childhood. Ochs (1988) argued that children acquire linguistic knowledge at the same time that they acquire sociocultural knowledge because linguistic "meanings and functions are to a large extent socioculturally organized" (1988, p. 14). Schieffelin and Ochs (1986) referred to this process as "socialization to use language" (p. 163). At the same time, Ochs (1988) explained that as children use language, they acquire "understandings of the social organization of everyday life, cultural ideologies, moral values, and structures of knowledge and interpretation" (1988, p. 14). Thus, children are not only socialized into using the language(s) of their speech community, but they are also socialized "through the use of language" (Schieffelin & Ochs, 1986, p. 163).

Watson-Gegeo and Nielsen (2003) explained that like the child acquiring her L1, an adult (or other) L2 learner acquires language that is necessarily constrained by cultural and situational influences that create and shape the language learning context. The authors explained that "there is no context-free language learning", including the context of a foreign or second language classroom, because "all communicative contexts involve social, cultural, and political dimensions affecting which linguistic forms are available or taught and how they are represented" (Watson-Gegeo & Nielsen, 2003, p. 157). Just as the process of socialization impacts the available linguistic forms and the context in which they are acquired, the language itself exerts an influence over the socialization process in both L1 and L2 socialization (see also Bayley & Schecter, 2003 for an overview of socialization in bi- and multilingual communities).

Like children who acquire cultural norms by participating in "linguistically marked events" (Watson-Gegeo & Nielsen, 2003, p. 158) with members of their L1 community, L2 learners also acquire linguistic and cultural knowledge simultaneously through their interactions in the TL with TL speakers. Thus, the application of SNA to L2 acquisition may be considered a logical extension of language socialization theory in SLA in which language learners gain access to socially and culturally appropriate language use through their social networks with TL speakers. A number of the Model Studies described in Chapters 5–9 draw heavily on language socialization theory to motivate the application of SNA to understand L2 development during SA. These include Model Study 9 by Kinginger and Carnine (2019), Model Study 10 by Diao (2017), and Model Study 11 by Hasegawa (2019).

The 'community of practice' (CoP) framework (Lave & Wenger, 1991) provides a useful means for understanding the process of language socialization through participation in group activities and shared outcomes, or "engagement in a matrix of interrelated social practices" (Meyerhoff & Strycharz, 2013, p. 428). In the CoP framework, inexperienced newcomers initially join the group as nonparticipants, or observers, and then engage in what Lave and Wenger (1991) called 'legitimate peripheral participation' where they are assisted by more experienced members of the group. Through continual interaction with 'expert' members of the group, and by assuming new and varied roles within the CoP, the newcomers eventually develop the necessary skills to become full participants in the shared pursuit of group goals.

Meyerhoff and Strycharz explained that the CoP is essentially a "domain defined by a process of social learning" (2013, p. 430) and because of this, it shares important similarities with social network theory and the concept of the speech community. At the same time, Meyerhoff and Strycharz emphasized that the original conception of the CoP included the following defining elements (Wenger, 1998): (1) there is *mutual engagement* of the CofP members (i.e., they come together for a specific purpose); (2) there is a *jointly negotiated enterprise* (i.e., the purpose of coming together is to engage in a shared 'practice'); and (3) there is a *shared repertoire* used by the CoP (i.e., the members of the CoP use linguistic, and other, resources in a way that differentiates them from other groups).

As explained by Meyerhoff and Strycharz (2013), the defining element of the CoP is the emphasis on 'practices', or "way[s] of doing things ... grounded in and shared by a community" (Eckert & Wenger, 2005, p. 583). Because these practices necessarily include linguistic resources, it is easy to see why the CoP framework has been adopted in studies of LVC that examine the stylistic choices that speakers make based on their CoP affiliations (Eckert, 2000; Mendoza-Denton, 2008). According to Eckert (2005), speakers create new patterns of linguistic variation within the CoP, and new form-meaning associations through the use of speech style, to index "stances, activities, [and] characteristics" (2005, p. 30).

Just as the CoP framework has provided a meaningful lens through which to examine stylistic variation among groups of L1 speakers, it has also been adopted by researchers working in SLA. A number of the Model Studies discussed in Chapters 5–9 combine the CoP framework with elements of SNA to motivate their analyses of L2 development during SA (Model Study 11 by Hasegawa, 2019), in the home-country context (Model Study 16 by Palfreyman, 2021), and in the host-country learning context (Model Study 14 by Bernstein, 2018). Both Palfreyman (2021) and Bernstein (2018) draw on an adapted version of the CoP, the Individual Network of Practice (INoP) proposed by Zappa-Hollman and Duff (2015), which specifically combines elements of social network theory (i.e., a focus on relationships) and elements of the CoP framework (i.e., a focus on shared practices). According to Zappa-Hollman and Duff (2015), an INoP draws on the concept of the Network of Practice (NoP, Brown, & Duguid, 2001), but is "more attuned to each individual's personal relationships within or beyond a social group, community, or institution" and "denotes all the social ties reported by a given individual, however weak/distant or strong/close, as relevant to the phenomenon under study" (2015, p. 339). In their own research, Zappa-Hollman and Duff (2015) used the INoP framework to examine patterns of language and academic socialization by a group of university students from Mexico during SA in Canada. Similarly, Model Study 16 by Palfreyman (2021) adopted the INoP framework to analyze the role of informal language learning networks in L2 English development among female Emirati university students in Dubai.

Model Study 14 by Bernstein (2018) proposed the Participation in Networks of Practice (P-NoP) framework that incorporates elements of both the NoP (Brown & Duguid, 2001), a framework that uses a whole network approach, and the INoP (Zappa-Hollman & Duff, 2015), a framework that uses an egocentric network approach. Specifically, Bernstein applied the P-NoP framework to examine "how a learner becomes part of a network of practice, how she becomes situated, however temporarily, in a particular place within that network, and how her position allows for particular kinds of participation" (2018, p. 809). What is unique about Model Study 14 by Bernstein (2018) is that it engages in the 'layering' of multiple theoretical perspectives (King & Mackey, 2016) to understand both the *process* through which a learner accesses opportunities for interaction in the L2 (using the P-NoP framework), but also the *products*, or the linguistic outcomes, of these opportunities for interaction. Model Study 14 by Bernstein (2018) thus provides an apt transition into the following section, which examines how theories of input and interaction inform and support the application of SNA in SLA.

Opportunities for Input, Output, and Interaction

Emergentist Theories of L2 Acquisition

This section considers how SNA aligns with theories of L2 acquisition that emphasize the critical role of input, output, and interaction in SLA. According to Mitchell et al. (2019), these 'emergentist' perspectives incorporate a number of usage- and frequency-based theories of language acquisition, construction grammar, and connectionism and posit that L2 learners rely on general learning mechanisms "in order to extract structure and patterns from the language input they are exposed to" (2019, p. 129), rather than on an innate language faculty such as Universal Grammar (UG; Chomsky, 1981). Because emergentist theories of L2 acquisition focus specifically on the linguistic environment of the learner, including the available linguistic input and the opportunities for interaction, feedback, and the co-creation of meaning, these approaches underscore the critical role of social networks in L2 acquisition—for it is within the bounds of these social networks that the learner's primary linguistic environment is created.

The Central Role of L2 Input and Output

When language learners create relationships with TL speakers, either by establishing first-order network ties (direct relationships) or second-order network ties (indirect, friend-of-a-friend network ties, see Chapter 2), they increase their potential access to two essential elements of both L1 and L2 acquisition: input and interaction. The central role of 'comprehensible input' in SLA was established in Krashen's (1985) Input Hypothesis, which argued that learners need only to be exposed to large amounts of linguistic input that is slightly more complex than their current level of linguistic competence in order to develop proficiency in the L2. More specifically, Krashen posited that the learner's linguistic environment needs to contain both input that allows the learner to comprehend the meaning and the general structure of the discourse, and enough new linguistic information that it prompts the learner to continually engage in the analysis of novel and more complex forms and structures. This specific combination of both familiar and unfamiliar linguistic information, in quantities that allow for both comprehension and development, is what Krashen deemed 'comprehensible input', or '$i + 1$' where i represents the learner's current level of comprehension.

The Central Role of L2 Input and Output

Krashen's (1985) Input Hypothesis further posited that through access to comprehensible input, the learner would deduce the rules of the L2 grammar and thus, these rules would not need to be taught explicitly in the language classroom. Gass (2003) provides a helpful explanation of how a language learner might deduce the rules of the L1 or L2 grammar from the various types of evidence available in the linguistic environment: positive evidence, negative evidence, and indirect negative evidence. Gass explained that positive evidence refers to the models of language available in the linguistic environment, "the set of well-formed sentences to which learners are exposed" (2003, p. 225). Gass further explained that in interactions with TL speakers, learners are also exposed to direct negative evidence. This direct negative evidence may be explicit, such as an overt correction of an ungrammatical form, or implicit, such as when a TL speaker does not understand the learner and requests clarification or provides a recast of the learner's utterance. Gass (2003) pointed out that indirect negative evidence, such as the absence of a particular form in the linguistic environment, also serves as a type of 'input' to the learner's developing grammar.

While Krashen's Input Hypothesis was highly influential among language teachers, it failed to consider the crucial role of learner output in acquisition. Moreover, it left a number of questions unanswered, such as how to determine if input is optimally comprehensible and how to verify the link between comprehensible input and L2 development. The research of Swain (1985, 1995) and Swain and Lapkin (1995, 1998) on students enrolled in English/French immersion programs in Canada argued for the critical role of output, in addition to input, in L2 development. Swain (1995) explained that "Output may stimulate learners to move from the semantic, open-ended, nondeterministic strategic processing prevalent in comprehension to the complete grammatical processing needed for accurate production" (1995, p. 128). Gass (2003) further argued that in addition to improving grammatical processing and providing opportunities for learners to receive feedback, the creation of output also allows learners to test hypotheses about the L2 (i.e., whether a particular form or structure is viable) and to develop automaticity which leads to greater L2 fluency.

It should be clear from the above discussion how research applying SNA to the L2 learning context draws heavily on SLA theory that argues for the critical role of L2 input and the production of L2 output in L2 development. That is, through their social networks with TL speakers,

L2 learners would be expected to have access to both higher levels of comprehensible and meaning-bearing (Lee & VanPatten, 2003) input, as well as increased opportunities for the creation of L2 output. It would also be expected that through their social networks with TL speakers, learners would be exposed to higher levels of both positive and negative evidence, as well as more plentiful opportunities to test hypotheses about the TL and to receive both implicit and explicit forms of corrective feedback that could potentially result in *uptake* (Lyster, 1998; Lyster & Ranta, 1997), which refers to the incorporation of feedback by the learner into their developing L2 grammar.

The Interaction Hypothesis

The Interaction Hypothesis (Long, 1980, 1996) proposed that collaborative conversational efforts and tactics such as repetitions, comprehension checks, and clarification requests are critical to the creation of comprehensible input that is essential for L2 acquisition. Long (1996) explained that such *negotiation for meaning*, and the *interactional* adjustments made by the TL speaker for the benefit of the learner, "facilitates acquisition because it connects input, internal learner capacities, particularly selective attention, and output in productive ways" (1996, pp. 451–452). Gass (2003) further explained that through negotiation for meaning, the learner has the opportunity to compare their own language with that of the TL speaker and to identify discrepancies between the two. Negotiation for meaning also draws the learner's attention to elements of the TL that they may not have any prior knowledge about. Gass noted that learning may occur within the interaction, as it unfolds, or learning may occur at a later point, with the interaction having served as a 'priming device' (Gass, 1997).

Long's (1980, 1996) Interaction Hypothesis thus motivates the role of social networks with TL speakers in L2 acquisition based on the expectation that the TL-speaking members of the learner's network will provide higher levels of comprehensible input than what the learner is exposed to outside of the social network and that the learner will gain access to increased opportunities to participate in the negotiation for meaning from this input. Moreover, as explained by Gass (2003), it would be expected that conversations with the TL speakers in their social networks would provide learners with increased opportunities to receive negative evidence, in the form of explicit corrections or recasts, as well as increased opportunities for producing output in the L2.

The majority of the Model Studies described in Chapters 5–9 emphasize the important role that social networks play in offering learners increased opportunities to be exposed to comprehensible input in the TL, to participate in negotiation for meaning with TL speakers, and to create output in the TL. These studies include: Model Study 3 by Mitchell et al. (2017); Model Study 4 by Dewey et al. (2012); Model Study 5 by Serrano et al. (2012); Model Study 6 by Kennedy Terry (2017, 2022a, 2022b); Model Study 7 by Pozzi (2021) and Pozzi and Bayley (2021); Model Study 8 by C. Li et al. (2021); Model Study 9 by Kinginger & Carnine (2019); Model Study 11 by Hasegawa (2019); and Model Study 14 by Bernstein (2018).

The Development of Communicative Competence

Hymes (1972) explained that children learning their L1 acquire not only grammatical competence, which refers to a child's ability to produce and understand any and all grammatical utterances of his or her language (Chomsky, 1965), but also notions of what is appropriate in that language—when, how, and with whom to speak. Communicative competence thus incorporates both the learning of linguistic structure and the "internalization of attitudes towards a language and its uses" through social experience (1972, p. 278).

The two components of communicative competence, grammaticality and acceptability, may be further separated into four categories. According to Hymes (1972), a speaker with communicative competence knows: (1) whether an utterance is formally *possible*; (2) whether an utterance is *feasible* given the linguistic tools available; (3) whether an utterance is *appropriate*; and (4) whether an utterance is actually *performed*. Knowing whether an utterance is possible or feasible (criteria 1 and 2) relates to the grammaticality of the utterance; knowing whether an utterance is appropriate and performed (criteria 3 and 4) relates to the acceptability of the utterance. Hymes explained that within their own L1 speech community, speakers have knowledge and capability with respect to all four categories and will assess the behavior of others according to this knowledge (1972, p. 281).

As Kanwit and Solon (2023) note, the construct of communicative competence has informed the field of SLA for more than five decades (see, e.g., Canale & Swain, 1980: Firth & Wagner, 1997, 2007; Geeslin & Long, 2014; Geeslin et al., 2018; Hymes, 1972; Kanwit, 2022; Regan, 2010; Spolsky, 1989; Swain, 1985). Communicative competence not only accounts for the ability to use language correctly, or grammatical competence, but also for the ability to use and interpret language appropriately in a variety of interactional contexts, or sociolinguistic competence (Canale & Swain, 1980). Thus, just as a child acquires communicative competence in their language(s) by learning to "accomplish a repertoire of speech acts" (Hymes 1972, p. 277), the L2 learner may seek to develop a similar repertoire leading to the acquisition of communicative, or sociolinguistic, competence in the L2. Classrooms are relatively formal environments, where particular forms and styles of speaking are considered appropriate; consequently, if learners are to acquire a full range of speech styles, they need opportunities to interact in a variety of situations with TL speakers. Thus, whether learners have the opportunities for interaction and negotiation for meaning that are a precursor to developing the ability "to accomplish a repertoire of speech acts" in the L2 is likely to depend on the social networks that learners are able to create and maintain with TL speakers. The development of communicative, or sociolinguistic, competence is the specific focus of Model Study 6 by Kennedy Terry (2017, 2022a, 2022b) and Model Study 7 by Pozzi (2021) and Pozzi & Bayley (2021), which are described in detail in Chapters 5–9.

Conclusion

Mitchell et al. (2019) proposed that there are three main perspectives on the language learner. The linguistic and psycholinguistic perspective views *the learner as language processor* and focuses on understanding the path of acquisition, finding universal mental processes among learners, and modeling inner mechanisms (2019, p. 21). According to the social psychological perspective, success in SLA depends on *differences among individual learners*, which may include attributes such as language aptitude, working memory, and learner strategies, as well as factors such as motivation, identity, and anxiety (2019, pp. 22–26). Finally, the third perspective, *the learner as social being*, posits that differences among learners are dynamic (rather than static) because learners operate in the social world and learning is impacted by socially constructed elements such as gender, ethnicity, social class, style, agency, and power (2019, pp. 26–27). As the current chapter demonstrates, SNA incorporates all three perspectives on the language learner—SNA links linguistic processing with the social context in which it occurs and, at the same time, demonstrates that individual learner characteristics intersect with, and often predict, opportunities for input, interaction, and output with TL speakers within social networks.

5

APPLICATIONS OF SOCIAL NETWORK ANALYSIS IN SECOND LANGUAGE RESEARCH

Introduction

This chapter examines the various second language (L2) learning contexts in which social network analysis (SNA) has made important contributions to our understanding of the L2 learning process. This chapter also introduces the reader to the diverse populations of L2 learners that have been examined through the lens of SNA: study abroad (SA) learners and others residing temporarily in the target-language (TL) environment, immigrant student groups in the TL educational system, and at-home language learners. Beginning with this chapter and extending through Chapter 9, 16 Model Studies have been selected for a close review of their research goals and questions, research methods, and data analysis and results. These Model Studies are representative of the flexibility and predictive power of SNA and can serve as a guide to researchers and students alike who are seeking to implement SNA in their own L2 research.

Language Learning during Study Abroad

SNA in the TL Environment

The most significant impact that SNA has had on L2 research has been in the area of L2 acquisition during SA or other temporary periods of residence in the TL community. This can be easily seen by the number of studies employing SNA to examine L2 acquisition in the SA context over the last 20 years and in the variety of linguistic outcomes considered in these

DOI: 10.4324/9781003174448-5

studies. The results from this growing body of research demonstrate why SNA has become a critical tool for analyzing, understanding, and predicting L2 acquisition patterns during a stay in the TL community. In these studies, SNA has been used to explain differences in learner gains during a period of time spent in the TL environment with a high level of accuracy and consistency.

Some of the first studies applying SNA to L2 acquisition (Isabelli-García, 2006; Lybeck, 2002) used primarily qualitative social network data to provide a critical enhancement to our understanding of L2 acquisition during SA or a period of time spent in the TL environment. These early studies demonstrated that just as SNA can identify and predict intracommunity linguistic patterns among L1 speakers who are not otherwise distinguishable by predefined categories of gender, age, and social class, SNA also has the ability to reveal and predict acquisition patterns in groups of L2 learners who appear to be relatively homogenous in terms of age, academic preparation, living arrangements, and time spent in the TL environment. This is especially important because, as the large body of research on SA indicates, no single learner characteristic or social factor has been exclusively associated with learner gains during a period of time in the TL environment (Isabelli-García et al., 2018).

Global Oral Proficiency and Fluency

Research using the Oral Proficiency Interview (OPI, American Council on the Teaching of Foreign Languages, ACTFL), or the Simulated OPI (SOPI), has clearly demonstrated the critical role of SA in the development of global L2 oral proficiency (Brecht et al., 1995; Dekeyser, 2010; Freed, 1995; Isabelli-García, 2010; Magnan & Back, 2007; Segalowitz & Freed, 2004). These results are supported by those from a number of other studies demonstrating that a period of SA contributes significantly to the development of oral proficiency in L2 Spanish (Huensch & Tracy-Ventura, 2017; Leonard & Shea, 2017), L2 Chinese (Wright, 2018), and L2 English (Llanes & Muñoz, 2009, 2013; Juan-Garau, 2018).

In one of the first studies to apply SNA to L2 acquisition, Lybeck (2002, Model Study 1) operationalized Schumann's acculturation model (1978) to examine the role of *cultural distance* (i.e., social and psychological distance) in the L2 acquisition of Norwegian pronunciation norms by a small group of American sojourners in Norway. Importantly, Lybeck incorporated the bidirectionality of acculturation in language learning; Lybeck acknowledged that both the language learner's attitude toward the target culture, as well as the attitudes of TL speakers toward the learner, impact the process of acculturation and, therefore, language acquisition. Lybeck focused on the acquisition of

Norwegian *r* by nine adult American women who had been living in Norway for one to three years. The participants represented a relatively homogenous group in age, educational background, professional experience, and language background in Norwegian. Lybeck hypothesized that participants who were able to overcome the difficulties associated with integrating into the highly cohesive Norwegian society (a potential barrier to acculturation) and able to form 'nurturing' exchange networks with TL speakers would achieve more native-like pronunciation than participants who did not.

Model Study 1: Lybeck (2002)

Context: Temporary/short-term residence in Norway (1–3 years)

Participants: Nine adult female L1 English speakers

Focus: Target-like pronunciation of Norwegian *r*

Methods: Oral interviews for qualitative social network and linguistic data

Results: Lower *cultural distance* and stronger social networks with TL speakers led to more native-like pronunciation

---

Model Study 2: Isabelli-García (2006)

Context: Semester of SA in Argentina

Participants: Four L1 English American university students

Focus: Oral proficiency in L2 Spanish

Methods: Pre-program questionnaire, informal interviews, diary entries, and social network logs for qualitative social network data; SOPI (ACTFL) for linguistic data

Results: A positive attitude, high motivation, and second-order network ties with TL speakers correlated with improved SOPI score for 2 of 4 learners

---

Similar to Lybeck (2002), Isabelli-García (2006, Model Study 2) used primarily qualitative data to reconstruct learners' social networks with TL speakers; however, in this study, Isabelli-García used SNA to examine L2 acquisition during a semester of SA, rather than during an extended period of residence in the TL community. In this study of four L2 Spanish learners in Argentina, Isabelli-García explored how the motivation and attitude of the learners impacted the social networks that they were able to create with TL speakers during SA, hypothesizing that dense networks with other L1 English speakers would inhibit contact with TL speakers and prevent language acquisition, whereas networks with TL speakers would facilitate L2 acquisition.

More recently, the LANGSNAP project ("Social networks, target language interaction, and second language acquisition during the year abroad: A longitudinal study"; McManus et al., 2014; Mitchell et al., 2017, Model Study 3) employed SNA to examine linguistic development in L2 French and Spanish during an academic year of SA, teaching assistantship, or work placement. As the project name indicates, this longitudinal study used qualitative social network data and quantitative network metrics to correlate learner gains in oral proficiency and fluency with the social networks that

Model Study 3:	LANGSNAP project (http://langsnap.soton.ac.uk); McManus et al. (2014), McManus (2019), Mitchell et al. (2015); Mitchell et al. (2017)
Context:	Academic year of SA, teaching assistantship, or work placement in France, Spain, or Mexico
Participants:	29 L1 English/L2 French learners; 27 L1 English/L2 Spanish learners
Focus:	Oral proficiency, lexical diversity and complexity, and fluency in L2 French and Spanish
Methods:	Language Engagement Questionnaire (LEQ) and Social Networks Questionnaire (SNQ) for L1/L2 use and interaction patterns; oral interviews and elicitation tasks for linguistic data
Results:	Most L2 contacts made within work or university context and represent 30–40% of total language contacts (McManus et al., 2014); placement type did not significantly influence general oral proficiency, lexical diversity, or oral fluency (Mitchell et al., 2015); positive correlation found between L2-speaking contacts and lexical complexity (McManus, 2019)

learners created with TL speakers during their time abroad. Linguistic data for this study were gathered using varied elicitation techniques (elicited imitation, monologic narratives, and semi-structured interviews) and social network data were gathered through online questionnaires both during and following the academic year abroad. Multiple analyses have been conducted and published from the results of the LANGSNAP project and these are summarized in Model Study 3.

The results of the LANGSNAP project (McManus et al., 2014; Mitchell et al., 2017) are supported by those of group of related studies that used SNA to examine both self-perceived oral proficiency gains in L2 Japanese (Dewey et al., 2012, Model Study 4) and L2 Arabic (Dewey et al., 2013; Dewey, Ring, et al., 2013), as well as actual gains on the OPI (Smemoe et al., 2014) in L2 Spanish, French, Russian, Arabic, Chinese following a period of SA.

Model Study 4:	Dewey et al. (2012); see also Dewey et al. (2013) and Dewey, Ring, et al. (2013) on L2 Arabic; Smemoe et al. (2014) on various L2s
Context:	8.4 months (average) of SA in Japan
Participants:	204 L1 English/L2 Japanese American university students
Focus:	Self-perceived oral proficiency gains in L2 Japanese
Methods:	Study Abroad Social Interaction Questionnaire (SASIQ) to measure social networks with TL speakers; self-assessment of changes to oral proficiency using a "then-now" design based on Clark (1981); modified version of the Language Contact Profile (LCP, Freed et al., 2004) for language use data
Results:	Learner's pre-departure proficiency, time in the TL environment, and social network *dispersion* (i.e., number of different groups within the social network) were strongest predictors of self-perceived oral proficiency gains

Grammatical Competence

In the area of L2 grammatical competence, the existing SA research provides a number of conflicting results on the benefits that L2 learners may experience during a period of SA or immersion (DeKeyser, 2014; Isabelli-García et al.,

2018; Kinginger, 2008; Llanes, 2011; Sanz & Morales-Front, 2018). For example, many studies comparing groups of at-home and SA learners in the acquisition of specific, categorical grammatical features of the L2 have not demonstrated a clear advantage for the SA context (Arnett, 2013 on L2 German; Collentine, 2004 on L2 Spanish; Howard, 2005, 2008 on L2 French; Isabelli-García, 2010 on L2 Spanish).

Model Study 5:	Serrano et al. (2012)
Context:	Academic year of SA in UK
Participants:	14 L1 Spanish/L2 English Spanish university students
Focus:	Oral and written fluency, complexity, lexical richness, accuracy
Methods:	Oral narrative retell, written descriptive essays for linguistic data; questionnaire focused on accommodations, language contact, and attitudes toward English people
Results:	Significant improvement in grammatical accuracy occurred in the second semester in both oral and written production; gains in lexical richness were predicted by living in an apartment or house (vs. a residence hall) and living with only English speakers

Serrano et al. (2012, Model Study 5) investigated language acquisition in L2 English over the course of an academic year of SA in the UK. In order to measure the impact of TL and L1 interactions within social networks, Serrano et al. focused on the accommodation type of learners (apartment or house vs. residence halls) and the nationality and language of communication of the four people with whom each learner had the most contact. The researchers focused on changes to fluency, complexity, lexical richness, and grammatical accuracy in both oral and written production over the course of the SA period.

The results of Serrano et al. (2012) are supported by those of Lundell and Arvidsson (2021) who used qualitative interview data to explore the role of social networks, among other factors, in grammatical proficiency and native-like pronunciation among long-term adult L1 Swedish/L2 French learners residing in France (between 5 and 54 years). Results of this study indicated that 'high performers' mainly socialized in French, or in both French and Swedish, and intentionally avoided co-nationals while residing in France.

Sociolinguistic Variation

While the research on SA is vast, relatively few studies have focused on the L2 acquisition of stylistic variation, commonly referred to as Type 2 variation (Rehner, 2002). Type 2 variation refers to the L2 learner's ability to alternate between two sounds or forms that have the same referential meaning (e.g., the alternation between *working* and *workin'* in English) but whose use by TL speakers is governed by a variety of linguistic and extralinguistic factors (Adamson & Regan, 1991; Bayley, 1996; Bayley & Regan, 2004; Bayley & Escalante, 2022). Participation in stylistic variation by L2 learners, even at very low levels, indicates the emergence of sociolinguistic competence in the L2 where the learner begins to internalize not only what is grammatically correct in the L2, but also what TL speakers view as culturally and socially appropriate language use (Hymes, 1972).

Studies on the L2 acquisition of stylistic and regional variation during SA indicate that learners benefit from the opportunity to interact with TL speakers and demonstrate incipient acquisition of TL variation patterns after a period of SA or immersion in the TL community. In a number of studies on L2 French, the length of time spent residing in the TL community was the strongest predictor of the acquisition of variation (Regan et al., 2009; Sax, 2003); however, studies on L2 Spanish have demonstrated that even short-term SA programs can contribute to the acquisition of regional TL speech norms (Geeslin et al., 2013; George, 2014; Knouse, 2013; Linford et al., 2018). Moreover, the role of interaction with TL speakers outside of the classroom has been positively correlated with the acquisition of regional phonological features in L2 Spanish both during SA (George, 2014) and after SA participants have returned home (Geeslin & Gudmestad, 2008). These results are supported by research on the acquisition of Type 2 variation in L2 French by Canadian immersion students (Nagy et al., 2003; Mougeon et al., 2010; Rehner et al., 2003) and in L2 Chinese by student residents spending 1–4 years in China (X. Li, 2010).

The growing body of research on the L2 acquisition of sociolinguistic variation demonstrates that extended interactions with TL speakers outside of the language classroom, such as those available to SA and immersion learners, facilitate the acquisition of an L2 variety that reflects target-like variation patterns, regional speech norms, and a sensitivity to TL pragmatic constraints. SNA provides a means to understand how these interactions occur, with whom, and in what contexts. SNA also facilitates the analysis of those linguistic features that are more readily influenced by participation in social networks with TL speakers and those that are either more resistant to development despite social networks or those that develop independently of social networks.

In order to identify the factors that contribute to the L2 acquisition of variation, Kennedy (2012) and Kennedy Terry (2017, 2022a, 2022b, Model Study 6) applied SNA to the acquisition of stylistic variation by 17 L2 French learners during SA in France. Kennedy (2012) designed a *social network strength scale* (SNSS; Milroy & Milroy, 1978) for SA that was used to: (1) measure the strength and breadth of the social networks that learners created with TL speakers during SA, and (2) determine the impact of social networks on the acquisition of three phonological variables showing stylistic variation in L1 French. Using naturalistic speech data gathered from sociolinguistic interviews (Labov, 1984) and a mixed-effects model (Rbrul; Johnson, 2009), the research by Kennedy Terry (2017, 2022a, 2022b) demonstrates the critical role that social networks play in the L2 acquisition of stylistic variation during SA.

Model Study 6:	Kennedy Terry (2017, 2022a, 2022b)
Context:	Academic semester or year of SA in France
Participants:	17 L1 English/L2 French American university students
Focus:	Target-like patterns of phonological variation (i.e., informal French)
Methods:	Social network strength scale for SA (SNSS) to measure social networks with TL speakers; oral interviews to gather linguistic data
Results:	SNSS score at final interview is a significant predictor of the acquisition of all three phonological variables studied

SNA has also been shown to predict the L2 acquisition of regional linguistic features during SA. Pozzi (2021, Model Study 7) examined the L2 acquisition of *vos*, the informal second-person singular form commonly used in place of *tú* 'you' in some Latin American countries, by 23 L1 English speakers during a semester of SA in Buenos Aires, Argentina. Additionally, Pozzi and Bayley (2021, Model Study 7) examined the L2 acquisition of a phonological, rather than morphological, feature of Buenos Aires Spanish (BAS) among the same group of 23 American learners studying in Argentina. In this study, Pozzi and Bayley focused on the acquisition of *sheísmo/zheísmo*, or the use of [ʃ] and [ʒ], respectively, for segments represented orthographically as "y" and "ll", such as in the pronunciation of the word llave [jaβe] 'key', pronounced as [ʃaβe] with *sheísmo* or [ʒaβe] with *zheísmo*.

Model Study 7: Pozzi (2021); Pozzi & Bayley (2021)

Context: Academic semester of SA in Argentina

Participants: 23 L1 English/L2 Spanish American university students

Focus: Acquisition of regional phonological (*sheísmo/zheísmo*) and morphological (*vos*) features

Methods: Social network strength scale for SA (SNSS, Kennedy 2012) to measure social networks with TL speakers; oral interviews and discourse completion task to gather linguistic data

Results: SNSS score at final interview is a significant predictor of the use of *vos*, but not for the use of *sheísmo/zheísmo*

Discourse and Pragmatic Competence

In addition to contributing to the acquisition of variable linguistic forms, existing research also demonstrates that a period of SA facilitates the acquisition of interlanguage pragmatics, or "those aspects of language that cannot be considered in isolation from its use, language in its situational context" (Isabelli-García et al., 2018, p. 456). The results from a number of studies (Bataller, 2010; Iwasaki, 2010; Kinginger & Farrell, 2004; Lafford, 1995, 2004; Marriott, 1995) demonstrate that L2 learners make progress toward the acquisition of pragmatic constraints during SA, although most fall short of target-like application (see Pérez Vidal & Shively, 2019 for a review).

To examine the role of social networks on the pragmatic choices made by L2 Chinese learners, C. Li et al. (2021, Model Study 8) examined *pragmatic subjectivity* (C. Li & Gao, 2017) among learners during SA in China. According to the authors, pragmatic subjectivity refers to a learner's awareness of the pragmatic resources available to them in the L2, as well as to the conscious pragmatic choices that learners make based on this metapragmatic awareness. Specifically, the authors looked at the changing use of request strategies (i.e., direct versus indirect strategies), external modifiers (e.g., greetings, thanks, sweeteners), and internal modifiers (e.g., sentence-final particles, tag-questions, politeness markers) by the learners over the one-year period.

Model Study 8:	C. Li et al. (2021)
Context:	Study conducted over one year of residence in China
Participants:	8 international L2 Chinese university students
Focus:	Changing use of request strategies and internal/external modifiers
Methods:	Study Abroad Network Questionnaire (SANQ) to measure social networks; role plays and retrospective verbal reports to gather linguistic data; observations, field notes, social media posts to supplement other data sources
Results:	Learners moved toward NS patterns of directness in making requests but varied widely in their use of external and internal modifiers

The results of C. Li et al. (2021) are complemented by those of Bracke and Aguerre (2015) who examined the communities of practice in which Erasmus SA participants interacted and the discursive strategies employed by 52 learners from 19 different countries during a semester or year in France. In this study, the authors created and distributed an online questionnaire focused on the students' social activities in three areas (personal, educational, and public) and on their attitudes toward language learning and use. Participants also indicated whether they employed a variety of discursive strategies in their interactions in French with TL speakers, such as adjusting their speech to the status of the TL speaker or organizing their utterance in advance of speaking.

Learner Stance, Identity, and Socialization

Many studies of how students in SA programs are socialized into the norms of the target culture have examined how staying with a host family can facilitate language acquisition (e.g., Iino, 2006; Kinginger, 2015; Kinginger & Carnine, 2019; Knight & Schmidt-Rinehart, 2002). While most do not rely specifically on traditional methods of SNA, the rich detail provided in these studies allows us to see how the learners' developing social networks, or in some cases lack of such networks, contribute to their overall L2 acquisition as well as to the acquisition of specific variable TL structures.

An example of this approach is Kinginger (2015) who examined the language socialization of two American high school students in a short-term (four-week) homestay program in China. In this study, Kinginger emphasized that because the students were in high school, the program operated *in loco parentis* meaning that the host family members, program directors and administrators, and local and home institution faculty were deeply invested in ensuring the success of the program and its participants. This differs from typical university SA programs in which college-aged students have access to program administrators and faculty during the SA abroad period, but also have a high level of freedom in terms of how, where, and with whom they spend their time.

Similarly, Kinginger and Carnine (2019, Model Study 9) focused on two university students living with French families in the southwest of France, one for an academic semester and the other for an academic year. The goal of the study was to apply Vygotsky's (1978) genetic method to trace "the history of language learning" (Kinginger & Carnine, 2019, p. 859) of these two SA participants with a specific focus on language socialization, in "zones of proximal development" (ZPD, Vygotsky, 1978, p. 85) through mealtime discussions with their host families.

Model Study 9:	Kinginger & Carnine (2019)
Context:	Academic semester or year of SA in France
Participants:	2 L1 English/L2 French American university students
Focus:	Mealtime language practices and language learning support in the homestay environment
Methods:	Social network interaction data gathered through pre- and post-SA questionnaires and a semi-structured interview at the end of the sojourn; socialization and linguistic data gathered through 4–8 hours of recorded mealtime conversations with host family members
Results:	Different language socialization practices among host families shape learners' experiences with, and abilities in, the L2

In another study that incorporated an analysis of both the language learners and the TL speakers in their social networks, Diao (2017, Model Study 10) analyzed the homestay environments of three American speakers of 'transnational Mandarin', a variety of Mandarin used by Chinese diaspora communities, during SA in Shanghai. Using interviews, surveys, and field observations, Diao analyzed the social and political stances of the members of the learners' social networks and examined how these TL speakers participated in the co-construction of each learner's identity in the TL. Moreover, Diao demonstrated how the learners' co-constructed TL identity contributed to their use (or nonuse) of a nonstandard phonological feature, a retroflex/dental merger, regularly used by speakers in the TL environment, but not by speakers of the standard Beijing variety.

Model Study 10: Diao (2017)	
Context:	Academic semester of SA in China
Participants:	3 American L1 English/transnational Mandarin speakers
Focus:	Socialization with host families/roommates; awareness of and participation in sociolinguistic norms (e.g., retroflex/ dental merger)
Methods:	Pre- and post-SA semi-structured interviews, language awareness questionnaires, Language Contact Profile (LCP, Freed et al., 2004), observations for social network interaction data; audio recordings of learners and host family members/roommates for linguistic data
Results:	Learners and TL speakers co-constructed the learner's TL identity which influenced their use (or nonuse) of the nonstandard phonological variant

We point out here that Model Studies 9 and 10 do not employ network modeling and do not attempt to trace the full extent of the interactions of the learners with TL speakers. Rather, they focus in great detail on learners' interactions with a relatively small number of TL interlocutors. However, as noted in the introductory chapter, SNA involves both quantitative and qualitative analysis and both Kinginger and Carnine (2019) and Diao (2017) provide illustrations of the richness of the data that can be obtained in naturalistic settings. We suggest that the type of recordings analyzed in these two studies could enrich SNA research in a number of ways, as elaborated on in Chapter 6. For example, sample recordings of learners' interactions provide a check on the validity of responses to the types of questionnaires about interactions used by many SNA researchers. In addition, for researchers examining the contribution of learners' social networks to the acquisition of vernacular variants, recordings are much more likely to offer unmonitored speech than interviews with a researcher.

SA Program Design and Opportunities for Interaction

Hasegawa (2019, Model Study 11) emphasized that most research on social networks in language learning during SA has focused on *egocentric* networks where all relationships are considered from the viewpoint of the language learner (*ego*); however, other research disciplines employing SNA focus on *sociocentric* networks which consider the viewpoints of all actors within a social network or networks. Hasegawa's study makes an important contribution to the field of SNA in terms of how social networks are formed during SA, with whom, and what opportunities they provide for interaction in the TL. Hasegawa's study also represents one of the first attempts to combine both conversation analysis and SNA.

Model Study 11:	Hasegawa (2019)
Context:	Short-term (2-month) SA in Japan
Participants:	91 L1 English/L2 Japanese university students
Focus:	Comparison of interaction and networking opportunities offered by three different SA programs; impact of local factors on socialization
Methods:	Participant observations, social network surveys, interviews, activity logs, audio/video recordings to gather social network and interaction data
Results:	SA program design influences the access that learners have to diverse interpersonal relationships that are critical to the development of interactional competence

Also employing a sociocentric (whole) network approach, Van Mol and Michielsen (2015) used an online survey to investigate and examine the interaction patterns and social network formation of European university students during SA with co-nationals, other nationals, and TL speakers. From a pool of over 5,000 responses, the authors selected 757 bachelor and master level students, under the age of 28, from six different countries who had participated in a short-term Erasmus SA program in another European country. The authors supplemented the quantitative survey data with qualitative data gathered through interviews and focus groups involving 71 university students in their final year of a master's program who had either participated in an Erasmus exchange program (49 students) or had decided not to participate in an exchange program (22 students).

Language Learning by Immigrant Students and Adults

This section provides an overview of studies of immigrant and immersion student populations that have used SNA to demonstrate the critical role of peer networks in L2 acquisition. These studies used a variety of methods, including questionnaires, direct classroom observation, and participant and teacher interviews, to examine the social networks of young children, adolescents, and university students in an educational setting and to link the interactions within these social networks to outcomes in both written and oral proficiency in the L2.

One of the key observations that can be made from a review of this research is that where clear trends may be seen related to participation in social networks with TL speakers by SA learners at the university level, studies focused on younger learners residing permanently in the TL environment, and entering the educational system at various ages, present a wider variety of results when the composition and strength of the peer network are compared to linguistic performance.

One example from this group of studies, Carhill-Poza (2015, Model Study 12), demonstrated that the most influential factor in predicting the oral academic proficiency of L2 English high school students was the academic orientation of the learner's peer network, regardless of whether the primary language of the network was L1 Spanish or L1 English.

Model Study 12: Carhill-Poza (2015)

Context:	New York public high schools
Participants:	102 L2 English/L1 Spanish students (high school sophomores/juniors)
Focus:	Role of peer social networks in academic English proficiency
Methods:	Oral interviews and modified version of the Longitudinal Immigrant Adaptation Study (Suárez-Orozco et al., 2008) to gather social network data; standardized oral academic English proficiency measure (IPTK-12) to gather linguistic data
Results:	Academic orientation of peer social network was strongest predictor of academic English proficiency (outweighing time in the US and mother's education level)

Model Study 13: Wiklund (2002)

Context:	Swedish secondary-school students
Participants:	54 Bilingual Swedish speakers; median length of residence 7–15.5 years
Focus:	Role of informal contact with L2 Swedish in verbal/written sophistication
Methods:	Social networks questionnaire focused on connections with three groups of speakers: L1 Swedish speakers, their own ethnic group, members of another ethnic group; interviews and written compositions for linguistic data
Results:	Demonstrated positive impact of social networks with L1 Swedish speakers and with other ethnic groups where Swedish is the language of communication

---

Similar to Carhill-Poza, Wiklund (2002, Model Study 13) examined the social networks of secondary-school students in Sweden in order to analyze the impact of Swedish peer networks on verbal and written sophistication in Swedish. For this study, Wiklund examined the peer networks of 54 bilingual Swedish speakers (aged 16–22 years) at two different upper-secondary schools: a suburban school where the L2 speakers represented a majority (90 percent) of the student population and a provincial school where the L2 speakers represented a small minority (12 percent). Wiklund hypothesized that informal contact with spoken Swedish would be required in order for these learners to achieve a high level of proficiency in written Swedish.

A number of studies have also focused on social networks among younger language learners who present different challenges and linguistic outcomes. For example, Bernstein (2018, Model Study 14) combined qualitative, ethnographic data on L2 English learners' participation in the complete social network of a single preschool classroom with quantitative data on L2 acquisition. Bernstein's results for specific focal students in the classroom contradict long standing beliefs about the interconnectedness of social position, interaction, and language learning opportunities by demonstrating that being a 'central' network member is not always a prerequisite to language learning and being a 'peripheral' network member does not always hinder linguistic development.

Model Study 14: Bernstein (2018)

Context: US Head Start preschool classroom

Participants: 11 L2 English learners aged 3;9–4;0 years

Focus: Participation in Networks of Practice (P-NoP) and L2 English acquisition

Methods: Classroom observations and video recordings, field notes, interviews with students and teachers, network diagrams

Results: A central network position may inhibit linguistic development because of the pressure it imposes on the learner to maintain authority; network peripherality provides opportunities to observe and notice language which can contribute to linguistic development

In another study of young L2 learners, Kibler et al. (2021) used SNA to examine how L1 and L2 English integration within US middle-school classrooms led to different levels of classroom participation by L2 English learners. Using a sociocentric approach to SNA, Kibler et al. analyzed peer-to-peer language support with a specific focus on peer support that transcended English learner (EL) proficiency classifications. That is, Kibler et al. sought to understand whether EL-classified students turned to other EL-classified students for assistance in the classroom more or less frequently than they turned to non-EL-classified students and what impact these 'academic helping relationships' have on overall classroom participation by EL-classified students.

Language Learning at Home

A final research strand has examined the impact of learners' social networks, both with TL speakers and with other L2 learners, on L2 socialization and L2 learning processes outside of the classroom and outside of the TL community, in the home environment. These studies demonstrate the central role that social networks play in facilitating access to sociocultural and sociolinguistic aspects of the L2 that are generally not present in instructed, at-home learning contexts.

Previous research on learners in L2 French immersion programs in an L1 English/bilingual environment, such as Nagy et al. (2003), has demonstrated that interaction with TL speakers outside of the classroom is positively correlated with the acquisition of sociolinguistic variation in L2 French. In their study, Nagy et al. (2003) examined the acquisition of subject doubling (e.g., *mes parents, ils sont* ... 'my parents, they are ...') in a corpus of spoken data of 29 Anglophone immersion students. Using multivariate analysis, the researchers demonstrated that the language used at work (English or French) and adult (versus adolescent) integration into the Francophone community were the only significant predictors of subject doubling by the L2 French speakers in the study. The researchers concluded that subject doubling "is only really acquired by people who actually speak French with Francophones" (Nagy et al., 2003, p. 92).

Similarly, in two case studies of adult L2 Japanese learners residing in Australia, Kurata (2010, 2021, Model Study 15) investigated how learners use social networks to scaffold their learning outside of the TL community. In the first study, Kurata (2010) used a conversation analytic approach to examine language alternation between English and Japanese in the conversations of one L1 German/L2 Japanese university student interacting with the L1 Japanese members of his social network. A second case study by Kurata (2021) used interviews and diary entries to examine one L2 Japanese learner's interactions over 2.5 years while living and studying the L2 in her own L1 English community.

Model Study 15: Kurata (2010, 2021)

Context:	Acquisition of L2 Japanese in an L1 English environment
Participants:	1 L1 English/L2 Japanese speaker; 1 L1 German/L2 Japanese speaker
Focus:	Role of social networks in providing scaffolding for L2 language learning
Methods:	Recorded conversations for linguistic and interaction data (Kurata, 2010); oral interviews and diary entries for interaction data (Kurata, 2021)
Results:	Conversations with TL speakers facilitated L2 acquisition in many ways (e.g., noticing practice, feedback, Kurata, 2010); sustained interactions with L2 speakers resulted in steady progression from lack of confidence in L2 to pursuing self-directed learning opportunities (Kurata, 2021)

In another study on adult L2 acquisition in the L1 environment, Palfreyman (2021, Model Study 16) analyzed the influence of informal language learning networks (ILLNs) on English language use by a group of Emirati females studying at a government university in Dubai. This study specifically examined longitudinal changes in opportunities for English language use by comparing data gathered in 2003 (Palfreyman, 2006) with data gathered in 2018 (Palfreyman, 2021) for a similar cohort of Emirati females. By comparing data from two similar cohorts of female students, separated by 15 years of social and technological evolution, Palfreyman (2021) makes an important contribution to the current understanding of who or what might serve as a linguistic resource within a learner's social network, as well as how learners make use of available network resources while also serving as a resource themselves.

Model Study 16: Palfreyman (2021)

Context: Acquisition of L2 English in an L1 Arabic environment (Dubai)

Participants: 41 L1 Arabic/L2 English female Emirati university students

Focus: Changes over time to L2 English learning opportunities offered by participation in ILLNs; changes to participant contributions to ILLNs

Methods: Online multiple-choice survey focused on English language use in social networks inside and outside of the home and proficiency of English speakers inside the home/family network

Results: Loose social networks contributed to increased use of English outside of the home in all four skills (speaking, listening, reading, writing) and a decreased reliance on brothers and teachers for assistance

---

Similar to Palfreyman, Ferenz (2005) examined the impact of at-home social networks on L2 English development among six Israeli graduate students. Ferenz used biographical questionnaires and sociolinguistic interviews to examine opportunities for access to the social practices of advanced academic literacy. Results demonstrated that some participants had greater access to academic literacy practices through a network of professors and advisors at the university, with advisors playing a key role in the acquisition of advanced L2 English literacy practices for four of the six participants.

Conclusion

The studies described in this chapter establish the central role of SNA in the L2 acquisition of categorical, variable, and regional linguistic elements during SA, immersion, or other temporary periods of residence in the TL community. Moreover, the results of these studies highlight two important aspects of social network theory as it applies to L2 acquisition. First, it is notable that social networks have most often been found to be a significant predictor of language gains in the acquisition of oral proficiency and L2 phonology, indicating that L2 phonology, like L1 phonology, is highly reflective of extralinguistic social forces (Labov, 1972b). Second, the studies discussed in this section provide evidence for the essential role that social networks play in more advanced stages of L2 development where learners demonstrate not only grammatical competence but also begin to demonstrate sociolinguistic, pragmatic, and discourse-level competence.

As a complement to numerous studies employing a quantitative approach to SNA, the studies described in this chapter utilizing fine-grained, qualitative discourse and conversation analysis, involving both L2 learners and TL speakers, also demonstrate the critical role of social networks in the language socialization process and in the development of L2 identity. Additionally, a number of the Model Studies demonstrate that peer social networks have a significant influence on the academic language proficiency of L2 learners in the secondary school context, and in some cases, outweigh individual learner characteristics such as age, gender, and time in the TL environment. Finally, the research described in this chapter clearly demonstrates that social networks with TL-speaking peers, classmates, host family members, and roommates are a significant predictor of opportunities for interaction in the TL and a critical component to multiple aspects of L2 development.

Discussion Questions

1. In terms of the influence of social networks, what differences would you expect to see in the results of studies focused on overall oral proficiency versus variable linguistic forms? Why?
2. What aspects of L2 acquisition do you believe would be most influenced by social networks with TL speakers?
3. How would you expect social networks with L1 speakers/co-nationals to impact L2 development during SA?
4. Are there certain aspects of L2 acquisition that have not been considered in the research discussed in this chapter? Describe these and explain how they might be influenced by participation in social networks.

6

DATA COLLECTION FOR SOCIAL NETWORK ANALYSIS IN SECOND LANGUAGE RESEARCH

Introduction

This chapter provides an overview of the data collection methods that have been widely used in social network analysis (SNA) in second language (L2) research with a specific focus on Model Studies 1–16 described in Chapter 5. This chapter is divided into four sub-sections based on the primary methods of gathering data related to learners' social networks: (1) Participant Interviews; (2) Diaries, Journals, and Contact Logs; (3) Surveys and Questionnaires, and; (4) Live Recordings and Observations. Although the majority of L2 research using SNA seeks to correlate participation in social networks with linguistic development, the current chapter focuses specifically on the collection of data related to participants' social networks for SNA. Methods of linguistic data collection are described in Chapters 8 and 9. The current chapter also focuses on defining key terms in SNA that are used throughout the remaining chapters.

Participant Interviews

To gather data about participation in social networks, motivation to learn the target language (TL), and attitudes toward TL speakers and the TL culture, researchers may choose to conduct interviews with their study participants at specific intervals before, during, and after a period of residence in the TL community. This approach to SNA is well suited to small-scale studies, with fewer than 25 participants, and this longitudinal data serves to paint a picture of the participant within the TL community—how, with whom, and in what contexts the participant interacts with and in the TL.

DOI: 10.4324/9781003174448-6

Participant interviews generally focus on the *egocentric* network, or those network members who have a direct connection to the participant (*ego*), commonly referred to as *first-order ties*, or network members that are removed from ego by one person, referred to as *second-order ties* (L. Milroy, 2002, see Chapter 2). Additionally, during their interviews, researchers may choose to gather data related to the social networks that participants create with TL speakers only, or they may also incorporate information about social networks with co-national, first language (L1), and/or international speakers. Moreover, participant interviews may be conducted in the TL, providing linguistic data at the same time, or in the participant's first language. Finally, participant interviews are often combined with social network and biographic data collected from online or in-person surveys and questionnaires. The decision about which type of social network data to gather during an interview and in which language will be based on the specific research questions of the study.

In Model Study 1, Lybeck (2002) used participant interviews to examine and compare the level of acculturation (Schumann, 1978) into Norwegian society achieved by nine adult female participants. In this study, Lybeck gathered speech data from two participant interviews in Norwegian at a six-month interval and analyzed these for overall target-like pronunciation, as well as for the use of American *r* instead of the native-like Norwegian trill/tap *r*. During these interviews, Lybeck also gathered social network data by asking participants to describe how well they identified with the TL and TL culture, how native speakers (NSs) reacted to their speech, how much social contact they had with Norwegians, and how satisfied they felt with their linguistic and social progress in Norway. During a third interview conducted in English, Lybeck informed the participants of the goal of the study and asked them to give their own assessments of their linguistic and social development, as well as their self-assessed levels of acculturation in Norwegian society. Using the qualitative data gathered during participant interviews, as well as network questionnaires at each interview, Lybeck was able to reconstruct each participant's social network and to categorize the clusters of TL speakers with direct ties to the participant as either a 'supportive', 'moderately supportive', or 'unsupportive' network. Additionally, Lybeck analyzed the interviews for participants' feelings about and impressions of Norwegians in general, especially those outside the social networks that participants had created. Table 6.1 provides a sample of questions from Lybeck's participant interviews.

Overall, Lybeck noted that few of the participants were able to create exchange-based social networks (Milardo, 1988, pp. 26–36, see Chapter 2) with TL speakers but those who did were more likely to express positive feelings about creating and assuming a new identity in the target culture.

TABLE 6.1 Sample of questions from Interview 1

How do you feel you fit into the Norwegian society? What kind of roles do you
  have? Do you feel integrated? How do you think Norwegians feel about you (as
  a foreigner)?
Have you participated in any Norwegian organizations or clubs?
Tell about the friends you've made in Norway. How have your relationships
  developed? Do you think it is easy or difficult to come into contact with
  Norwegians? Are you satisfied with the social network you have now? Do you
  want to change the situation? How?
What are your feelings about Norwegian culture and behaviors? Have you had
  someone to help you learn about and understand Norwegian culture?
Who has helped you most to learn the language?
Would you like to be taken for a Norwegian?

Source: Translated from the Norwegian (adapted from Lybeck, 2002, p. 185)

Lybeck's results also confirmed that lower *cultural distance* (see Chapter 4)
and stronger social networks with TL speakers led to more native-like
pronunciation: the two speakers who formed strong, exchange-based
networks had the highest levels of native-like pronunciation (above
80 percent) and the highest use of Norwegian r (above 90 percent).
Similarly, the participants with the weakest social networks and highest levels
of cultural distance had the lowest levels of native-like pronunciation (below
61 percent) and the least frequent use of Norwegian r (below 5 percent).
Lybeck's research affirms the central role that social networks play in L2
language acquisition and underscores the ability of SNA to predict linguistic
patterns for L2 learners, just as they do for L1 learners.

Similar to Lybeck (2002), Lundell and Arvidsson (2021) used qualitative
interview data to examine the impact of social networks on grammatical
proficiency and native-like pronunciation among ten 'long-term' adult L1
Swedish/L2 French learners. Nine of the ten focal participants had arrived
in France between the ages of 12 and 18 and had resided in France for a
minimum of five years (up to a maximum of 54 years). In their analysis,
Lundell and Arvidsson used qualitative interviews to target five specific
factors that they hypothesized would impact language acquisition. These
five factors included the participants' migratory experience, language use/
social networks, language learning experience, identity, and attitude toward
the host community. Qualitative interview data were then coded using
a thematic analysis based on the work of Braun and Clarke (2006), who
explained that a theme "captures something important about the data in
relation to the research question and represents some level of patterned
response or meaning within the data set" (Braun & Clarke, 2006, p. 82). In
addition to the interview data, Lundell and Arvidsson incorporated linguistic

data from a prior assessment which included a verb–noun collocation task and an evaluation of the 'nativelikeness' of the participants' spoken French by a group of ten NSs. Using this linguistic data, the participants were divided into two categories: high and low performers.

The qualitative interview data for the language use/social networks category from Lundell and Arvidsson (2021) revealed that the high performers mainly socialized in French, or in both French and Swedish, but intentionally avoided co-nationals and did not socialize with international groups where English was commonly used as a lingua franca. In contrast, the low performers reported socializing primarily in international groups and speaking either English or Swedish. The efforts of the high performers to create social networks with TL speakers and to avoid co-nationals were also reflected in their discussions about the language learning experience during which they expressed making conscious efforts to meet and interact with French speakers and to attain native-like pronunciation. While the positive influence of social networks on the L2 French proficiency of high-performing participants is clearly indicated in the interview data, this study also highlights the interconnectedness of social networks with a variety of individual factors, such as identity, affiliation with the target culture, and motivation which may contribute to, or inhibit, adult L2 acquisition. Table 6.2 provides sample data from the thematic analysis of

TABLE 6.2 Identified themes—high performers

Category: Language use/social networks	Category: Language learning experience
• Predominantly French use in everyday life • Socializing mainly with French people in the beginning • Socializing mainly with Swedish people and other expats in the beginning • Currently socializing mainly with French people and interacting mainly in French • Currently socializing with equal proportions of French-speaking and Swedish-speaking people • Actively avoiding co-nationals in the beginning	• Having studied French at school • Having chosen French in a conscious manner • Had always had an interest in or liked languages • Self-reported language learning aptitude • University studies in French • Self-regulation • Agency • Extensive media consumption • Active listening • Efforts to sound like a native speaker • Language learning experience perceived as an enjoyment

Source: Adapted from Lundell & Arvidsson, 2021, pp. 10–11

the interview data for two of the five predetermined categories (Language Use/Social Networks and Language Learning Experience) for the high performers only.

In addition to using interviews to gather data on social network formation and participation, a number of studies have used participant interviews to better understand how student placements and activities may impact access to the TL and to TL speakers. These studies employ SNA in a novel way in order to provide important insights into program design which can benefit universities and other organizations offering both study abroad (SA) and at-home language learning opportunities.

For example, as part of the LANGSNAP project, Model Study 3 ("Social networks, target language interaction, and second language acquisition during the year abroad: A longitudinal study", McManus et al., 2014; Mitchell et al., 2017), researchers examined the oral proficiency development of 29 advanced L2 French learners during an academic year in France with a specific focus on how their placement in either a teaching assistantship, work placement, or university exchange impacted the social networks that they created with TL speakers, their perceived language development, and their actual language development as measured by a number of oral production tasks. The researchers conducted six oral interviews in French over a 23-month period: once before residence abroad, three times during the academic year abroad, and twice upon return to the UK (at a three-month interval). These interviews were used to gather both qualitative social network and TL interaction data, as well as linguistic data. An additional interview, conducted in English and focused on reflections related to the participant's experience in France, was also conducted during the academic year.

The qualitative interview data from this project reported in Mitchell et al. (2015) indicated that the university exchange students generally found it difficult to make French friends, but did report some interactions with conversation partners or other international students. The teaching assistants had many opportunities to speak French in the lunch or staff room, but many found that the other teachers wanted to practice their English. For example, during one of the interviews, a student working as a teaching assistant reported:

In one of the schools the teachers were quite keen on speaking English, because sort of having an English person there helped them, and then in the other school my teachers were like "well we're going to speak to you in French, because we know you are here to learn French, so we will speak French unless you mind in which case we can speak English to you", and I said "no, speak French to me and if I don't understand we can work around it", and that really helped, having people that sort of only spoke to me in French.

(Mitchell et al., 2015, p. 125)

Most of the learners who were in work placements had opportunities to eat lunch and participate in other social events with workmates and they also used French most of the time at work. For all three placement types, the researchers noted that in many cases, students had to "trade English" in order to access French speaking opportunities and many or most formed multilingual relationships with the members of their social networks.

In terms of linguistic development, learners in all three placement types from Mitchell et al. (2015) perceived improvement in their L2 French skills, especially in the areas of oral fluency and listening comprehension. Workplace interns also noted improvements in their written French because of various tasks related to their work duties (e.g., writing emails, completing forms, taking notes). For example, during interview 1, a student in a work placement described various tasks that required the use of the L2:

I answer the phone, I do translations, and I take the minutes in the meetings. I organise deliveries for parcels and for equipment, I make hotel reservations and train reservations for staff travel, and lots of other tasks, the tasks that other people don't want to do.

(Mitchell et al., 2015, p. 125)

The perceptions of the learners in Mitchell et al. (2015) were supported by their documented gains over time in oral proficiency (measured by an elicited imitation task), lexical diversity (measured by an oral interview), and oral fluency (measured by a narrative retell task). While the learners showed improvement in all three areas over the course of the residence abroad period, the main effect for time achieved statistical significance for oral proficiency only and placement type was not shown to be a significant predictor of any of the oral production measures. At the same time, the qualitative data gathered through the participant interviews in both French and English elucidate important elements of the residence abroad experience, especially the role of English as a lingua franca and the many ways in which L2 learners abroad must negotiate 'mixed networks' characterized by communication in both their L1 and the TL.

As the studies described in this section clearly demonstrate, participant interviews are a rich source of qualitative data that can be used to explain and predict linguistic development during a period of residence in the TL community (Lundell & Arvidsson, 2021; Lybeck, 2002) and to describe how opportunities for interactions in the TL are shaped by the structure and nature of the language learning context available to SA learners (Mitchell et al., 2015). Moreover, participant interview data offer the researcher opportunities to analyze any number of TL features to assess learner proficiency and, if the researcher is interested in examining the acquisition of informal registers, the degree to which participants have moved beyond the relatively formal language that characterizes the classroom environment. An additional benefit of participant interviews is that they can be used at a later date to examine linguistic features that were not part of the original study. For example, Langman (1998) originally focused on communication strategies used by Chinese migrants in Budapest, Hungary. Several years later, Langman returned to the original interviews, which provided the data for a study of the untutored acquisition of the complex Hungarian verbal system (Langman & Bayley, 2002).

Diaries, Journals, and Contact Logs

In addition to oral interviews in which participants describe their language learning experiences and participation in social networks, researchers also rely on participant self-reporting to characterize the nature and frequency of their interactions in the TL, as well as to understand the impact of individual characteristics and social network composition on linguistic development.

In Model Study 2, Isabelli-García (2006) used diary entries and social network contact logs, in addition to informal interviews, to assess the motivation, attitudes, and social integration into the TL culture of four L2 Spanish learners during SA in Argentina. In this study, participants were given notebooks in which they wrote weekly entries in English about their progress in Spanish and important events during the week in order to achieve the researcher's goal of identifying "the environments, activities, and sociocultural views that lend themselves to more or less successful language acquisition" (Isabelli-García, 2006, p. 240). From the diary entries and informal interviews, Isabelli-García assigned an overall rating for each learner's social attitude toward the TL culture (positive, negative, or neutral) and used their attitude rating and the results of a pre-program questionnaire to categorize each learner as having high or low motivation to learn the TL.

Diary entries (a) and (b) from Isabelli-García (2006) characterize what the researcher considered to be an example of a positive attitude (a) and a negative attitude (b) toward the TL culture:

(a) This past weekend I went to Cordoba [...] I spent two days in a friend of a friend's home, which was really nice [...] It was good to spend a weekend with a family. I think I have a better idea of Argentina, of course more trips are necessary to improve the idea even more (Stan, p. 242).

(b) I have noticed Argentine men are not at all shy about telling a girl she is fat. Several times I have been walking on the street or with friends and someone has pointed out the fact that I am not stick thin. I can't imagine being an Argentine woman and putting up with that [...] (Jennifer, p. 252).

Additionally, Isabelli-García provided the students with daily social network contact logs in which to track their TL interactions over a seven-day period. The participants completed the seven-day logs at three different points during the SA period: week 1, week 8, and week 15. From these logs, Isabelli-García reconstructed the social network of each L2 learner. The qualitative and quantitative data gathered from the diary entries, informal interviews, and social network contact logs are discussed in more detail in Chapter 7.

In another small-scale study of seven learners who spent an academic year studying at a French university and living with a French host family, Gautier and Chevrot (2015) evaluated learners' social networks using data gathered through contact diaries and questionnaires. In the contact diaries, learners recorded all of their interactions outside the French classroom for an entire week, including the name of the person, the length of the exchange, and the language used in the exchange. This approach, which was also used by Isabelli-García (2006), is referred to as a *name-generator* approach to SNA because it requires the learners to create a list of contact names based on their interactions.

In the same study, Gautier and Chevrot (2015) created a questionnaire using the contact names provided in the diary entries. In these questionnaires, participants responded to a series of questions about each network contact mentioned in their diary entries. Participants were asked to provide the age, sex, and nationality of each network contact and to describe the type of relationship and language(s) spoken with the contact. Participants also quantified the frequency of their interactions with the contact and described the connections between the network members. In this way, the questionnaires served as a *name-interpretor* whereby participants are provided with a preset list of network contacts and they 'interpret' their relationship with this contact for the researcher. As shown in the following section of this chapter (Surveys and Questionnaires), questionnaires often combine both the name generator and name interpreter approaches to accurately depict learners' social networks.

Case studies of language learners, such as Model Study 15 by Kurata (2021), have also used diary entries, in conjunction with other methods of data collection, to conduct a close examination of participation in social networks by individual language learners. In this study, Kurata (2021) examined the interactions of one L2 Japanese learner over 2.5 years while living and studying the L2 in her own L1 English community. Using a combination of interviews and diary entries, Kurata examined the learner's attitude and approach toward language learning and her evolving feelings about the L2 and the L2 culture.

Qualitative data from Kurata (2021) demonstrated a steady progression from a deep lack of confidence in her own L2 competence in year one to engagement in self-directed learning opportunities by the third year. This progression was facilitated by a personal trip to the TL community, a supportive network of fellow L2 Japanese students, and participation in online language learning communities. Moreover, in the third year, the learner began volunteering at Japanese cultural events and became a committee member of the university Japan club. The learner also benefited from interactions with an L1 Japanese speaker through a second-order network tie (friend of a friend). Finally, the learner developed a relationship with a bilingual English/ Japanese boyfriend with whom she spent at least one day each week speaking exclusively Japanese and with whom she felt comfortable making mistakes and receiving corrective feedback. At the final interview, the L2 learner also indicated that she regularly sought out naturalistic language learning opportunities like watching Japanese films and spontaneous interactions with TL speakers. From this longitudinal case study, Kurata concluded that although learners often face difficulties in accessing opportunities for TL interactions at lower levels of language proficiency, social networks, motivation, and a long-term investment in the language learning process can lead to increased opportunities for socialization in and acquisition of the L2.

Like participant interviews, diary entries, activity journals, and social network contact logs make important qualitative and quantitative data available to researchers that would be otherwise difficult to obtain on a longitudinal and/or large scale. While it is acknowledged that self-reported language use data may be prone to inaccuracies, as the studies described here demonstrate, researchers often combine qualitative diary entries with other forms of data (e.g., activity and social network logs, questionnaires) in order reduce the potential for learners to overstate or underestimate their interactions in the TL. Moreover, as studies such as Isabelli-García (2006) and Kurata (2021) demonstrate, qualitative reflections recorded in a longitudinal format provide valuable insights into the language learning experience as it is being 'lived by the learners'.

Surveys and Questionnaires

Benefits and Applications

Surveys and Questionnaires are by far the most common method of gathering social network and interactional data from SA and at-home learners alike. One reason that surveys and questionnaires are widely used is because they are relatively easy to distribute to large numbers of language learners in an online format and thus lend themselves to large-scale projects in a way that participant interviews, diary entries, and observations do not. Moreover, surveys and questionnaires are extremely flexible to the needs and goals of the researchers, as demonstrated by the variety of questionnaires described in this section. Finally, given the advances in technology and in network diagramming software programs, in particular, the conversion of participant responses into social network diagrams and calculations of important social network metrics have become increasingly popular.

As the research described in this section demonstrates, creating a comprehensive questionnaire that accurately documents, quantifies, and characterizes interactions between language learners and TL speakers, or between language learners and co-nationals or international speakers, is not a simple task. For example, the Language Contact Profile (LCP, Freed et al., 2004) has been widely used in research on L2 acquisition during SA, but because it requires learners to make retrospective generalizations about their total TL use in multiple categories (e.g., speaking, reading, writing, listening), most studies have not been able to correlate scores on the LCP with proficiency gains during SA (Isabelli-García, 2010; Issa et al., 2020; Magnan & Back, 2007; Segalowitz & Freed, 2004; c.f., Hernández, 2010). Since the creation of the LCP, many researchers have sought to incorporate its overarching goal, the close examination of interactions in the TL, into surveys and questionnaires informed by SNA. That is, the questionnaires described in this section aim to quantify, characterize, and analyze linguistic and social development within the structure of the social networks that language learners form and maintain with others. Here, we describe four different questionnaires that are representative of the variety of data points that researchers seek to gather when employing SNA in L2 research.

Social Network Questionnaire (SNQ)

In Model Study 3, the LANGSNAP project ("Social networks, target language interaction, and second language acquisition during the year abroad: A longitudinal study") the researchers used the *Social Networks Questionnaire* (SNQ, McManus et al., 2014; Mitchell et al., 2017) to gather information on participants' social networks during their stay in the TL environment. This questionnaire focused on active L1 or L2 contacts across five different social contexts, where 'active' meant that the participant had interacted with this contact within the last month. These five contexts -included: work/university, organized free time, general free time, home, and virtual social activities. For each network member listed as an active contact (i.e., name generator), learners answered follow-up questions (i.e., name interpreter) describing the nature of their relationship with the network member, the frequency of their contact with this person, the language(s) used during interactions with this person, and the activities that the participant and network member engaged in together. Participants were also asked to nominate five people, 'Top 5', with whom they had the highest levels of interaction across all social contexts. Table 6.3 provides a sample of the follow-up questions that participants answered for each active social network contact identified in the name-generator portion of the SNQ.

In addition to the SNQ, participants in McManus et al. (2014) completed the *Language Engagement Questionnaire* (LEQ), which focused on L1 and TL use during a nine-month period of residence in France. The 29

TABLE 6.3 Follow-up questions by person

Source: SNQ, reprinted with permission from McManus, 2019, p. 275

TABLE 6.4 Follow-up questions by language

How often do you do the following in French?

	Everyday	Several times a week	A few times a week	Couple times a month	Rarely	Never
Watch television	●	o	o	o	o	o
Watch films	●	o	o	o	o	o
Browse the internet (e.g., read news, etc.)	●·	o	o	o	o	o
Use social networking sites (e.g., Facebook/ Twitter)	●	o	o	o	o	o
Read or write emails	●	o	o	o	o	o
Listen to music or talk radio	●	o	o	o	o	o

Source: LEQ, adapted from McManus et al., 2014, p. 104

L2 French learners were first asked which languages they used regularly while residing in France and for each language, they indicated whether they used that language to engage in any of the 26 provided activities and how frequently. Participants completed the SNQ and the LEQ at interviews 1–3 during the SA period (in November, February, and May, respectively). Table 6.4 provides an extract from the LEQ for the use of French in a subset of the 26 activities.

Study Abroad Social Interaction Questionnaire (SASIQ)

The Study Abroad Social Interaction Questionnaire (SASIQ) was first used in Dewey et al. (2012, Model Study 4) in their study of L2 Japanese learners during SA in Japan and Dewey et al. (2013) in their study of L2 Arabic learners in Morocco and Jordan. The SASIQ was developed by the first author of both studies (Dewey) and was modeled on the Montreal Index of Linguistic Integration (Segalowitz & Ryder, 2006) and the General Social Survey (Burt, 1985). The SASIQ combines both a name generator and a name interpreter approach, similar to the SNQ (McManus et al., 2014) described in the previous section. Participants completed the SASIQ at the end of the SA period.

Although the SASIQ has been modified a number of times in subsequent studies, the original version used in Model Study 4 by Dewey et al. (2012) included 13 questions designed to gather data that would allow the researchers to calculate a number of important metrics related to learners' social networks. These key metrics are discussed in more detail in Chapter 7 but are included here because they serve to illustrate the research goals that inform the design of the questionnaire. The participant responses to the SASIQ questionnaire can be used to calculate the following social network metrics: (a) the *size* of the learner's networks with TL speakers, (b) the *intensity* or strength of each relationship, (c) the *durability* of the network connections based on the frequency of TL interactions, (d) the *density* of the network based on the interconnectedness of network members, and (e) the *dispersion* of the network based on the number of different groups within the network.

The SASIQ measures the *size* of a learner's social network in the TL community by asking the learner to list all of the TL speakers with whom they associate on a regular basis. From this list, the SASIQ then asks learners to characterize the *intensity* of their relationship with each person (ranging from acquaintance to very close friend) on a numerical scale. The *durability* of each relationship is assessed with questions related to how often the learner associates with each person included in their social network, and in what language (TL or L1). Learners are then asked to arrange the members of their social network into social groups and to indicate which members are connected to other members. Understanding the connections between social network members allows the researchers to calculate network *density*, as dense social networks have been shown to reinforce linguistic norms in studies of L1 communities (Milroy & Milroy, 1978). Using the participant responses related to network density, the researchers are able to calculate the *dispersion* of the network which represents the number of different social groups (e.g., host family, school or athletic club, etc.) that exist within the learner's overall network. Additionally, the SASIQ asks learners a variety of general questions related to social network formation during SA. Table 6.5 includes a sample of the general questions included in the SASIQ used in Dewey, Ring, et al. (2013) in their study of 71 L2 Arabic learners in Jordan and Egypt.

TABLE 6.5 Sample SASIQ questions

1. What did you do to meet native speaker (NS) friends?
2. What factors facilitate deeper friendships with NS friends?
3. What factors inhibit deeper friendships with NS friends?
4. How did the SA program help you to make NS friends?
5. What more could the SA program have done to help you meet NS friends?

Source: Adapted from Dewey, Ring, et al., 2013, Tables 1–6, pp. 279–281

Social Network Strength Scale (SNSS) for SA

The Social Network Strength Scale (SNSS, Kennedy, 2012) for SA used in Model Study 6 by Kennedy Terry (2017, 2022a, 2022b) on L2 French acquisition during SA in France also uses the name generator and name interpreter approaches to SNA; however, unlike the SASIQ (Dewey et al., 2013; Dewey et al., 2012; Dewey, Ring, et al., 2013) and the SNQ (McManus et al., 2014), the SNSS for SA does not include all TL contacts made during the SA period—the SNSS for SA includes only those TL speakers with whom the learner speaks the TL for at least 30 minutes consecutively each week and with whom the participants have an ongoing relationship. The SNSS for SA is also differentiated from the LCP (Freed et al., 2004) that seeks to capture total TL language use in all modalities (e.g., speaking, reading, writing, listening) because the SNSS for SA focuses on one activity only: speaking the TL with TL speakers.

The scoring procedure for the SNSS for SA is described in detail in Chapter 7, but the overall goal of the questionnaire is to yield a single global measure of social network strength on a numerical scale. To this end, the SNSS for SA first asks the learners to list all of the native French speakers with whom they speak French for at least 30 minutes each week (as well as the TL speaker's age and their relationship to the learner). Using this list of network members, participants are asked to estimate how many hours per week they speak French with this person and to indicate whether these interactions include only the learner and the TL speaker, or multiple TL speakers at the same time (see Figure 6.1, Question 1). Using the same list of TL speakers, participants are asked to draw their social network and to indicate any connections between the TL speakers in their list from Question 1 (see Figure 6.1, Question 2). Learners are then provided with a list of common social activities (see Figure 6.1, Question 3), and they are asked to indicate whether they engage in these activities with each of the TL speakers in their social network and, if so, to estimate the number of hours spent doing each activity. Finally, in Question 4, learners are provided with a list of potential conversation topics and they are asked to indicate which ones they discuss regularly with the TL speakers in their network (Figure 6.1, Question 4).

In Kennedy Terry's (2017, 2022a, 2022b) studies of 17 American university students in France, year-long SA participants completed the SNSS for SA twice, at interviews 2 and 3 (January and April, respectively), and semester participants completed the SNSS for SA once at the end of their SA period (January or April). Participants completed the SNSS for SA in person and in hardcopy. The SNSS for SA (Kennedy, 2012) is shown in Figure 6.1 on the following pages.

Name: _____

Question #1 (Density Measure #1)

Name each French (or native French-speaking) person with whom you have *at least 30 minutes of consecutive conversation in French* each week. List the number of hours spent speaking French with each person and what their relationship is to you (friend, host family member, roommate, etc...).

Note: Do not double count hours spent with two+ people at the same time. In this case, place the total number of hours next to one name only, place a "G" in the Hours column for the others, and draw an arrow to the name of the person on whose line you listed the hours.

Name (+ age)	Hours per week	Relationship
1)		
2)		
3)		
4)		
5)		

Question #2 (Density Measure #2)

Now use the names listed above to draw a social network grid. Place your name in the first box, the name of each person in a separate box, and connect the boxes with a line to show who knows whom. An example is provided for you:

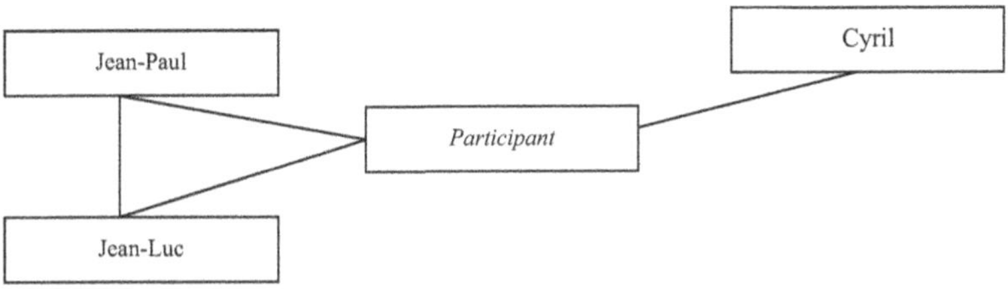

Jean-Paul

Cyril

Participant

Jean-Luc

Create your drawing here:

FIGURE 6.1 Social Network Strength Scale (SNSS) for SA (reprinted with permission from Kennedy, 2012, pp. 205–208)

Question #3 (Multiplexity Measure #1)
Using the number associated with each name above (from Question #1), indicate the activities you do with each person. List the number of *hours per week* (or *per month* for monthly activities) that you spend doing each activity with each person.

As in question 1, do not double count hours spent with two+ people at the same time. In this case, place the total number of hours in one column only, place a "G" in the Hours column for the others, and draw an arrow to the person in whose column you placed the hours.

Weekly activities	(1)	(2)	(3)	(4)	(5)	(6)	(7)	(8)	(9)	(10)
Share a meal	—	—	—	—	—	—	—	—	—	—
Have coffee/drink	—	—	—	—	—	—	—	—	—	—
Exercise or play a sport	—	—	—	—	—	—	—	—	—	—
Play board games or cards	—	—	—	—	—	—	—	—	—	—
Go shopping	—	—	—	—	—	—	—	—	—	—
Go out (bars/clubs/events)	—	—	—	—	—	—	—	—	—	—
Other _____	—	—	—	—	—	—	—	—	—	—

Question #4 (Multiplexity Measure #2)

In the last week (or in a typical week if last week was atypical), I spent _____ hours discussing one or more of the topics listed below with at least one native French speaker.

Indicate which topics you have discussed in the last (or in a typical) week:

Discussion Topics:	Yes
French vs. American culture	□
French politics	□
American politics	□
Clothing	□
Sports	□
Vacations	□
Love interests	□
Television & movies	□
Trivia	□
Problems I am having (e.g., being homesick)	□
Future plans (jobs, trips, advanced degrees)	□
Technology	□
Schoolwork/classes	□

FIGURE 6.1 (Continued)

Snowball Sampling

In addition to sharing a common data collection tool for SNA, the three Model Studies reviewed in this section (Model Studies 3, 4, and 6) share another commonality—all three included study participants who were selected from specific SA programs and/or who had been specifically recruited by the researchers to participate in the project. In cases where researchers do not have ready access to the population of language learners they intend to study, they must find another means of contacting and recruiting participants.

Model Study 16 by Palfreyman (2021) provides an example of how this can be accomplished using a technique called 'snowball sampling'. As the goal of this study was to examine longitudinal changes in opportunities for English language use by Emirati females from 2003 to 2018, Palfreyman (2021) identified a small group of study participants who were then asked to forward the multiple-choice survey to others in their network, thereby creating a 'snowball' effect resulting in a total of 102 study participants.

From the 102 participants recruited for the comparison study, Palfreyman (2021) focused on the English language learning activities of 41 Emirati females studying at the same government university in Dubai as the original cohort from Palfreyman (2006) in order to identify changes over time to the learning opportunities afforded by participation in informal language learning networks (ILLNs). Using the online questionnaire, Palfreyman (2021) gathered qualitative and quantitative data about the frequency and type of English language use inside and outside of the home, social networks inside and outside of the home, and the education level and English proficiency of family members living with the participant. The online survey questions also focused on how participants sought assistance from their ILLNs in their study of English (Palfreyman refers to this as 'co-regulation' of their learning in the network) and how participants assisted others in their ILLNs with the study of English. The results of Palfreyman (2021) are discussed in Chapter 9.

Conclusions about Surveys and Questionnaires

As demonstrated by the studies reviewed in this section, surveys and questionnaires for SNA generally rely on a name generator and/or name interpreter approach in which study participants are prompted to first identify the members of their social networks and then to characterize their relationship with each member in terms of the frequency and nature of their interactions in the TL (and often the L1). Surveys and questionnaires are popular among researchers working in SNA because they are both a flexible means of meeting the specific goals of the research project and they provide a rich source of data about how learners form and maintain relationships with TL speakers, as well as with co-national and international speakers, and how they access opportunities to use the TL. This flexibility is demonstrated by the number of Model Studies using surveys and questionnaires to gather social network data. In addition to the Model Studies described in detail in this section, the following Model Studies also relied on surveys and questionnaires, in conjunction with other forms of data, to gather social network data from their study participants: Model Study 5 (Serrano et al., 2012), Model Study 7 (Pozzi, 2021; Pozzi & Bayley, 2021), Model Study 8

(C. Li et al., 2021), Model Study 9 (Kinginger & Carnine, 2019), Model Study 10 (Diao, 2017), Model Study 11 (Hasegawa, 2019), and Model Study 12 (Carhill-Poza, 2015).

Live Recordings and Participant Observations

Live Recordings

In more recent studies, including Model Study 9 (Kinginger & Carnine, 2019) and Model Study 10 (Diao, 2017), researchers have gathered social network interaction data and linguistic data simultaneously through the use of live audio recordings. In these studies, participants are instructed to record a certain number of interactions, at specific intervals, with the TL speakers in their social networks. This data collection method provides a number of advantages over retrospective interviews, diary entries, and questionnaires: live recordings eliminate the potential inaccuracies of self-reported data and they mitigate (although do not completely eliminate) problems associated with the 'observer's paradox' (Labov, 1972b) whereby a researcher must be present to record naturalistic linguistic data, but their presence renders the situation unnatural and likely impacts the behavior of the speakers being recorded. The disadvantages of relying on live recordings are related to the lack of control that the researcher has over the timing and content of the recordings, as well as the reliance on the study participants to ensure that research guidelines are being followed throughout the recording process.

Nonetheless, live recordings of language learners and TL speakers provide a rich qualitative data source that is especially useful in studies of language socialization and identity formation. They are also very useful in studies focusing on the acquisition of patterns of sociolinguistic variation, particularly if study participants are recorded during interactions with speakers with whom they have different relationships or with speakers of varying social statuses. For example, a more proficient learner of Spanish or French would be expected to use *usted* 'you (formal)' or *vous* 'you (formal)' with an acquaintance or with a person in a position of authority, but *tú* 'you (informal)' or *tu* 'you (informal)' with a friend or with a child.

Because it is difficult to separate the data collection tool from the actual data collected when using live recordings in SNA, this section focuses on both the data collection process and the results of Model Study 9 (Kinginger & Carnine, 2019). In their study, Kinginger and Carnine (2019) analyzed 4–8 hours of recorded mealtime conversations with host family members to examine the language socialization process of two L2 French learners participating in a university homestay program in France. In addition to the recorded conversations, each learner completed pre- and post-questionnaires and a semi-structured interview at the end of the sojourn, and one member of each host family also completed a post-sojourn interview with the researchers.

The first student in Kinginger and Carnine (2019), Amelia, requested a semester homestay with two adults in a quiet atmosphere, which she found with Aladin and Capucine, who were experienced hosts of international university students. According to the authors, the analysis of Amelia's mealtime conversations with her host family revealed many "intensive, cordial mealtime interactions" focused on Amelia's activities and interests and in which Aladin and Capucine "displayed remarkable skill in managing conversations with a language learner on a wide variety of topics" (Kinginger & Carnine, 2019, p. 860). The researchers noted that these conversations included everyday events, elements of cultural significance, and discussions of a more abstract, humanistic, or linguistic nature, such as the meaning of the word 'friend' in both French and English. The authors noted that just as Amelia expressed gratitude for the time and effort that her hosts had invested in her language acquisition and social and cultural education during her time abroad, so too did her hosts appreciate the opportunity to learn about American culture and to see their own culture from a different perspective. Table 6.6 is an excerpt of the mealtime conversation in which Capucine (the French homestay mother) asks Amelia (the SA learner)

TABLE 6.6 Excerpt of conversation between Capucine (C) and Amelia (A) about the word 'friend'

1. C: ouais je voulais je je voulais euh qu'on parle de:: de quelque chose d'un mot.	yeah I wanted I I wanted uh for us to talk abou:: t about something about a word.
2. Am: @oui?	@ yes?
3. C: d'un mot que: vous les étudiants depuis qu'on a des étudiants vous utilisez beaucoup quand vous rencontrez quelqu'un?	about a word tha:t you students since we have had students you use a lot when you meet someone
4. Am: um um @@@@	um um @@@@
5. C: vous dîtes tout de suite je me suis fait un ami.	you say right away I have made a friend
6. Am: ou::I	ye:s
7. C: alors, je voulais savoir, en anglais,	so, I wanted to know, in English,
8. Am: um hm?	um hm?
9. C: est-ce qu'on fait la différence entre un copain, un camarade, un ami. est-ce que c'est tout le même mot?	do you differentiate between a *copain*, a *camarade*, an *ami*. is it all the same word?
Am: ah	ah

Source: Reprinted with permission from Kinginger & Carnine, 2019, p. 860

about the word 'friend' in English and whether English, like French, has other words to distinguish between levels of intimacy in relationships with 'friends'.

The second student in Kinginger and Carnine (2019), Irène, stayed a full year in France and lived with a host family of four people, including two children, aged 16 and 12. In contrast to Amelia's mealtime conversations where both TL speakers were primarily focused on Amelia and her contributions to their discussions, the authors pointed out that Irène's mealtime conversations were characterized by rapid speech, frequent topic shifts, and regular interruptions and overlapping discourse. The researchers described this conversation style as having a low level of 'considerateness' and a high level of engagement. Using live recordings, the analysis of Irène's mealtime recordings shows that, initially, Irène needed to be prompted or invited to join in the conversations (usually by her host mother), but that by the end of the academic year, she was participating in 'cooperative overlap' with her host family members, was able to joke with them in the TL, and was also able to provide culturally relevant interjections, without assistance, to the unfolding discussion. Table 6.7 provides an excerpt of a

TABLE 6.7 Excerpt of conversation between Irène (I), Jean (J), and Corrine (C)

1. J: Lionel Jospin, qui était un premier ministre, il se faisait toujours prendre en photo euh:: quand il faisait du vélo, sur l'Île de Ré,	Lionel Jospin, who was a Prime Minister, he had photos taken of him euh:: when he was on his bike, on Ré island,
2. I: mm	mm
3. J: p'is l'Île de Ré, c'est quand même une:: une île très riche hein? mai:s euh pour montrer que lui, il faisait du vél[o::, il était SI:::MPLE	and Ré island, it's after all a:: a very rich island right? but to show that he travels by bi::[ke, he was SI:::MPLE
4. I: je suis normal @]	I am normal @]
5. J: ouais, [tu montres que t'es écolo- ÉCOLOGI:::STE::	yeah, [you show that you're an ECOLOGI:::ST::
6. C: qu'il passait ses vacances en France]	that he took his vacations in France]
7. J: voilà::: que t'es en Fra:::nce, tu:: voilà. et inversement, Sarkozy dès qu'il a été élu, le lendemain- c'est Sarko- ouais, on l'a vu sur u::n un voilie::r euh de lu::xe tu vois, un- un bateau de [luxe::	that's i:::t that you are in France, you:: that's it. and on the contrary, Sarkozy as soon as he was elected, the next day- it's Sarko-yeah, we saw him on a:: a luxury sailboa::t, a [delu::xe ship
8. I: bon] ça c'est- ÇA C'EST SARKOZY [@	well] that's- THAT'S SARKOZY [@

Source: Reprinted with permission from Kinginger & Carnine, 2019, p. 865

conversation at the end of the academic year (in May) involving Irène (I), her host father, Jean (J), and one interjection by her host mother, Corrine (C). This discussion centers on French politicians and their attempts to appear simple and relatable to their constituents and demonstrates that Irène has developed the ability to fully participate in the family's mealtime discussions.

Model Study 9 by Kinginger and Carnine (2019) uses live mealtime recordings of two SA learners and their homestay families to draw important conclusions about the role of host families in language socialization during SA. First, because both the host families and the learners were invested in developing the relationships, all parties benefited from the increased cultural awareness afforded by the experience, and both learners benefitted linguistically. Second, because Amelia's mealtime conversations did not involve the type of high-engagement, overlapping discourse that Irène's host family used, and Amelia did not have learn how to take the floor during these discussions, the researchers noted that Amelia's French remained formal and "bookish", and she did not show evidence of having acquired certain common characteristics of informal French. In contrast, the authors noted that Irène was exposed to many different speech registers at the dinner table, including the speech of her young host brother and sister, and that this allowed her to develop a more conversational speech style in French, as well as the ability to participate in the fast-paced, unmodified discourse that occurs between two, or more, TL speakers who know each other well. Finally, the researchers pointed out the importance of including this type of fine-grained, qualitative analysis of language learners and the TL speakers within their social networks in order to better understand how interactions within these networks contribute to linguistic development and language socialization in the SA context.

The methods and results of Model Study 9 (Kinginger & Carnine, 2019) are supported by those of Kinginger (2015) who used recorded conversations at the dinner table between two language learners and their Chinese host families to examine socialization related to two specific areas of language use, or 'routine speech events': teasing and discussions of food and taste. The first student, David, whose host family engaged in regular acts of teasing at the dinner table, had studied Chinese for only two years before participating in the homestay program. Although David's proficiency in Chinese was limited, the analysis of his conversations with his host family shows that these interactions facilitated the development of language skills that allowed him to both participate in teasing (e.g., of his host sister) and to also be the focus of teasing (e.g., his distaste for seafood). Kinginger concluded that through the social practice of teasing, a higher level of intimacy between David and his host family members was created.

The second student in Kinginger (2015), Sam, had studied Chinese for 11 years, had participated in a Chinese immersion program in elementary school, and had completed Advanced Placement coursework in Chinese in high school. Kinginger pointed out that because Sam started with a higher level of Chinese, he was able to actively participate in more complex conversations with his host mother about food, food aesthetics, and health. For example, many of the mealtime conversations included interactions between Sam and his host mother in which she would ask Sam to name the ingredients in a dish and, if he did not know them, she would provide the vocabulary words and ask him to repeat them until he pronounced them correctly. Sam also engaged in discussions about American and Chinese eating habits and preferences and was thereby socialized into understanding certain Chinese cultural values and beliefs surrounding food and meals. Through the analysis of recorded conversations between learners and their host families, Kinginger was able to 'extract' qualitative data about the relationships that learners developed in and through the L2 and to provide empirical evidence of the 'two-way enrichment' (Iino, 2006) that can occur within the reinforcing boundaries of social networks with TL speakers during SA.

The type of live participant recordings that Kinginger and Carnine (2019) used are most suitable for studies with a relatively small number of participants, and for that reason are not often found in SNA studies. We suggest, however, that such recordings could be part of the data analyzed in larger SNA studies. It is possible, for example, to collect participant-recorded data from several focal participants, including a small number with more elaborate social networks and a small number with fewer connections with TL speakers. As noted in the previous chapter, such data would be particularly valuable in studies examining the relationship between the acquisition of patterns of sociolinguistic variation and the depth and breadth of learners' social networks.

In Model Study 10, Diao (2017) also used audio recordings of three SA participants and their host family members (or roommates) to examine how the social and political stances of the members of the learners' social networks influenced the development of each learner's identity in the TL. Diao specifically focused on how learners co-constructed their TL identity with the TL speakers in their social networks and how this identity was reflected in their use (or nonuse) of a nonstandard phonological feature regularly used by speakers in the TL environment. In this study, participants were provided with audio recorders and were asked to record their routine conversations with their host families or roommates. Participants also completed semi-structured interviews, a background survey, and a language awareness questionnaire and the researcher supplemented this participant data with observations made during participant field trips and other social events. The results of Diao (2017) are discussed in Chapter 9.

Although not explicitly employed by the studies described in this section, another tool that can provide a useful supplement to qualitative SNA data gathered through live recordings with TL speakers is the 'walking interview' (Emmel & Clark, 2009). This data collection tool, which is described in Paradowski et al. (2021a), involves the researcher visiting the participant's neighborhood in order to create a visual representation of the participant's daily social network interactions.

Participant Observations

For studies involving young learners, participant observations and video recordings in classroom settings provide valuable data on social network formation and interaction. For example, Model Study 14 by Bernstein (2018) relied on weekly classroom observations and student and teacher interviews to reconstruct the egocentric student networks, as well as the sociocentric (see Chapter 7) classroom-level network, within a US Head Start preschool classroom with over 50 percent L2 English learners at the early stages of acquisition. Over the course of an academic year, Bernstein acted as an adult volunteer in the preschool classroom in which the research was conducted. Once a week (162 hours total), the researcher spent a full day in the classroom and participated in all classroom activities—snack time, circle, play time—with the exception of formally teaching or disciplining the students. Bernstein explained the need for the students to see her as an adult figure who would not report them to the teachers for breaking the rules in order to have access to a full range of interactions between the students (even those that would normally be considered against the rules).

For this study, Bernstein (2018) recorded 40 hours of classroom interactions, had extensive discussions with the two female preschool teachers, and conducted final interviews with the students at the end of the year in order to examine both the process of becoming a participating member of a classroom social network and the linguistic outcomes of such participation. The interviews consisted of asking each student who they "liked to play with the most" from a set of class photos. That is, instead of using a name generator approach whereby participants create their own list of network members, Bernstein used a name interpreter approach whereby participants interpret the relationship that they have with each person based on a predefined list of network members. Bernstein noted that although the preschool day was tightly structured by the teachers (i.e., breakfast, circle time, outside time, etc.), the teachers never specifically paired or grouped students together, with the exception of whole-class activities, leaving

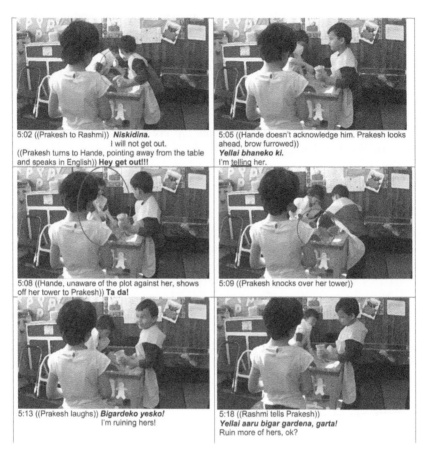

5:02 ((Prakesh to Rashmi)) **Niskidina.**
I will not get out.
((Prakesh turns to Hande, pointing away from the table and speaks in English)) **Hey get out!!!**

5:05 ((Hande doesn't acknowledge him. Prakesh looks ahead, brow furrowed))
Yellai bhaneko ki.
I'm telling her.

5:08 ((Hande, unaware of the plot against her, shows off her tower to Prakesh)) **Ta da!**

5:09 ((Prakesh knocks over her tower))

5:13 ((Prakesh laughs)) **Bigardeko yesko!**
I'm ruining hers!

5:18 ((Rashmi tells Prakesh))
Yellai aaru bigar gardena, garta!
Ruin more of hers, ok?

FIGURE 6.2 Video recording and transcript of free play time (reprinted with permission from Bernstein, 2018, p. 824)

approximately 4–6 hours per day during which students could choose with whom they interacted. This freedom of interaction was the focus of Bernstein's classroom observations, which sometimes included children being unkind to each other, such as the example depicted in Figure 6.2 in which Prakesh and Rashmi attempt to kick Hande off the sand table by knocking down her tower and yelling at her to leave. The results of Model Study 14 by Bernstein (2018) using participant observations to analyze classroom social networks are discussed in detail in Chapter 9.

Conclusion

The studies described in this chapter underscore the importance of using a variety of data collection methods in SNA, including: participant interviews; diaries, journals, and contact logs; surveys and questionnaires; and recordings and observations in order to meet the specific goals of the research project. Moreover, as demonstrated by the majority of the studies discussed here, a combination of data collection methods is often required in order for the researcher to have a complete picture of how the language learner uses the TL with TL speakers, as well as how the use of the L1 with co-nationals and international speakers may influence L2 acquisition. Finally, as this chapter highlights approaches to both qualitative and quantitative data collection, and the many potential uses of both types of data in SNA, it is critical that researchers continue to leverage both in their applications of SNA to L2 research.

Discussion Questions

1. Think about the qualitative and quantitative data gathered using the methods reviewed in this chapter. What are the advantages and disadvantages of each type?
2. Consider a population of learners that you would like to study using SNA. What data collection methods would you use and why?
3. Choose one of the questionnaires described in this chapter (Surveys and Questionnaires) and make some improvements to it. What would you add? What would you remove?
4. Create and maintain a log of 'important linguistic events' for a seven-day period. Analyze your data for common themes and report back on these.

7

MEASURING AND DEPICTING SOCIAL NETWORKS IN SECOND LANGUAGE RESEARCH

Introduction

Chapter 6 examined the types of social network data that L2 researchers collect and the most common methods that they use to gather this data. The current chapter focuses on what happens after the data is collected—how researchers use this quantitative and qualitative data to measure and depict learners' social networks with TL speakers, and others, and how these measurements may be correlated with specific linguistic outcomes. This chapter is divided into three sections: Quantitative Social Network Analysis (SNA), Network Diagrams, and Qualitative Assessments. As in previous chapters, this chapter uses Model Studies 1–16 and supplemental research to exemplify the methods described in each section.

Quantitative Social Network Analysis

Social Network Metrics and Scales

Quantitative network metrics and scales seek to characterize learners' social networks with target-language (TL) speakers, and others, based on a number of factors related to the strength and breadth of learners' social networks, such as the number of TL speakers in the network, the amount of time spent or frequency of interactions with TL speakers, the number of connections between network members, and the number of different groups within the overall network. Most studies using quantitative assessments of learner social networks take one of two approaches: (1) researchers analyze learner

DOI: 10.4324/9781003174448-7

networks for a variety of well-known metrics, or (2) researchers calculate an overall 'network strength score' for each learner's network. Both network metrics and network strength scores can be compared to those of other learners or compared to other factors contributing to L2 acquisition, such as time in the TL community, and then correlated with specific aspects of L2 development.

Network Metrics: Density and Multiplexity

Two of the most common network metrics used in both first language (L1) and second language (L2) research are network *density* and *multiplexity*. As described in Chapter 2, the ties that an individual (*ego*) forms with others may be characterized as strong or weak ties and strong ties may be *multiplex*, *dense*, or both (L. Milroy, 2002). *Multiplex* ties refer to the multiple ways that one individual may be linked to another (e.g., they are neighbors and co-workers). *Dense* ties are those that link many of the same people to each other thereby forming a closed circle or network. Conversely, weak ties are neither dense, nor multiplex—they refer to the type of uniplex, or singular, relationship that one might have with a local merchant or an acquaintance. Both of these metrics, network *density* and network *multiplexity*, have been shown to reinforce local linguistic norms in research on L1 and bilingual communities (Edwards, 1992; Lippi-Green, 1989; W. Li, 1994; Milroy & Milroy, 1978) and have also become important metrics in SNA in L2 research.

In this section, Model Study 13 by Wiklund (2002) is presented as a case study demonstrating how researchers use social network data to calculate important network metrics like network density and multiplexity and to correlate these metrics with L2 acquisition. Wiklund's study also demonstrates how calculations of network density and multiplexity can be adapted to reflect the specific characteristics of a community of learners and their linguistic environment, such as the adolescent L2 Swedish immigrant students in Wiklund's study. In this study, Wiklund examined the social networks of 54 learners at two different upper-secondary schools in Sweden in order to analyze the impact of Swedish peer networks on verbal and written sophistication in L2 Swedish. Wiklund selected participants from a suburban school where the L2 speakers represented a majority (90 percent) of the student population, as well as a provincial school where the L2 speakers represented a small minority (12 percent). It is important to note that the participant groups were not homogenous in their length of residence in Sweden: the participants from the suburban school included a number of second- and third-generation immigrants and their median length of residence in Sweden was 15.5 years compared to 7 years for the participants from the provincial school. Of the original 54 participants, 39 participants completed all of the research tasks.

To measure the density (i.e., level of interconnectedness) of the participants' networks, Wiklund (2002) used a questionnaire that asked each participant to first report all of the people with whom they interacted on a regular basis, and in what language, according to three categories: (1) friends, family, and countrymen from their own ethnic group; (2) Swedes (born in Sweden with Swedish parents); and (3) members of another, non-Swedish ethnic group. From each of these three categories, participants selected their "three best friends", which resulted in a list of nine total contacts (interactants), three from each category. Based on these nine interactants, Wiklund measured the *network density* of each participant based on a total possible density score of 45 points (i.e., if all nine interactants knew each other and interacted on a regular basis). Participant density scores were calculated by dividing the number of existing links among members by 45 possible links and reported as a percentage of the total possible score. For example, if a learner reported 18 existing links among their network members, 18 divided by 45 possible links would yield a network density score of 40 percent.

Figure 7.1 provides a visual representation of Wiklund's density calculation. In this diagram for learner S36, interactants A-B-C from the learner's own ethnic group all know each other—this is represented by the six connections within this group of three people. Similarly, interactants D-E-F (Swedes with Swedish parents) all know each other and interactants G-H-I (contacts from another ethnic group) know each other. In addition to these 18 network within-group connections, interactant B from the

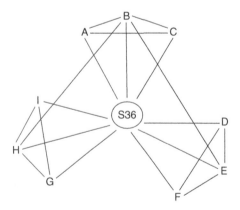

FIGURE 7.1   Network density calculation for learner S36 (reprinted with permission from Wiklund, 2002, p. 67)

learner's own ethnic group knows interactant E from the Swedish group and interactant H from the other ethnic group resulting in a total of 20 network connections or ties. Wiklund then divided these 20 ties by a total possible score of 45 ties, resulting in a network density score of 44.4 percent for learner S36.

In addition to network density, Wiklund calculated a *friendship multiplexity score* for each participant using the same nine interactants from the density calculation. Friendship multiplexity was calculated based on whether each interactant was a schoolmate (*school*), lived in the same neighborhood (*proximity*), and/or was a relative in addition to being a friend (*kinship*). In Wiklund's calculation, each of the nine interactants contributed up to three points to the overall multiplexity score if they met all three criteria (*school, proximity, kinship*), resulting in a total possible multiplexity score of 27 points. Network multiplexity scores were then calculated for each participant as a percentage of the total possible 27 points. The friendship multiplexity score for learner S36 is shown in Figure 7.2.

In Figure 7.2, each of the nine interactants (A-I) has been assigned a score of 1–3 depending on the way (or ways) in which learner S36 interacts with these contacts. For example, interactants A and C contribute one point each to the multiplexity score because they live in the same neighborhood as learner S36, but they are not schoolmates or members of the learner's family. In contrast, interactant B lives in the same neighborhood and is also a cousin, so this interactant contributes 2 points to the multiplexity score. Similarly, interactants G-H-I live in the same neighborhood and are also schoolmates, so they each contribute 2 points to the overall multiplexity score of 13 points. The overall friendship multiplexity score of learner S36 would then be calculated as 13/27 total points or 48 percent.

To the friendship multiplexity calculation, Wiklund added an activity calculation (*additional scoring for nuancing: activities*) to incorporate the diversity of activities that the participants engaged in with each interactant. The maximum activity score per learner was 13.5 points (1.5 points per interactant, or 0.5 points per activity for up to three activities). Wiklund explained that the activity calculation was added to balance the friendship multiplexity score—to account for the fact that although interactants may only contribute one point to the multiplexity score, as schoolmates for example, they may spend a significant amount of time with the learner if they engage in many activities together. Additionally, Wiklund calculated a *frequency score* for each learner-interactant relationship based on whether the participant saw the interactant three or more times per week (contributing one point) or at least once a month, but less than three times per week (contributing 0.5 points). The maximum frequency score was nine points,

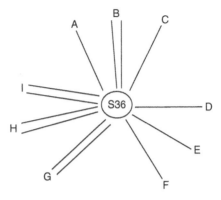

Network capacities: | Scores:

A: proximity — 1
B: proximity, kinship (cousin) — 2
C: proximity — 1
Total A–C — 4

D: proximity — 1
E: proximity — 1
F: proximity — 1
Total D–F — 3

G: proximity, school — 2
H: proximity, school — 2
I: proximity, school — 2
Total G–I — 6

FIGURE 7.2 Friendship multiplexity calculation for learner S36 (reprinted with permission from Wiklund, 2002, p. 70)

TABLE 7.1 Network effect calculation for learner S36

Network orientation	Friendship multiplexity	Nuancing scoring: activities	Frequency	Total: resp. network
A–C	4.0	4.5	3.0	11.5
D–F	3.0	3.0	1.5	7.5
G–I	6.0	3.0	2.5	11.5
Total: A–I	13.0	10.5	7.0	30.5

Source: Reprinted with permission from Wiklund, 2002, p. 74

or one point per interactant. Together, the friendship multiplexity score, the activity score, and the frequency score contributed to a *potential network effect* out of a possible 49.5 points for each learner. The calculation for network effect for learner S36 is shown in Table 7.1.

Wiklund then correlated the *potential network effect* score with a composite L2 proficiency score related to written and verbal sophistication, using a written language sample from a school composition and a recorded 30-minute oral interview in Swedish. The compositions were analyzed for a variety of features related to 'verbal sophistication', including the mean word length and number of nonrecurring words and the use of nominalizations and passive constructions. Wiklund also examined the participants' ability to alternate repertoires between the written and verbal tasks where a higher frequency of nominalizations and passive constructions in the written composition versus the oral interview was considered evidence of such ability. Wiklund calculated four different verbal-sophistication indices based on the criteria listed above (long-word index, mean-length index, nonrecurring index, word-variation index), as well as the number of nominalizations and passives for each learner, and compared the composite score (out of 21 points possible) against the group average (8.33) and the average for the L1 Swedish control group (9.5).

For social network orientation, Wiklund categorized the 39 participants into five different groups based on whether the participant primarily associated with: (1) members of their own ethnic group; (2) Swedes; (3) members of another ethnic group; (4) their own ethnic group and other ethnic groups; or (5) Swedes and other ethnic groups. Results demonstrated that the participants in category 5, those whose social networks were comprised primarily of Swedes and members of other ethnic groups where Swedish serves as a lingua franca, had the highest composite proficiency scores (average L2 proficiency = 10.93) and the highest scores on the verbal sophistication indices. This group was followed closely by the participants in category 2 (average L2 proficiency = 10.12), whose social networks were comprised primarily of Swedes. The participants with the third highest proficiency scores (average L2 proficiency = 8.73) had social networks comprised of members from their own ethnic group and other ethnic groups (category 4). Other notable results include the fact that the participants with primarily Swedish networks (category 2) achieved the highest scores for the ability to alternate between the norms of a written and spoken repertoire and that all participants performed at higher levels of verbal sophistication in the oral interviews than in the compositions. Additionally, the highest social network density and multiplexity scores were achieved by participants with mixed networks of either Swedes and other ethnic groups (category 5) or their own ethnic group and other ethnic groups (category 4).

Overall, Wiklund's results demonstrate the positive impact of social networks with L1 Swedish speakers, and with other ethnic groups where Swedish is the language of communication, on the acquisition of L2 Swedish—as the participants with mixed networks of Swedes and other ethnic groups had the highest scores for social network density and multiplexity, as well as the highest proficiency scores in L2 Swedish. At the same time, only five of Wiklund's 39 final participants reported having primarily L1 Swedish networks, and only two participants reported having mixed networks of Swedes and other ethnic groups, results which underscore the difficulties that immigrants often face in integrating themselves into the host community and in creating social networks with TL speakers, even after a long-term residence in the TL environment.

Network Metrics: Intensity, Durability, and Dispersion

As described in Chapter 6, The Study Abroad Social Interaction Questionnaire (SASIQ) was first used by Dewey et al. (2012, Model Study 4) in their study of L2 Japanese learners during study abroad (SA) in Japan and Dewey et al. (2013) in their study of L2 Arabic learners in Morocco and Jordan. In both of these studies, the participant responses to the SASIQ questionnaire contributed to the calculation of five key social network metrics: (a) the *size* of the learner's networks with TL speakers, (b) the *intensity*, or strength, of each relationship, (c) the *durability* of the network connections based on the frequency of TL interactions, (d) the *density* of the network based on the interconnectedness of network members, and (e) the *dispersion* of the network based on the number of different groups within the network.

Model Study 4 by Dewey et al. (2012) provides one example of how learner networks with TL speakers may contribute to oral proficiency gains during SA. In this study, Dewey et al. examined self-perceived proficiency gains using a *then-now* questionnaire that asks learners to rate their abilities to complete various real-life speech acts in the TL at the beginning and end of their sojourn abroad. Examples of speech acts from the then-now self-assessment include the ability to "respond to simple questions on the most common aspects of daily life" (novice level), "obtain and give information by asking and answering questions" (intermediate level), and "describe events and objects in the past, present, and future" (advanced level). At the beginning and at the end of the SA period, the participants rated their ability to complete each speech act on a scale of 1–5 points where 1 point indicated 'not at all' and 5 points indicated 'quite easily'. According to Dewey et al., then-now analyses are effective because they provide a direct assessment of the learner's perceived linguistic change and the effectiveness of the SA program, as experienced by the learner.

The goals of Model Study 4 were to understand the self-perceived oral proficiency gains of SA learners and to correlate these self-perceived gains with language contact and social networks with TL speakers during SA. Using the results of the SASIQ, a modified version of the Language

Contact Profile (LCP, Freed et al., 2004), and the results of the then-now self-assessment, Dewey et al. (2012) identified three primary predictors of perceived gains during SA. The strongest predictor of perceived gains was the learner's pre-departure proficiency self-assessment where a lower assessment correlated with greater self-perceived gains following the SA period. Time spent in the TL was also a significant predictor of self-perceived gains. Finally, the *dispersion* of social networks with TL speakers (i.e., the number of different social groups within the social network) was also found to be a significant predictor of self-perceived gains. These results demonstrate that social networks with TL speakers play a central role in the SA experience while also facilitating two additional predictors of self-perceived gains reported in the study: total time spent speaking the TL and time spent speaking the TL with TL speakers.

A subsequent study by Dewey et al. (2013) also used the LCP, the SASIQ, and a then-now questionnaire to examine self-perceived proficiency gains by 30 L2 Arabic learners during SA in Morocco and Jordan. The results from this study indicated that the learners spoke Arabic and English in nearly equal amounts during the SA period, but that most of the English was spoken with L1 Arabic speakers. Moreover, the third highest category of language use by these L2 learners was speaking Arabic with TL speakers, which may have been a direct result of the L2 learners using "English to access Arabic" (p. 97) by offering English tutoring or conversation exchanges to meet and interact with TL speakers. In terms of self-perceived gains, results indicated that the strongest predictor was the English proficiency of the Arabic speakers in the learner's social network, likely because the interactions in English provided a gateway to interactions in Arabic.

Additionally, the analysis of the learners' social networks by Dewey et al. (2013) revealed that the *intensity* (i.e., strength on a scale from acquaintance to very close friend) of the relationships with TL speakers was positively correlated with self-perceived proficiency gains. Finally, interactions with TL speakers outside of the social network were also positively correlated with self-perceived gains in L2 Arabic indicating that frequent exchanges in service and other public contexts provide opportunities for TL use that may contribute to overall L2 acquisition. The descriptive statistics from the SASIQ responses of 29 study participants are shown in Table 7.2. Table 7.2 includes the five key social network metrics included in Dewey et al. (2012) and Dewey et al. (2013): network *size* (number of TL speakers), *durability* (frequency), *intensity* (strength), *density* (interconnectedness), and *dispersion* (number of different groups).

The results of Dewey et al. (2013) highlight the importance of understanding both the size and the density of the social network, but also the composition of the network and the L1/L2 usage patterns among

TABLE 7.2 Descriptive statistics from SASIQ responses from 29 participants

	Minimum	Maximum	Mean	SD
Size				
Number of friends and acquaintances	3	20	8.8	4.00
Number of friends and acquaintances outside of host family	0	15	5.9	3.96
Durability				
Frequency of Arabic use	3 (Sometimes)	5 (Very often)	4.0	0.59
Frequency of English use	2 (Rarely)	5 (Very often)	3.2	0.85
Intensity				
Percent friends	0	100	60.0	24.10
Number friends	0	14	5.6	3.05
Density				
Size of largest social group	1	5	3.5	1.57
Average size of social group	1	6	2.40	1.01
Size of two largest social groups	1	5.5	2.60	1.15
Average size of social groups excluding host family	1	3.5	1.80	0.76
Dispersion				
Number of social groups	1	6	3.0	1.29

Source: Adapted from Dewey et al., 2013, p. 93

the network members. In their study, speaking English with L1 Arabic network members was positively (rather than negatively) correlated with self-perceived gains in L2 Arabic because establishing the relationships with L1 Arabic speakers presumably led to increased opportunities to use the L2 alongside English. Thus, this study makes an important contribution to our current understanding of L2 acquisition during SA indicating that speaking one's L1 during a period of SA does not *automatically* reduce the potential gains to be made in the L2 as long as the L2 is also being used with TL speakers.

In a related study, Smemoe et al. (2014) compared the results of the SASIQ and an intercultural sensitivity measure with oral proficiency gains on the Oral Proficiency Interview (OPI, American Council on the Teaching of Foreign Languages, ACTFL). In this large-scale study of L1 English participants, the researchers examined proficiency gains in L2

Spanish, French, Russian, Arabic, Chinese during a period of SA of 8–16 weeks. Results demonstrated that the SASIQ measures of network *intensity* (relationship strength) and network *dispersion* (number of social groups in the network) were the strongest predictors of language proficiency of all factors considered in the analysis.

Network Dispersion: A Key Indicator

The studies by Wiklund (2002), Dewey et al. (2012, 2013), and Smemoe et al. (2014) discussed in the previous sections exemplify how researchers use social network data to quantify specific components of a language learner's social networks, including network density, multiplexity, frequency, and dispersion. The analysis involves first identifying the primary contacts within a learner's network and the language(s) spoken with each contact, as well as determining the division of language use in the case of a bilingual or multilingual relationship. Additionally, researchers have created various means for establishing how active or meaningful the contact is in the learner's life—whether the learner and the contact are close friends or merely acquaintances, whether they engage in diverse and frequent activities together, or whether they only see each other occasionally or in a single situational context like work or school. By combining the social network data collected using the methods described in Chapter 6 with the network metrics described in this section of Chapter 7, researchers are able to characterize the relationships that the learner has with TL speakers (and others) and to quantify the impact that these relationships have on the learner's acquisition of the TL.

While network density and multiplexity may be considered 'classic' network metrics that have been used in sociolinguistics since the foundational studies by Milroy and Milroy (1978) were published, three of the four studies of L2 acquisition reviewed in this section (Dewey et al., 2012; Smemoe et al., 2014; Wiklund, 2002) highlight the importance of network dispersion, or the number of different social groups within the overall network. In the study by Dewey et al. (2012), network dispersion was a significant predictor of self-perceived oral proficiency gains. In the study by Smemoe et al. (2014), network dispersion, in addition to network intensity, was a significant predictor of oral proficiency gains on the ACTFL OPI post-test. In Wiklund's (2002) study, the analysis of the ethnic orientation of the nine social network members of each learner revealed that learners with 'mixed' networks of Swedes and other ethnic groups achieved the highest levels of verbal sophistication, as well as the highest potential network effect scores incorporating network density, multiplexity, and frequency. The results of these three studies indicate that the number of different social groups in which the learner uses the TL, as measured by network dispersion, is a critical component of L2 acquisition.

The important role of network dispersion in L2 acquisition is exemplified by Model Study 8 (C. Li et al., 2021) on the acquisition of L2 Chinese during residence in China. In this study, C. Li et al. (2021) used SNA to examine *pragmatic subjectivity* (C. Li & Gao, 2017) where pragmatic subjectivity refers to a learner's awareness of the pragmatic resources available to them in the L2, as well as to the conscious pragmatic choices that learners make based on this metapragmatic awareness. The authors explain that a learner's pragmatic subjectivity leads them to accommodate or resist specific norms in their L2 production. Specifically, the authors looked at the changing use of request strategies (i.e., direct versus indirect strategies), external modifiers (e.g., greetings, thanks, sweeteners), and internal modifiers (e.g., sentence-final particles, tag-questions, politeness markers) by the learners over a one-year period.

C. Li et al. (2021) gathered speech data through open role-play activities that required the eight L2 Chinese learners to employ various requests and request strategies. One week later, the authors gathered reflective data from the learners that included explanations for their specific pragmatic choices in the role-play activities. Social network data for this study was gathered using the Study Abroad Network Questionnaire (SANQ) modeled on the questionnaires developed by Dewey et al. (2012) and Gautier and Chevrot (2015). Social network data included biographical information, a list of the 20 most frequent contacts during SA for each learner, and detailed information about each of these contacts. From this social network data, each learner's network was drawn using E-Net (Borgatti, 2006) and measures of network density and *heterogeneity* (i.e., the number of different nationalities within a network) were calculated. Additionally, the authors identified 'structural holes' (Burt, 1992, 2000) in the learners' networks which refer to network members that are connected to the learner (*ego*), but not to any other network members. Finally, the authors used ethnographic interviews and field notes to identify patterns of interactions among the learner and the members of their social network, as well as to complement the quantitative social network data gathered via the SANQ.

As a group, the eight learners in C. Li et al. (2021) moved toward NS patterns of directness in making requests over the one-year period, but results demonstrated that the learners varied widely, among themselves and as compared to native speakers (NSs), in their use of external and internal modifiers. These results are supported by the social network data gathered for the learners which demonstrated wide ranges in both network heterogeneity and network density.

To better understand their results, C. Li et al. selected two learners, Kent and Camille, as case studies to exemplify the role of dense or loose social networks, including co-nationals, other nationals, and L1 speakers, in the use of internal and external modifiers in the production of requests in L2 Chinese. The first learner, Kent, had a relatively 'balanced' social network made up of both co-nationals and locals with an average level of network density. Through this relatively dense network structure, Kent was exposed to high levels of L1 Chinese input, especially in the academic context. At the same time, Kent's reflective interviews indicated that he often received conflicting messages from his network members about the required or desired level of politeness or directness in making requests and, therefore, his production of requests was variable, or 'hybrid', in its alignment with NS norms.

In contrast, the second learner, Camille, had a social network characterized by the highest level of heterogeneity of all eight learners, as well as the lowest level of network density of all eight learners. That is, where Kent approached the group averages for both heterogeneity and density, Camille's network represented the extremes for both measures. The authors point out that Camille worked part-time in the Office of International Student Affairs, which gave her access to both local and international contacts and numerous opportunities to socialize with peers in Chinese. Camille also volunteered at a local retirement community where she interacted with elderly speakers, an experience which offered her the opportunity to compare linguistic norms across different segments of Chinese society.

The changes to Kent and Camille's use of external and internal modifiers over the course of the year, as well as the network diagrams for the 20 most frequent contacts in each learner's social network, are shown in Figure 7.3 (Kent) and Figure 7.4 (Camille). In Figures 7.3 and 7.4, the left column shows the rate of use of the modifier during the first set of role-plays and interviews (left) and during the second set of role-plays and interviews six months later (right). These rates were then compared to NS rates of use in order to determine whether the learner showed a closer alignment with NS patterns over time. The social network diagrams in the right column include all 20 speakers in the learner's network, their nationality, and their connections to other speakers. Kent's diagram in Figure 7.3 clearly shows a higher level of network density whereas Camille's network shows minimal density.

According to the authors, the result of Camille's loose, but extensive network of locals and international contacts shown in Figure 7.4 was an overall trend toward making more "situationally appropriate requests" over the course of the year (p. 412). Additionally, Camille's reflective interviews indicated a high level of metapragmatic awareness and engagement in a

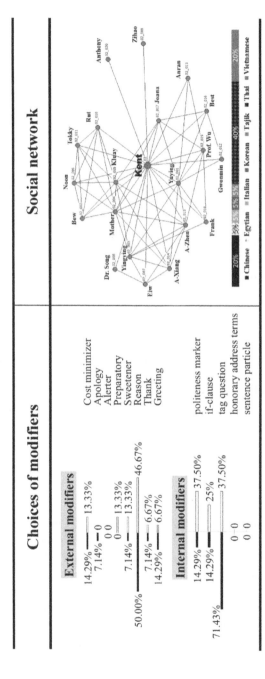

FIGURE 7.3 Kent—change in modifier use and network diagram (reprinted with permission from C. Li et al., 2021, p. 407)

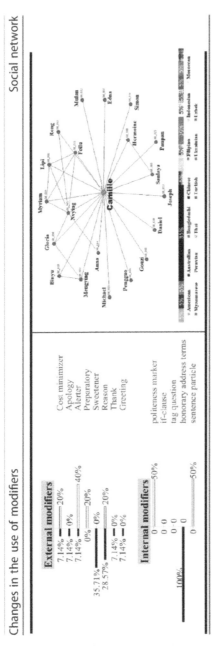

FIGURE 7.4   Camille—change in modifier use and network diagram (reprinted with permission from C. Li et al., 2021, p. 410)

"self-directed socialization process" (p. 413) in which she played the role of agent rather than that of a passive recipient.

The results of Model Study 8 by C. Li et al. (2021) highlight an important aspect of SNA in the context of L2 learners during a period of SA: where network density has repeatedly been shown to reinforce local speech norms in L1 and bilingual speech communities (see Chapters 2 and 3), network density may not have the same impact on L2 learners residing in the TL community and may in fact, hinder the L2 acquisition of pragmatic norms that show high levels of variation within the local community. These results are supported by those of Model Study 4 by Dewey et al. (2012), Model Study 13 by Wiklund (2002), and a supplementary study by Smemoe et al. (2014), all of which demonstrate that a social network incorporating different groups of TL speakers, or speakers with whom the learners use the TL, facilitates L2 acquisition.

Quantitative Network Scales

Model Study 6 (Kennedy Terry (2017, 2022a, 2022b) and Model Study 7 (Pozzi, 2021; Pozzi & Bayley, 2021) approach the assessment of social network strength somewhat differently than the studies described in the previous sections. Unlike the SASIQ first used in Model Study 4 by Dewey et al. (2012), the Social Network Strength Scale (SNSS, Kennedy, 2012) for SA used in Model Study 6 (Kennedy Terry 2017, 2022a, 2022b) and adapted for use in Model Study 7 (Pozzi, 2021; Pozzi & Bayley, 2021) includes only one global measure of social network strength on a scale of 1–10 points. Moreover, while the SASIQ includes all TL contacts in the learner's network, the SNSS for SA includes only those TL speakers with whom the learner speaks the TL for at least 30 minutes consecutively each week and with whom the learner has an ongoing relationship. Additionally, Dewey et al. (2012) used a separate questionnaire, the LCP, to gather TL use data in all modalities, but the SNSS for SA focuses on one activity only, speaking the TL with TL speakers, and incorporates this metric into the overall strength score.

The procedure for social network data collection using the SNSS for SA, including a visual presentation of the main sections of the questionnaire (Figure 6.1), is described in Chapter 6. The objective of this section is to explain how the SNSS for SA measures network density, multiplexity, and frequency, and to examine, in detail, the scoring procedure for the SNSS for SA.

The SNSS for SA (Kennedy, 2012) includes two density measures to characterize the overall level of TL interactions and two multiplexity measures to assess the 'richness' of these TL interactions. In Density Measure 1, the learner (e.g., Marissa) lists all of the native TL speakers with whom she speaks the TL for at least 30 minutes each week and receives one point for each contact and one point per hour (per week) spent speaking the TL with this contact. For example, if Marissa lists three TL speakers (speakers A, B, C), with whom she speaks the TL for two hours (speaker A), one hour (speaker B), and three hours (speaker C) per week, Marissa would earn nine points (3 points for the three contacts + 2 + 1 + 3 points for the hours spent speaking the TL = 9 points). For Density Measure 2, the participants use the list from Density Measure 1 to draw their social network and the learners receive one point for each network tie connecting the participant to a TL speaker or connecting TL speakers to each other. In the previous example, if Marissa knows three speakers (A, B, C) and speakers B and C also know each other, then Marissa would receive 4 points for a total of four network connections.

Multiplexity Measures 1 and 2 of the SNSS for SA investigate what activities the participant engages in with TL speakers (e.g., play sports, watch a movie, go to a bar) and what they talk about with these TL speakers (e.g., current events, sports, friends, classes). Multiplexity Measure 1 asks the learner to identify (from a provided list of six activities) the activities done with each of the TL speakers listed in Density Measure 1: learners receive one point for each different weekly activity shared with a TL speaker. In the example above, if Marissa indicates that she engages in four different activities with speaker A, two with speaker B, and all six with speaker C, then Marissa would receive a total of 12 points for this question. Finally, Multiplexity Measure 2 asks the learner what subjects they discuss regularly with TL speakers in order to assess the level of complexity and the potential for new vocabulary acquisition in the learner's TL interactions. In this question, learners review a list of 13 conversation topics and indicate (with a checkmark) which ones they discuss regularly with the TL speakers in their network, receiving one point for each different topic, up to a maximum of 13 points. For the sample learner described here, if Marissa regularly discusses 10 of the 13 topics with the speakers in her network, she would receive 10 points for this question. Up to this point in the questionnaire, Marissa has a score of 35 points (9 points for Density Measure 1; 4 points for Density Measure 2; 12 points for Multiplexity Measure 1; 10 points for Multiplexity Measure 2).

In addition to the Density and Multiplexity measures, the SNSS for SA also awards points for interactions with TL speakers outside of the network (e.g., in service or academic contexts), as well as for weekend activities and special events/occasions that are not captured in the weekly calculation (e.g., a day trip or holiday spent with a TL speaker). Additionally, for both Density Measure 1 and Multiplexity Measure 1, participants receive 1.5 points per hour spent with multiple TL speakers at the same time (vs. one point per hour spent with a single TL speaker) to account for the potentially beneficial exposure to unmodified TL interactions between TL speakers (Long, 1983). In the example of the learner Marissa, if Marissa receives an additional 5 points for out-of-network/weekend activities, and if she spends two hours per week with speaker C and some of speaker C's friends at the same time (+ one point on Density Measure 1), Marissa's overall score on the SNSS for SA would be 41 points out of a possible 100. Marissa's adjusted score on a scale of 1–10 points would be 4 out of 10 points.

The results by individual learner for the SNSS for SA at the final interview from Kennedy Terry (2017, 2022a, 2022b) are presented in Table 7.3. In these studies, Kennedy Terry examined the L2 acquisition of phonological variables characteristic of informal French. In Table 7.3, the learners are listed in the first column (using pseudonyms) and their length of stay in France (semester or year) is listed in the second column. Columns 3 and 4 indicate the rate of use of two phonological variables examined by Kennedy Terry: /l/ deletion in subject pronouns and schwa deletion in clitics. The final column includes the learner's score on the SNSS for SA at the final interview (after one semester or a full academic year in France). With very few exceptions, Table 7.3 demonstrates that higher scores on the SNSS for SA are associated with higher usage rates for both of the phonological variables studied. These results are discussed in more detail in Chapter 8.

TABLE 7.3 Final SNSS for SA scores by speaker

Speaker	Year/Sem.	/l/ deletion % at final interview	Schwa deletion % at final interview	Final SNSS
Claire	Sem.	68.2	17.1	9
Miranda	Year	29.6	14.2	8
Sasha	Year	30.0	5.3	6
Cassie	Year	54.1	12.3	5
Julie	Sem.	48.3	11.5	5
Jennifer	Year	34.0	32.4	5
Katherine	Year	31.6	21.4	5
Tiffany	Year	21.6	15.6	5
Ericka	Sem.	15.0	6.2	5
Marissa	Year	3.4	14.7	4
Brittany	Sem.	0.0	5.2	4
Tyler	Year	40.0	5.7	3
Eric	Year	15.2	10.6	3
Adam	Sem.	2.6	1.6	3
Audrey	Year	3.8	1.4	3
Melissa	Sem.	0.0	0.0	2
Jade	Sem.	1.9	6.5	0

Source: Reprinted with permission from Kennedy Terry, 2022a, p. 257

TABLE 7.4 Social Network Strength Scale

Name:
Date:
(1) List each native Spanish-speaking person with whom you have maintained at least a 30-min. conversation in Spanish over the last couple of weeks. List the number of hours per week (if you spent time with two+ people at the same time just write the number of hours next to one name), your relationship to this person (e.g., host mom, conversation partner, etc.), where each person is from (country, city, neighborhood), and their approximate age.
(2) Check and/or list all activities in which you participated with this person (e.g., sharing a meal/drink, taking a trip, exercising, celebrating an occasion, playing a sport/board game/ cards, going to an event/bar/club) and all of the topic(s) you discussed with this person (e.g., culture, current events, politics, sports, music, movies, tv, problems, plans, school, daily life).

Name	Hours /week	Relationship (e.g., host mom, roommate)	Place of origin (neighborhood, city, country)	Age	Activities in which you have participated with this person (Check all that apply / list all others.)	Topic(s) discussed with this person (Check all that apply / list all others.)
					[] Share a meal/ drink [] Take a trip [] Exercise [] Celebrate an occasion [] Play a sport / board game/ cards [] Go to event/ bar/club [] Other:	[] Culture [] Daily life [] TV [] Politics [] Sports [] School [] Music [] Movies [] Problems [] Events [] Plans [] Other:
					[] Share a meal/ drink [] Take a trip [] Exercise [] Celebrate an occasion [] Play a sport / board game / cards [] Go to event/ bar/club [] Other:	[] Culture [] Daily life [] TV [] Politics [] Sports [] School [] Music [] Movies [] Problems [] Events [] Plans [] Other:

(Continued)

TABLE 7.4 (Continued)

[ ] Share a meal/ drink	[ ] Culture
	[ ] Daily life
[ ] Take a trip	[ ] TV
[ ] Exercise	[ ] Politics
[ ] Celebrate an occasion	[ ] Sports
	[ ] School
[ ] Play a sport / board game/ cards	[ ] Music
	[ ] Movies
	[ ] Problems
[ ] Go to event/ bar/club	[ ] Events
	[ ] Plans
[ ] Other:	[ ] Other:

If the native speakers here know each other, which ones and how?

Source: Adapted from Kennedy, 2012; reprinted with permission from Pozzi, 2021, p. 16

Model Study 7, Pozzi (2021) and Pozzi and Bayley (2021), used a modified version of the SNSS for SA (Kennedy, 2012) to examine the influence of social networks with TL speakers on the L2 acquisition of *vos*, the informal second-person singular form commonly used in place of *tú* 'you' in some Latin American countries, by 23 L1 English speakers during a semester of SA in Buenos Aires, Argentina. The modified SNSS used in Pozzi (2021) and Pozzi and Bayley (2021), shown in Table 7.4, included Density Measure 1 where the learner listed all of the native Spanish speakers with whom they had spoken Spanish for at least 30 minutes over the preceding two weeks and the total number of hours spent speaking Spanish with this person. Density measure 1 also included biographical information related to each NS such as their age, relationship to the learner, and their place of origin (i.e., neighborhood, city, and country). Although Pozzi (2021) and Pozzi and Bayley (2021) did not ask learners to draw their social network diagrams from the contacts listed in Density Measure 1, learners were asked whether the NSs in their networks knew each other and, if so, how. These studies also incorporated Multiplexity Measures 1 and 2 which asked what activities the learner engaged in with NSs and what the learner talked about with these NSs. As shown in Table 7.4, learners were supplied with a list of activities and conversation topics and were asked to indicate which ones they would engage in regularly with the TL speakers in their network. Using a point system similar to Kennedy Terry (2017, 2022a, 2022b), learners were classified into three categories of social network strength: low (0–19 points); mid (20–49 points), and; high

(40 points and above). The results of Pozzi (2021) and Pozzi and Bayley (2021) are discussed in Chapter 8.

Network Diagrams

Egocentric Network Diagrams

As shown in Figures 7.3 and 7.4 from Model Study 8 (C. Li et al., 2021), visual representations of *egocentric* social networks, or the direct connections between the learner and their social network members (see Chapter 2), can provide useful information regarding network density and multiplexity that can supplement quantitative metrics and network strength scales. For example, Model Study 2 by Isabelli-García (2006) used egocentric social network diagrams to examine the role of social networks with TL speakers in L2 Spanish acquisition during a semester of SA in Argentina. Using three sets of 7-day contact logs completed in week 1, week 8, and week 15 by four study participants, Isabelli-García reconstructed the social network of each L2 learner in order to establish the number of network ties with TL speakers in the first and second-order zones of the network (i.e., direct relationships and friend-of-a-friend relationships, respectively). Isabelli-García further differentiated learner experiences based on uniplex networks, where the participant interacted individually with TL speakers (in the first-order zone only), and multiplex networks where the learner interacted with multiple TL speakers at the same time (accessing both the first and second-order zones of the network). Figure 7.5 depicts the first- and second-order network zones of one learner (Stan) who increased his score on the Simulated OPI (SOPI) from Intermediate High to Advanced over the course of the SA period. According to the author, because of his positive attitude toward the TL culture and his high motivation to learn the TL, Stan was able to grow his social network from a single TL speaker in the first-order zone after one month in Argentina to three TL speakers in the first-order zone and five TL speakers in the second-order zone at the end of the semester (shown in Figure 7.5).

Overall, Isabelli-García's results demonstrated that for two of the four learners, including Stan, a positive attitude, high motivation, and second-order network ties with TL speakers correlated with improved grammatical accuracy and communicative competence on the SOPI. In contrast, a third learner also improved one level on the SOPI despite having a negative attitude, low motivation, and only three members in his first-order social network; however, a final learner with a generally negative attitude toward the TL culture, low motivation to learn the TL,

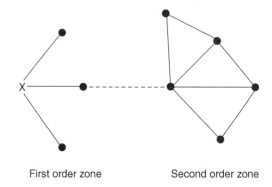

First order zone   Second order zone

FIGURE 7.5   Stan's first- and second-order network zones (reprinted with permission from Isabelli-García, 2006, p. 243)

and a restricted social network did not improve her post-test SOPI rating. Overall, the data from this study demonstrate a link between the learner's success in integrating into social networks and their ongoing motivation to learn the TL.

Similar to Isabelli-García (2006), Trentman (2017) used egocentric network diagrams to analyze the role of social networks in the acquisition of L2 Arabic by 21 American learners during a semester of SA in Cairo. In this study, Trentman examined the acquisition of both sociolinguistic competence (i.e., features of the Egyptian dialect of Arabic) and speed fluency in L2 Arabic. Trentman used sociolinguistic interviews (Labov, 1984), designed to promote a casual speech style from participants, at the beginning and end of the SA period to gather both linguistic and social network data. Learners were also interviewed once or twice about their SA experience (in English or Arabic) and 19 of the 21 participants completed a modified version of the LCP (Freed et al., 2004) to provide language contact and use data.

Trentman's results demonstrated that while all learners made some progress in acquiring features of Egyptian Arabic, the 'high gainers' who made gains on all three measures examined in the study (e.g., speech rate, mean length of run, percent of Egyptian dialect), had social networks that included both SA students and Egyptians and they used Arabic, rather than English, to communicate with both groups. In contrast, the learners who demonstrated the smallest (or negative) gains in one or more measures used English in their interactions with fellow SA participants and Egyptians. In the discussion of these results, Trentman references Coleman's (2013, 2015) concentric circles model in which other L1 English/co-nationals form the

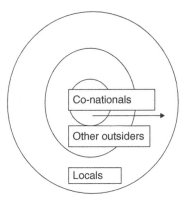

FIGURE 7.6   Concentric circles representation of social networks during study abroad (reprinted with permission from Coleman, 2013, p. 31)

inner circle of a learner's social network, other outsiders form the middle circle, and local TL speakers represent the third or outer circle. Coleman's concentric circles model is shown in Figure 7.6.

Using Coleman's (2013, 2015) concentric circles model, Trentman (2017) explained that the 'high gainers' had social networks that encompassed all three circles and these learners reported speaking Arabic with contacts in each of the three circles. The 'low gainers' had social networks that were limited to the first two circles only (co-nationals and other outsiders) and within these circles, the learners reported speaking primarily English. As many of the learners in this study reported speaking Arabic within their SA programs, in accordance with a language pledge that they had signed as part of the program requirements, Trentman's research underscores the critical role that SA program design and other program interventions, such as coordinated language partners and guided participation in local activities, can have on the formation of effective social networks with TL speakers during SA.

Sociocentric Network Diagrams

In Model Study 11, Hasegawa (2019) encourages researchers in SLA to take advantage of the sophisticated network modeling tools that allow for *sociocentric* analysis of L2 learners during SA, where a sociocentric (i.e., macro-level, full) network analysis considers the viewpoints of all actors within a social network or networks, rather than focusing solely on the egocentric network. For example, Hasegawa used Gephi (Bastian et al., 2009) to conduct a macro-level, sociocentric network analysis of the social networks of three different groups of L2 Japanese learners (91 learners total) enrolled in three different short-term SA programs in Japan (Programs A–C described below). Using multiple sources of data (e.g., participant observations, social network surveys, interviews, activity logs, recordings, documents) gathered at multiple research sites allowed Hasegawa to conduct a close examination of the impact of local factors on socialization and network formation during SA. For SNA, Hasegawa used both a name generator approach and a name interpreter approach (see Chapter 6) in which learners were provided with the names of other SA participants and asked to describe their relationship with each participant. Interviews were conducted in both Japanese and English and Hasegawa asked participants three specific questions about each network relationship: the role that the person played (e.g., friend), how close they felt to this person, and how often they interacted with the person.

Hasegawa described Program A as taking place on an insulated university campus where the sociocentric network structure remained fairly closed for the length of SA and where most relationships were formed along the lines of residence since SA learners were housed with Japanese students in three different residences. For this program, students signed a language pledge regarding their use of L2 Japanese and Hasegawa noted that although there was a high density of network ties, the number of network members reported as 'friends' did not change as much as the level of closeness and interaction over time. Figure 7.7 provides a visual representation of the sociocentric network analysis of Program A, during week 8 of the program, where colors indicate clusters (Blondel et al., 2008) or groups of close-knit students.

In contrast to Program A, Program B was associated with a large university, on the campus of the School of Foreign Studies. This program had a 'supporters' program where Japanese students could volunteer to help or hang out with the international students and the International Friendship Club planned events for both local and international students. Housing for Program B was either in a family homestay, far from campus, or in an apartment within walking distance to campus. Sociocentric network analysis revealed that the network density for Program B was much lower than for Program A, and it remained the same over the course of SA. Figure 7.8 provides a visual representation of the sociocentric network analysis of Program B during week 8 of the program.

Unlike Program A, many of the students in Program B formed unique relationships with local students. Hasegawa noted that Program B allowed for more agency among L2 learners but questioned whether this level of independence would benefit shy students as much as students with a more outward orientation. That is, would shyer students achieve more success

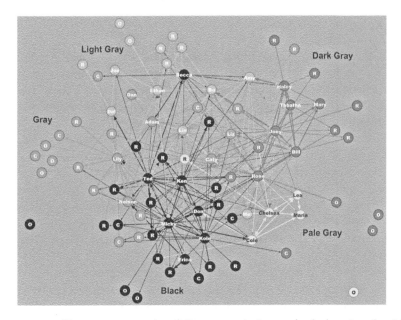

FIGURE 7.7   Closeness network of Program A in week 8 (reprinted with permission from Hasegawa, 2019, p. 57)

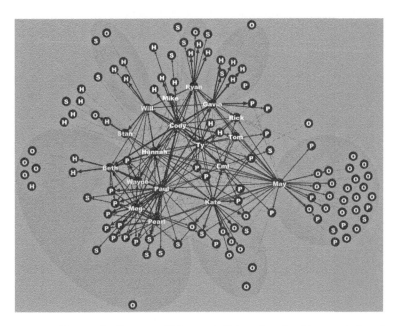

FIGURE 7.8   Clusters in Program B in week 8 (reprinted with permission from Hasegawa, 2019, p. 74)

in a program like Program A where their connections are more structured and/or forced?

Finally, Program C took place at a Center for International Studies and had a heavy focus on the use of English. The Japanese students were encouraged to interact with international students and through a university-sponsored conversation exchange program. The students in this program had a lighter work load than students in the other two programs and had more free time. All students in Program C lived in an international student dorm with a Japanese roommate. Hasegawa referred to Program C as a 'collapsed' network because of the low level of interaction between the participants in this program but did point out that the sociocentric analysis showed that the total number of network actors and ties increased significantly over the course of the SA period. Figure 7.9 provides a visual representation of the sociocentric network analysis of Program C during week 5 of the program.

Hasegawa's study also represents one of first attempts to combine both conversation analysis (CA) and SNA, and makes an important contribution to the field of SNA in terms of how social networks are formed during SA, with whom, and what opportunities they provide for interaction in the TL. Hasegawa concluded that while opportunities for interaction initially create the social network, the relationships within the network ultimately shape the scope and variety of interactions that SA learners will have with TL speakers. Hasegawa provided the example of "Rose" who

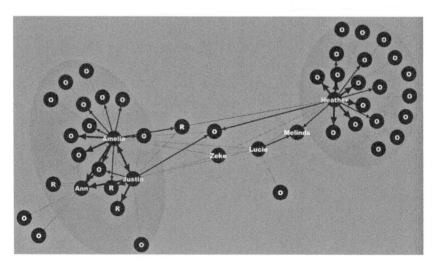

FIGURE 7.9   Closeness network of Program C in week 5 (reprinted with permission from Hasegawa, 2019, p. 85)

was usually found in groups and was diligent about not using English, but had mostly short interactional stretches. That is, Rose seemed to be interacting a lot with others, but her interactions remained short and superficial. Hasegawa contrasted Rose with "Joe" who appeared to be a loner in terms of the size and density of his social network, but who had high levels of closeness with a small number of Japanese speakers and therefore often engaged in conversations that were both meaningful and diverse. Using sociocentric SNA focused on three different groups of SA learners, Hasegawa explained that in order to develop interactional competence in the L2, SA learners need access to a diverse network of TL speakers. Hasegawa further concluded that "diversified interactional occasions require diversified interpersonal relationships" (2019, p. 197) and that SA program design has an important role to play in whether learners will have access to such "diversified interpersonal relationships" with TL speakers.[1]

Model Study 14 by Bernstein (2018) also used sociocentric network diagramming to analyze the role of network centrality and peripherality in L2 English acquisition by immigrant children in a US preschool. The results of this study are discussed in detail in Chapter 9.

Qualitative Network Assessments

Network Composition

In Model Study 12, Carhill-Poza (2015) applied SNA to investigate the role of peer support networks in the development of oral academic English during adolescence. This study used an ecological model to examine the environmental impacts of the high school learning context, including the formation of peer social networks, on emergent bilingual immigrant adolescent English learners in the United States. Carhill-Poza hypothesized that academic English proficiency could be correlated with individual characteristics such as time in the US and the mother's education level, as well as with the peer scaffolding and interaction opportunities offered to English learners through peer social networks.

Participants in Carhill-Poza's study included 102 L1 Spanish students enrolled in public high schools in New York who had been in the US for an average of 3.5 years. All students had immigrated to the US within the previous seven years and had attended their current school for at least one year. The participants included equal numbers of male and female students and the average age was 16.5 years. Over 60 percent of the participants immigrated from the Dominican Republic and the remaining 40 percent of the participants came from Ecuador, Mexico, and Central America.

Participants attended four different public high schools that were selected for similarities in size, educational quality (based on graduation rates), density of newcomers, and ethnic composition (all over 50 percent Latino). Volunteer student participants were recruited from sophomore and junior courses that included a variety of proficiency levels (e.g., Global History) and interviews were conducted in English or Spanish depending on the preference of the participants.

Carhill-Poza (2015) used oral interviews, including both open-ended questions and Likert scales, to gather biographical information related to immigration history and qualitative social network data. To measure linguistic development, participants also completed a standardized oral academic English proficiency measure (IPTK-12; Ballard & Tighe, 2006), which has been shown to correlate closely with the NY State English as a Second Language Assessment Test (NYSESLAT; Pearson, 2009). Both participant gender and mother's education level (completion or noncompletion of high school) were coded in the data set. Additionally, four focal students were chosen for qualitative analysis, including observations and audio recordings of conversations with peers which were then analyzed for speech context, conversation topic (social, academic, or metalinguistic), language choice (Spanish or English), and for the use of academic language (i.e., the use of specific lexical, syntactic, and discourse features associated with an academic register).

To measure participants' peer social networks, Carhill-Poza used a modified version of the Longitudinal Immigrant Adaptation Study (Suárez-Orozco et al., 2008), which employs a name generator approach to SNA. Participants were asked to name all of the important people in their lives, including family and friends from both school and outside activities, and then to indicate the level of interactions in Spanish and English with each network member. Network members were then categorized as *English-oriented* (if English was used 50 percent or more of the time) or *Spanish-oriented* (if English was used 25 percent or less of the time). Academic peers (both English- and Spanish-oriented) were also identified on the basis of whether they engaged in academic oriented activities with the participant (e.g., helping with homework, studying for a test) and interactions were rated based on frequency. From this data, Carhill-Poza then categorized each student's composite network as: Academic English-Oriented, Academic Spanish-Oriented, Nonacademic English-Oriented, and Nonacademic Spanish-Oriented.

Carhill-Poza's results demonstrated that the orientation of the learner's peer network (Academic or Nonacademic), regardless of the primary language used within the network, was the most influential factor in the oral academic proficiency of the participants in this study. These results are discussed in more detail in Chapter 8.

Integration and Engagement

In a small-scale study by Chamot et al. (2021) on the acquisition of L2 French during SA, the analysis of qualitative social network data and levels of 'integration' revealed a hierarchy of acquisition for three sociolinguistic variables characteristic of informal French. This study focused on nine Irish undergraduate L2 French learners who spent 6–10 months in a Francophone country and used qualitative data from participant interviews to categorize students into two groups based on their level of socialization and integration with TL speakers during the SA period. Based on the social network data gathered in the sociolinguistic interviews, learners were classified as '+/– integrated' into the TL community and these integration levels were compared to the learners' use of three sociolinguistic variables: *ne* (negative particle) deletion, schwa deletion, and /l/ deletion.

The results for Chamot et al. demonstrated that variable *ne* deletion was used at high rates by both groups of participants: + integrated learners deleted *ne* at a rate of 62.38 percent and –integrated learners deleted *ne* at only a slightly lower rate of 59.26 percent. At the same time, the results for the phonological variables examined in Chamot et al. (schwa deletion and /l/ deletion) demonstrated that acquisition is highly dependent on socialization with TL speakers. For example, learners in the +integrated group deleted schwa 25 percent of the time and deleted /l/ 26.81 percent of the time after SA. In contrast, learners in the –integrated group deleted schwa only 2.7 percent of the time and did not delete /l/ at all following a period of SA. These results support those of Pozzi (2021) discussed in Chapter 8 which demonstrated that for certain regional variables in L2 Spanish like *vos*, the informal second-person singular form commonly used in some Latin American countries and *s* weakening (Pozzi, 2022), only learners with strong social networks with TL speakers will acquire these forms. Similarly, the results of Chamot et al. (2021) for *ne* deletion align with those of Pozzi & Bayley (2021) which indicate that for certain very salient variables, such as *sheísmo/zheísmo* in Buenos Aires Spanish, learners will generally acquire the variable form regardless of the strength of their social networks.

Similar to Chamot et al. (2021), Mougeon and Rehner (2015) gathered qualitative data from surveys, questionnaires, and semidirected sociolinguistic interviews for 61 L2 French university learners in Ontario, Canada, in order to establish learner 'engagement portraits' based on three factors: (1) learners' reflections on their own French as a second language

TABLE 7.5 Measurement of overall engagement in French according to profile portrait

Measures of engagement	Engaged multilinguals	Engaged bilinguals	Moderately engaged bilinguals	Moderately engaged multilinguals	Minimally engaged bilinguals	Minimally engaged multilinguals
Year abroad or long-term stays	++	+	+	=	=	=
University French-medium courses	++	++	+	=	+	–
Jobs and careers	++	++	+	+	=	–
Curricular exposure	++	++	+	+	=	–
Extracurricular activities	++	++	+	++	–	–
Immersion experiences	++	++	+	=	–	–
Regular contact with Francophones	++	++	+	=	–	– –

Note: The most active commitments are indicated by "++" and the least active commitments are indicated by "– –", with "+" and "–" indicating intermediate levels of commitment; "=" indicates average levels of commitment. The gray-shaded characteristics take into account actual engagement and intentions to engage, whereas the nonshaded characteristics include only actual commitments or performance.

Source: Table 2, reprinted with permission from Mougeon & Rehner, 2015, p. 441

(FSL) learning; (2) learners' reflections on bilingualism, multilingualism, and language education in Canada, and; (3) *active commitments* to FSL learning that required the learner to make an extracurricular lifestyle change and to assume responsibility for their own language learning (e.g., a decision to study abroad in a Francophone environment). From this qualitative data, the researchers identified three different learner engagement portraits ranging from 'engaged', to 'moderately engaged', and finally, 'minimally engaged' learners. Each of these three learner portraits was further divided for multilingual and bilingual learners, for a total of six learner profile portraits.

In terms of linguistic data, the researchers focused on the overall length of the interviews in French (excluding the speech of the interviewers), the use of positive or negative language about French and/or English and about bilingualism in general, and the use of six specific sociolinguistic variables that are characteristic of informal French that is generally acquired outside of the language classroom. In order to examine changes to learners' linguistic development over time, the researchers interviewed 19 of the original 61 learners after a three-year interval, when these learners were completing their fourth year of L2 French study. While this study did not employ a formal SNA approach, the focus on active commitments to L2 learning, commitments that include working and socializing with TL speakers, participating in an immersion experience or residence abroad, and speaking the TL in extracurricular contexts, provides a useful example of how qualitative data related to learner activities and interactions within TL social networks underscore the role of social networks in L2 acquisition, especially in the acquisition of informal language. Results from Mougeon and Rehner (2015) are discussed in Chapter 9.

Conclusion

The Model Studies reviewed in this chapter demonstrate the variety of quantitative and qualitative assessments that researchers create and use to transform and analyze the social network data gathered through the questionnaires, interviews, observations, and recordings described in Chapter 6. The quantitative assessments described in section 1 include specific metrics, such as network density, multiplexity, and dispersion, as well as global network strength scales that combine network metrics into a single quantitative indicator that can be compared to linguistic development. The predictive power of these quantitative metrics and scales is supported by the network diagramming techniques and qualitative assessments of network strength described in sections 2 and 3 of this chapter. In all of the Model Studies and supplemental research discussed in this chapter, strong correlations between social networks and L2 development, especially in the area of L2 oral proficiency and sociolinguistic variation, have been identified.

Discussion Questions

1. Compare the social network measurement tools described in this chapter (SASIQ, Dewey et al., 2012; SNSS for SA, Kennedy, 2012). What are the strengths and weaknesses of each tool?
2. If you were designing your own measurement tool, what aspects of SNA would you focus on (e.g., dispersion, density, frequency, intensity) and why?
3. Review the quantitative metrics and qualitative assessments described in this chapter and make a list of learner attributes/activities that have not been explored or considered in these studies. What questions or techniques would you use to gather this additional information?

Note

1 The description of Model Study 11 by Hasegawa (2019) provided here was previously published in a modified form in Kennedy Terry (2023).

8

USING SOCIAL NETWORK ANALYSIS TO EXAMINE LINGUISTIC OUTCOMES

Inferential Statistics

Introduction

This chapter provides an overview of the current methods used to incorporate social network analysis (SNA) into linguistic analysis using inferential statistics. As a review, Chapter 5 presented the research questions and goals of Model Studies 1–16 and Chapter 6 outlined the primary means of social network data collection used in these studies. Chapter 7 discussed how social network data can be analyzed using quantitative metrics and scales, network diagramming, and qualitative assessments. In the current chapter, we discuss the linguistic outcomes of Model Studies 1–16 with a specific focus on how researchers have used inferential statistical analysis to investigate the relationship between social networks and second language (L2) acquisition.

Overview: Using Inferential Statistics in Linguistic Analysis

A main goal of statistical analysis is to determine whether the results that we see in descriptive statistics represent genuine differences between groups or whether they could have come about by chance. That is, if we find that students participating in a study abroad (SA) program who have more contacts with people in the host community perform better on a language proficiency test than students with fewer local contacts, can we attribute the difference to the learners' social networks with a reasonable degree of assurance? To do so, we turn to inferential statistics that enable us to generalize from the sample in our study to the broader population that the

DOI: 10.4324/9781003174448-8

sample represents. We want to know the likelihood that we would achieve similar results if we repeated the study with a different population. In second language acquisition (SLA), as in most other social sciences, researchers are satisfied with a significance level of .05. That is, we are satisfied if there is only a 5 percent chance that a difference between speakers or groups came about by chance.

As shown in detail in the following sections, to achieve that level of assurance, researchers use a variety of statistical procedures, based on the size of the sample, whether the different groups are evenly distributed, and the nature of the variables being examined. For example, if a researcher is investigating whether the extent of interactions between SA students and target-language (TL) speakers is significantly associated with the outcome on an overall test of L2 proficiency, a simple measure of correlation might well suffice. However, if a researcher is investigating the relationship between the strength of SA learners' social networks and the acquisition of the constraints (i.e., predictors) on sociolinguistic variation, such as French schwa deletion in Kennedy Terry (2022a, 2022b) or Spanish /s/ weakening in Pozzi (2022), more complex procedures such as logistic regression analysis are normally required. This is because sociolinguistic variables are not usually evenly distributed across different linguistic environments. For example, in Spanish, word-final /s/ occurs more frequently as a plural marker than as part of a monomorpheme. Thus, any study based on relatively informal speech is likely to have far more tokens of plural /s/ than of monomorphemic /s/. Second, variables of interest such as those discussed here are normally subject to many different constraints, both linguistic (e.g., the influence of the preceding or following segment) and social (e.g., gender, ethnicity, sexual orientation, etc.) and we want to examine the relative strength of those different constraints. Finally, unlike what we might find in a proficiency test where study participants are required to produce the same number of responses, participants in a study of the acquisition of sociolinguistic competence produce widely differing amounts of speech data. This means that our samples will typically be unbalanced. As shown in the following sections, researchers using SNA have adapted a wide range of statistical methods to deal with all of these questions.

Statistical Significance and Correlations

One of the primary goals of researchers applying SNA to studies of L2 acquisition is to determine the extent to which participation in social networks is associated with L2 acquisition and development. To do this, researchers most often use a combination of descriptive and inferential statistics. Descriptive statistics include social network metrics such as the total number of TL or first language (L1) speakers in a learner's network, the amount of time spent with these speakers, and calculations related to the density or multiplexity of the learner's network (see Chapters 6 and 7 for a discussion of data collection and assessment methods). Researchers also gather descriptive statistics related to linguistic performance. Oral Proficiency Interview (OPI, American Council on the Teaching of Foreign Languages, ACTFL) scores, usage rates of specific linguistic elements or variables, and syntactic or lexical complexity scores and grammatical accuracy rates are all examples of descriptive statistics that researchers use to assess L2 development. These descriptive statistics are critical to understanding how learners interact within their social networks and important comparisons can be made between individual learners or groups of learners in relation to social network patterns and L2 development. However, descriptive statistics alone will not tell us whether there is a significant correlation between social network interaction patterns and L2 development—whether the correlation between the features of a learner's social network and L2 development is greater than what is likely to occur by chance. Descriptive statistics also cannot tell us how strong the influence of social networks is on L2 development compared to other influences such as prior coursework in the L2, learner attitude and motivation, and time in the TL environment. To this end, researchers use a variety of inferential statistics to understand the specific role of social networks in L2 acquisition and development.

We begin our examination of the various statistical procedures available to SLA researchers with Model Study 3 by McManus (2019), which forms part of the LANGSNAP project ("Social networks, target language interaction, and second language acquisition during the year abroad: A longitudinal study"; Mitchell et al., 2017) and exemplifies how inferential statistics may be combined with descriptive statistics and linguistic data to explore correlations between participation in social networks and L2 development. In this study, McManus (2019) examined the social networks of 29 undergraduates from an English university who were either studying (n = 8), completing a workplace internship (n = 6), or serving as teaching assistants (n = 15) in France for nine months with a specific focus on the different social contexts that might favor or disfavor social network formation with TL and L1 speakers. McManus focused on the development of lexical complexity in French using a combination of three measures to ensure a reliable evaluation of complexity (2019, p. 276): Guiraud's Index (Guiraud, 1954), the moving-average type-token ratio (MATTR; Köhler & Galle, 1993) and D (Malvern & Richards, 2002).

Social network data for McManus (2019) were gathered using the *Social Networks Questionnaire* (SNQ, McManus et al., 2014; Mitchell et al.,

2017; see Chapter 6) and semi-structured oral interviews in French of approximately 20 minutes. The oral interviews were also used as the source of linguistic data and both the SNQ and the oral interviews were completed three times during the academic year in France (in November, February, and May).

Regarding the learners' social networks, one of the first notable results from McManus (2019) is that the total number of L2-speaking contacts in the learners' networks did not increase over time; in fact, it decreased slightly from time 1 to time 3. At the same time, data also showed that the number of L1-speaking contacts and the number of Mixed-language contacts also decreased steadily over the nine-month period resulting in relatively stable proportions of L1-L2-Mixed contacts in the learners' networks (average L1 contacts = 45 percent of total contacts). As shown in Figure 8.1, the learners did increase their proportion of TL contacts from 32 percent to 38 percent over the nine-month period with the increase coming from a decrease in Mixed-language contacts (from 23 percent to 18 percent).

Another important result from McManus (2019) was found in the social context of the L1 and TL contacts: L1 contacts took place primarily online (e.g., virtual social interactions) and TL contacts took place in person (e.g., work/university and organized social activities). Additionally, in terms of their 'Top 5' contacts (the five people with whom

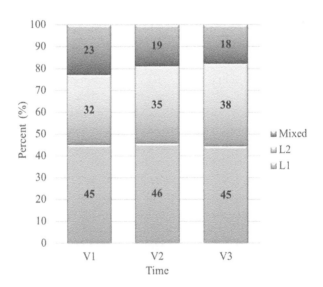

FIGURE 8.1 Learner network composition (L1, L2, Mixed) over nine months in France (reprinted with permission from McManus, 2019, p. 277)

the learner interacted the most across all contexts), learners increased their proportion of L1-speaking contacts from time 1 to time 3 (from 47 percent to 53 percent) with the increase coming from a reduction in Mixed contacts (from 29 percent to 22 percent) while the proportion of L2-speaking contacts within the learners' 'Top 5' remained approximately the same over time (McManus, 2019, p. 278). These results indicate that while learners may increase their overall level of L2 contact during the SA period, the amount of L2 contact within their 'Top 5', or with their closest network members, was established at the beginning of the SA period and did not change over time.

To understand the relationship between lexical complexity and social network formation during study abroad, McManus (2019) used inferential statistics and calculated Spearman's rank order correlations between each type of network contact (L1, L2, and Mixed contacts) within the participant's 'Top 5' list and lexical complexity. The Spearman rank order correlation is similar to the Pearson Correlation Coefficient, which provides a means for quantifying a linear relationship between two variables; however, the Spearman's rank order correlation is preferred when the relationship between the variables is not completely linear, when the focus is on the 'rank' of the two variables (i.e., identifying a positive or negative relationship), and when there are outliers present in the data (Statology, 2022). Results at time 3 for lexical complexity scores using the three complexity measures (Guiraud's Index, MATTR, and D) demonstrated a positive relationship (medium-to-strong correlations) between L2-speaking contacts and lexical complexity and a negative relationship (medium correlations) with L1-speaking contacts. These results are shown in Figure 8.2, which demonstrates that for all three lexical complexity measures, the more L2 contacts in the learner's network, the greater their complexity scores and the more L1 contacts in the network, the lower their complexity scores. Interestingly, these correlations were not found at time 1 or time 2, suggesting that the positive influence of L2-speaking contacts and the negative influence of L1-speaking contacts do not appear in L2 speech until later in the SA period after learners have spent more time in the TL environment.

Overall, the results from McManus (2019) indicate that learner networks do not change significantly during the SA period with L1 contacts representing the largest portion of total language interactions during SA both at the beginning and the end of the SA period. Additionally, while this study shows that L1 interactions occur primarily in virtual contexts, the study results demonstrate that L2 interactions occur primarily in person—either at work or at the university. The results from this study also demonstrate that interactions with L2-speaking contacts, if frequent enough to place the L2 contact into a learner's 'Top 5', will ultimately assist the learner in

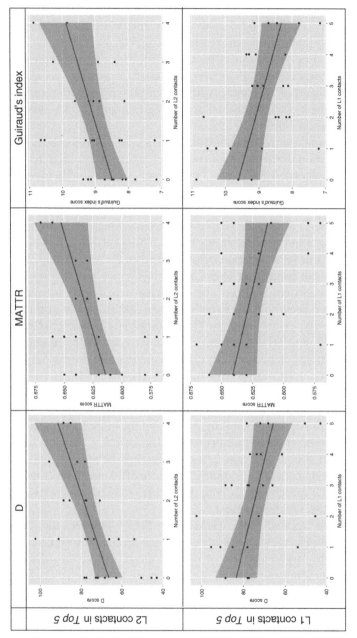

FIGURE 8.2 Correlations between lexical complexity and 'Top 5' contacts in learner networks at time 3 (reprinted with permission from McManus, 2019, p. 280)

developing higher levels of lexical complexity in the L2 after a full nine months in the TL environment.

Model Study 5 by Serrano et al. (2012) also used inferential statistics and a full network approach to investigate L2 English acquisition by 14 L1 Spanish students over the course of an academic year in the UK. In this study of L1 interactions within learner social networks, Serrano et al. focused on the learner's accommodation type and the nationality and language of communication of the four people with whom the learner had the most contact. With respect to linguistic development, Serrano et al. focused on changes to fluency, complexity, lexical richness, and grammatical accuracy in both oral and written production over the course of the SA period.

The 14 participants in Model Study 5 were university students from Spain participating in a one-year Erasmus European Exchange program. All participants began studying English between the ages of six and ten and they rated themselves between lower intermediate and advanced at the beginning of the SA period. These self-assessments were corroborated by a pre-test upon arrival in the UK that included an oral narrative (based on a series of pictures), a written narrative essay, and a questionnaire. The questionnaire inquired about the participant's English language background, their attitudes toward the English language and English people, and where the participants were living (e.g., shared or private accommodation in a residence hall, student apartment/house, or a private home). To understand the participants' social networks, the questionnaire also asked about the four people with whom the participants spent the most time while abroad and if they did "almost everything" with one of these people. Figure 8.3 shows an excerpt from the questionnaire used by Serrano et al. (2012) to gather participant social network data. As this was a longitudinal study, the participants completed the linguistic tasks and the questionnaire upon

7. **Make a list of the four people you've had the most contact with while abroad (at home, university, or weekends).**

Relationship (classmate, friend, roommate, etc.)	How much contact have you had with this person? A little/some/a lot	Nationality	Language used for interaction

8. **Among these people, is there anyone you've done almost everything with? If the answer is 'yes', add an 'X' next to her/him.**

FIGURE 8.3 Social network interaction data gathered by Serrano et al. (reprinted with permission from Serrano et al., 2012, p. 163)

arrival in the UK in September, in December, and again in May at the end of the academic year.

Linguistic data in Serrano et al. (2012) were analyzed for all of the following: oral fluency (syllables per minute) or written fluency (words per T-unit), syntactic complexity (clauses per T-unit), lexical richness (Guiraud's Index; Guiraud, 1954), and grammatical accuracy (errors per T-unit). The written essays were coded using the Computerized Language Analysis Program (CLAN; MacWhinney, 2000), and oral data were coded manually by multiple researchers.

The descriptive statistics for the oral production task used in Serrano et al. (2012) are shown in Table 8.1. From these descriptive statistics alone, it is clear that as a group, the learners made improvements in oral fluency, syntactic complexity, and lexical richness from time 1 to time 2, and again from time 2 to time 3. Similarly, the learners improved in the area of grammatical accuracy from time 1 to time 2, and again from time 2 to time 3. What the descriptive statistics do not tell us is whether these improvements are statistically significant, that is, whether the results are likely to be due to a specific influence, or influences, and unlikely to be due to chance.

To know whether results are statistically significant, researchers must incorporate inferential statistics into their analysis. Although it is beyond the scope of this volume to provide a full review of the statistical analysis tools

TABLE 8.1 Group results from oral production task

	Time 1	*Time 2*	*Time 3*
Fluency: syllables/minute			
Mean (standard deviation)	119.89 (25.81)	146.22 (30.48)	152.45 (33.57)
Median	122.42	145.61	147.25
Syntactic complexity: clauses/T-unit			
Mean (standard deviation)	1.89 (0.20)	1.77 (0.30)	1.81 (0.27)
Median	1.64	1.72	1.74
Lexical richness: Guiraud's index			
Mean (standard deviation)	5.66 (0.01)	6.13 (0.83)	6.16 (0.58)
Median	5.83	5.92	6.11
Accuracy: errors/T-unit			
Mean (standard deviation)	1.45 (0.95)	1.23 (0.72)	0.51 (0.33)
Median	1.07	1.29	0.50

Source: Reprinted with permission from Serrano et al., 2012, p. 147

and programs available to researchers in linguistics, this chapter highlights a number of approaches to inferential statistical analysis (e.g., significance testing, correlation analysis, and logistic regression) that are frequently used in studies applying SNA to linguistic performance.

To determine whether the changes to learners' fluency, complexity, lexical richness, and grammatical accuracy were statistically significant and not due to chance (i.e., the *null hypothesis*), Serrano et al. (2012) conducted significance testing using the Wilcoxon Signed Rank Tests in the Statistical Package for the Social Sciences (SPSS, 2007) to compare the time 1 and time 2 results, the time 2 and time 3 results, and the time 1 and time 3 results for each of the dependent variables (e.g., fluency, syntactic complexity, lexical richness, accuracy) and for both the oral and the written production tasks. Additionally, the researchers used a different test, the Mann Whitney-U test, to analyze the significance of the social network, background, and attitudinal data gathered via the questionnaire. Both the Wilcoxon Signed Rank Test and the Mann Whitney-U test are 'non-parametric tests' which means that the distribution for the participating population is not known up front and must be tested. Nonparametric tests are also preferred for small sample sizes.

The results of the Wilcoxon Signed Rank tests for the oral production task are shown in Table 8.2. In this table, the test results for each time period are provided as Z-values with the p-value directly below, where the p-value indicates the probability of these results occurring by chance. A p-value of less than 0.05 (5 percent) is considered statistically significant and

TABLE 8.2 Inferential statistics: oral production task results

	Time 1–time 2	*Time 2–time 3*	*Time 1–time 3*
Fluency syllables/minute	$Z = -3.18$ $p = .001*$ Cohen's $d = 0.93$	$Z = -1.01$ $p = .311$ Cohen's $d = 0.10$	$Z = -2.90$ $p = .004$ Cohen's $d = 1.08$
Syntactic complexity (clauses/T-unit)	$Z = -0.80$ $p = .424$ Cohen's $d = 0.31$	$Z = -0.31$ $p = .763$ Cohen's $d = 0.14$	$Z = -1.64$ $p = .101$ Cohen's $d = 0.50$
Lexical richness (Guiraud's index)	$Z = -2.48$ $p = .013$ Cohen's $d = 0.54$	$Z = -0.25$ $p = .807$ Cohen's $d = 0.04$	$Z = -1.99$ $p = .046$ Cohen's $d = 0.66$
Accuracy (errors/T-unit)	$Z = -1.25$ $p = .209$ Cohen's $d = -0.43$	$Z = -2.34$ $p = .019$ Cohen's $d = -1.28$	$Z = -2.55$ $p = .011$ Cohen's $d = -1.33$

Source: Reprinted with permission from Serrano et al., 2012, p. 148

these are shown in bold type in Table 8.2. Finally, Table 8.2 also includes calculations of Cohen's d for each of the significance tests where Cohen's d measures the *effect size* (i.e., how large or small the differences in the results are when compared to the null hypothesis). A measure of effect size is important in studies using small sample populations as it provides a single, interpretable number that can be used to compare the results of different research studies testing different hypotheses.

The results shown in Table 8.2 demonstrate that, as a group, the learners in Serrano et al. (2012) made statistically significant gains in oral fluency and lexical richness during the first semester (time 1 to time 2). In contrast, learners did not show significant improvement in syntactic complexity in oral production over the course of the year (time 1 to time 3). Moreover, significant improvement in grammatical accuracy did not occur until the second semester (time 2 to time 3). Although not shown here, the results for the written task demonstrated significant gains in fluency and lexical richness from time 1 to time 3 and significant gains in syntactic complexity and accuracy in the second semester.

These results from Model Study 5 by Serrano et al. (2012) make a substantial contribution to our current understanding of L2 acquisition during SA because they highlight the areas of oral production where learners make the quickest gains during a single semester abroad: oral fluency and lexical richness. The results of Serrano et al. also underscore the findings of previous research in which SA learners do not show greater gains in grammatical accuracy than at-home learners (Arnett, 2013; Collentine, 2004; Howard, 2005, 2008; Isabelli–García, 2010); in Serrano et al., significant improvements in grammatical accuracy were slow to appear and did not occur until the second semester of SA. Moreover, syntactic complexity in oral production remained static among learners even after a year of SA; however, it showed improvement in written production in the second semester. The results for the role of attitude were also statistically significant demonstrating that learners who found English speakers to be "more sociable than unsociable" and "more humble than snobbish" made greater improvements in grammatical accuracy in their written production. Additionally, learners who rated the English language as being "more complex than simple" made greater gains in lexical richness in both the oral and the written production tasks.

In terms of social networks, the results of the statistical analysis in Serrano et al. (2012) demonstrated that learners living in apartments or houses made significantly more gains in lexical richness in oral production (from time 1 to time 3) than those living in residence halls. Moreover, learners who reported doing almost everything with another Spanish speaker made significantly fewer gains in lexical richness in written production, and fewer gains in grammatical accuracy in oral production, than learners who did not spend the majority of their time with a co-national. Finally, learners who reported living only with English speakers made significantly greater gains in lexical richness in written production from time 2 to time 3 than learners living with one or more Spanish speakers.

Logistic Regression

Model Study 12 by Carhill-Poza (2015) exemplifies how results from SNA may be incorporated into analyses of linguistic data using logistic regression in order to isolate the impact of social networks from other potential influences such as age, gender, and time in the TL environment on L2 acquisition. In this study, Carhill-Poza examined the role of peer social networks in the acquisition of oral academic English proficiency (AEP) by 102 L1 Spanish-speaking high school students in New York. As described in Chapter 7, Carhill-Poza used interviews and questionnaires to determine the composition of participants' social networks and first differentiated network relationships based on the primary language of communication (i.e., English-Oriented or Spanish-Oriented) and later on the basis of their engagement in academic oriented tasks such as doing homework together and preparing for tests (i.e., Academic or Nonacademic Peers).

Descriptive social network statistics from Carhill-Poza's study revealed that the majority of the participants' English-language and academic support came from peers rather than from adults. On average, participants included 6.2 peers in their networks with over half (55.6 percent) of these relationships originating at school and another 30 percent provided by kin. Although fewer than 10 percent of the participants included monolingual or native English speakers in their networks, participants reported a higher average number of peers with whom they spoke English at least 50 percent of the time (3.59 peers) than peers with whom they spoke Spanish more than 50 percent of the time (2.56 peers). Additionally, over half of the participants reported at least one peer with whom they spoke English at least 75 percent of the time. Overall, participants reported an average of 2.13 Academic Peers; however, 25.5 percent of the participants had no Academic Peers and 22.5 percent reported only one Academic Peer in their social network.

To assesses the relative influence of peer social networks on AEP, Carhill-Poza used hierarchical multiple regression analysis incorporating variables that had been previously shown to contribute to L2 acquisition (e.g., participant age and gender, time in the US, and maternal education level), as well as two variables related to peer social networks: English-Oriented Peers and Academic Peers. In the regression analysis,

Carhill-Poza created an initial model that included only the individual control variables of participant age and gender, time in the US, and maternal education and then adjusted the model by adding additional social network variables. In the initial model (Model 1, Table 8.3), three of the four variables were shown to be significant (all but participant age), and the model predicted 29 percent of the variance in the participants' AEP. In Model 2, also shown in Table 8.3, the addition of the first social network variable (English-Oriented Peers) explained an additional 5 percent of the variance. Model 2 also shows that when the variable of English-Oriented Peers is added to the model, the variable of maternal education is no longer a significant predictor of AEP. Only the variables of time in US, gender, and English-Oriented peers remain significant in Model 2.

Finally, when the second social network variable of Academic Peers is added to Model 3 in Table 8.3, an additional 7 percent of the variance in AEP scores is explained, for a total of 41 percent ($p < .001$). Additionally, once the variable of Academic Peers is added to the model, the variable of English-Oriented Peers is no longer a significant contributor to AEP (The author noted that the interaction between these two variables was tested but did not reach significance). That is, using hierarchical multiple regression, Carhill-Poza determined that three variables contributed significantly to the variance in the participants' AEP scores: time in US, gender, and Academic Peers, with Academic Peers explaining 12 percent of the variance overall.

TABLE 8.3 Hierarchical regression analysis: Contributors to AEP

Independent variable	Model 1		Model 2		Model 3	
	B (SE B)	β	B (SE B)	β	B (SE B)	β
Age	−0.54 (0.46)	−.10	−0.20 (0.46)	−.04	0.02 (0.45)	.00
Time in US	1.84 (0.53)	.48***	1.60 (0.33)	.42***	1.46 (0.33)	.38***
Gender	−2.37 (1.15)	−.18*	−2.72 (1.12)	−.20*	−3.31 (1.10)	−.25*
Maternal education	2.50 (1.18)	.18*	2.10 (1.15)	.16	1.79 (1.12)	.13
English-oriented peers			0.49 (0.18)	.25**	0.20 (0.20)	.10
Academic peers					0.96 (0.53)	.30***
R^2		.29***		.35***		.41***
ΔR^2				.05**		.07**

Note: * $p < .05$. ** $p < .01$. *** $p < .001$.

Source: Reprinted with permission from Carhill-Poza, 2015, p. 687

In addition to the hierarchical multiple regression analysis, Carhill-Poza (2015) conducted an analysis of variance on the relationship between AEP and the four social network types identified in the study: Academic English-Oriented, Academic Spanish-Oriented, Nonacademic English-Oriented, and Nonacademic Spanish-Oriented. The analysis of variance revealed that the proficiency scores of students with Academic English-Oriented peer networks were significantly higher than all other groups, including Academic Spanish-Oriented and Nonacademic English-Oriented peers. The analysis did not reveal any other significant differences among the groups related to age, time in the US, or gender; however, the maternal education level of participants with Academic English-Oriented networks was found to be significantly higher than for the participants with Academic Spanish-Oriented networks.

The results of Model Study 12 by Carhill-Poza (2015) underscore the critical role that peer social networks, especially those that support interaction and collaboration related to academic tasks, play in the development of AEP among adolescent immigrant students. In this study, interactions with peers who provided academic support, either in the L1 or the L2, far outweighed the role of individual factors such as age, time in the US, gender, and maternal education level, in predicting AEP development. Given that 25.5 percent of the participants did not include any Academic-Oriented peers at all in their networks, these results underscore the important role that these network members play in the lives of the L2 English learners who do receive academic support from their peers.

Carhill-Poza's (2015) results also have important implications for SNA as a research tool and approach because they demonstrate that SNA has the potential to reveal influences on L2 acquisition that have been previously ignored or misunderstood, such as the contribution of bilingual academic peer support in the development of AEP. Moreover, Carhill-Poza's results underscore the critical role of social networks in the academic success of language learners— a role which could and should be understood by educational policymakers whose decisions about the placement of language learners in L1-dominant classrooms can have a direct impact on the social networking and language learning opportunities available to immigrant students.

Rbrul—A Specialized Application of Logistic Regression

According to Bayley (2013), multivariate analysis using the Varbrul programs (e.g., GoldVarb X; Sankoff et al., 2005) has been preferred to analysis of variance in studies of language variation because it was specifically developed to handle natural language data that is not uniform. At the same time, Bayley argued that one criticism of Varbrul is that it can be difficult to identify interactions among contributing influences on variation using Varbrul, especially when extralinguistic, or social, factors are incorporated into the analysis (Bayley, 2013; Gorman & Johnson, 2013; Roy, 2011). Because of this, mixed-effects models such as Rbrul (Johnson, 2009), that incorporate fixed-effects predictors, as well as 'continuous' variables such as time, and random effects such as individual speaker and word, have been adopted in more recent variationist research.

In L2 studies of language variation such as Model Study 6 (Kennedy Terry, 2017, 2022a, 2022b) and Model Study 7 (Pozzi, 2021; Pozzi & Bayley, 2021), Rbrul analysis is used to quantify the influence that individual variables (known as 'factors') within a given category (a 'factor group') have on the occurrence of particular linguistic forms. Most often, studies of language variation incorporate both linguistic and extralinguistic, or social, factor groups in the Rbrul analysis. For example, the linguistic factor groups in Kennedy Terry (2017) on the acquisition of variable /l/ deletion in L2 French included subject pronoun ('token') type, preceding phonological context, and following phonological context. The extralinguistic factor groups included time in the TL environment, French coursework prior to SA, and the final score on the Social Network Strength Scale (SNSS) for SA, among others.

Within each factor group, there exists a pre-determined set of possible linguistic environments, or factors, and raw data are coded according to these factors in preparation for the statistical analysis. The factors selected by the researcher are normally based on previous research on TL and L2 speakers (if available), linguistic theory, and observations made by the researcher in the course of the study. For example, the linguistic factor group of 'token type' in Kennedy Terry (2017) included five subject pronouns that are potential sites for /l/ deletion by TL speakers: *ils* (3p. masc.) 'they', *il* (3s. impersonal) 'it', *il* (3s. masc. personal) 'he', *elle* (3s. fem.) 'she', and *elles* (3p. fem.) 'they'. Kennedy Terry selected these token types based on previous research indicating that the deletion of /l/ in third-person subject clitic pronouns (/l/ realized as [l] or null, as in *il vient* [il vjɛ̃] ~[i vjɛ̃] 'he comes/is coming') by TL speakers follows a hierarchy with the subject pronoun *il* (3s. impersonal) 'it' providing the most favorable context for deletion and the subject pronoun *elle* (3s. fem.) 'she' providing the least favorable context. Previous research also demonstrates that TL speaker rates of /l/ deletion range from approximately 90–100 percent in the most favorable context to 15–30 percent in the least favorable context (Armstrong, 1996; Ashby, 1984; Laks, 1980; Poplack & Walker, 1986; Sankoff & Cedergren, 1976). These token types, along with the factors associated with the factor groups of preceding and following phonological context, are shown in Table 8.4.

TABLE 8.4 Rbrul analysis for /l/ deletion by linguistic factor group

Linguistic factor groups*	N	Deletion %	Factor weight	Log-odds
Token type				
ils (3p. masc.) 'they'	257	31.9	.80	1.384
il (3s. impersonal) 'it'	511	23.7	.67	0.714
il (3s. masc. personal) 'he'	333	6.9	.36	−0.571
elle (3s. fem.) 'she', elles (3p. fem.) 'they'[a]	434	3.2	.18	−1.527
Range			.62	
Following phonological context [b][c]				
Following consonant	718	17.3	.55	0.182
Following vowel / glide	817	14.2	.46	−0.182
Range			.09	
Preceding phonological context				
Preceding vowel / glide	986	16.1	[.55]	0.187
Preceding consonant	415	15.9	[.51]	0.029
Preceding pause	134	11.2	[.45]	−0.217
Total/Input (corrected mean)	1535	15.6	.05	

Note: Factor groups not selected as significant in square brackets.

[a] Includes 5 tokens of *elles* (3p. feminine).
[b] Excludes 15 tokens of a following pause.
[c] Factor group of Following phonological context originally included five separate factors (nasal consonant, fricative, glide, vowel, stop); however, an interaction between the factor group of Token type and Following phonological context was noted (97% of all following glides were associated with one subject pronoun—*il* 3s. impersonal). The five factors were thus collapsed into two factors only. NB: this factor group was found to be significant in both cases—with all five factors and with only two factors.
*p < .05.

Source: Reprinted with permission from Kennedy Terry, 2017, p. 563

Given a data set coded for specific factors, the Rbrul program calculates a 'factor weight' for each factor which "provides a numerical measure of the strength or influence of each factor, relative to other factors in the same group, on the occurrence of the linguistic variable under investigation" (Bayley, 2013, p. 92). Rbrul factor weights range from zero to one with weights above 0.50 indicating that a factor *favors* the use of a variant relative to the other factors within the same group, and weights below 0.50 indicating that a factor *disfavors* the use of a variant relative to other factors within the same group. For example, as shown in Table 8.4 for the factor group of token type, the subject pronoun *ils* (3p. masc.) 'they' has a factor weight of 0.80, which means that the learners in Kennedy Terry's study were far more likely to delete /l/ in this pronoun type as compared to the others. Alternately, the learners were extremely unlikely to delete /l/ in the pronoun types of *elle* (3s. fem.) 'she' and *elles* (3p. fem.) 'they' which is indicated by the low factor weight of 0.18 for this factor.

Significance testing in Rbrul is achieved through a *step-up/step-down analysis* in which a 'full model' is created containing only those factor groups that are significant at the level of 0.05 or above (Bayley, 2013). Table 8.4 from Kennedy Terry (2017) shows that the linguistic factor groups of token type and following phonological context were statistically significant predictors of variable /l/ deletion by L2 learners; however, preceding phonological context was not a significant predictor and this is indicated by the brackets around the factor weights for this factor group.

In addition to the linguistic factors shown in Table 8.4, Kennedy Terry (2017) also used Rbrul analysis to determine the influence of extralinguistic, or social, factors on the L2 acquisition of /l/ deletion in French. Kennedy Terry included six extralinguistic factors that could potentially influence acquisition based on previous research on both L2 acquisition during SA and the L2 acquisition of sociolinguistic variation. As shown in Table 8.5, Kennedy Terry included the final SNSS for SA score as a factor group, with score ranges from 0 to 100 points (adjusted to a scale of 1–10 points) and coded as individual factors, as well as the factor groups of period of SA/interview number (i.e., time in the TL community), languages spoken at home, previous experience with French (i.e., contact with French native speakers, NSs), prior coursework in French, and study center in France.

Using the Rbrul *step-up/step-down analysis*, only the learner's final SNSS score was found to be a significant predictor of variable /l/ deletion at $p <$ .05. As shown in Table 8.5, learners with a score of 5–6 on the final SNSS were very likely to demonstrate /l/ deletion based on the favorable factor weight of 0.79 and a deletion rate of 31.9 percent. Learners scoring 8–9 points and 3–4 points on the SNSS were somewhat likely to delete /l/ with factor weights of 0.67 and 0.66, respectively. Finally, learners scoring 0 or 1–2 points on the final SNSS were unlikely to demonstrate /l/ deletion with unfavorable factor weights of 0.35 and 0.11, respectively.

Table 8.5 also provides the results of the Rbrul analysis for the other five extralinguistic factor groups, none of which was identified as a significant predictor of /l/ deletion for the learners in this study (factor weights shown in brackets). It is important to note here this does not mean that these factor groups did not play any role at all in acquisition, but it does indicate that in the statistical analysis, these extralinguistic factors were overshadowed by the stronger influence of social networks represented by the SNSS score, as well as the linguistic factor groups of token type and following phonological context.

TABLE 8.5 Rbrul analysis for /l/ deletion by extralinguistic factor group

Extralinguistic factor groups*	N	Deletion %	Factor weight	Log-odds
SNSS score[a]				
5–6 (50–69 points)	339	31.9	.79	1.325
8–9 (80–99 points)	150	19.3	.67	0.713
3–4 (30–49 points)	549	15.5	.66	0.679
1–2 (10–29 points)	209	7.7	.35	−0.611
0 (0–9 points) [b][c]	288	0.7	.11	−2.106
Range			.68	
Period of SA / interview #				
Interview #1 (year-long)	249	11.2	[.63]	0.513
Interview #3 (year-long)	399	26.8	[.58]	0.305
Interview #2 (year-long)	455	13.8	[.56]	0.249
Interview #2 (semester)	248	14.9	[.59]	0.356
Interview #1 (semester)	184	2.7	[.19]	−1.423
Languages spoken at home				
English only	1025	16.5	[.50]	0.014
English + additional language	510	13.9	[.50]	−0.014
Previous experience with French				
Little/no contact	1046	16.3	[.50]	0.013
Some contact with NSs (2–4 weeks)	489	14.3	[.50]	−0.013
Prior coursework in French				
1+ year upper division	81	27.2	[.59]	0.345
Lower division only	821	12.9	[.46]	−0.153
Some upper division	633	17.7	[.45]	−0.192
Study center				
Toulon	98	28.6	[.75]	1.121
Lyon	573	21.5	[.51]	0.026
Paris	300	14.0	[.46]	−0.174
Bordeaux	364	8.3	[.27]	−0.974
Total/Input (corrected mean)	1535	15.6	.05	

Note: Factor groups not selected as significant in square brackets.

[a] SNSS results include both mid-year scores (for year-long students) and final scores (for year-long and semester students).

[b] SNSS scores of "0" include interview #1 results for learners who did not demonstrate any instance of /l/ deletion at the first interview and results for one semester learner who had no regular contact with NSs at the final interview (Jade).

[c] Tokens from the initial interviews were assigned SNSS scores based on group averages for interviews #2 and #3. For example, if a learner deleted at 1–9% during interview #1, these tokens were assigned a SNSS score of "1". If a learner deleted at 10–19% during interview #1, these tokens were assigned a SNSS score of "2", and so on.

*p < .05.

Source: Reprinted with permission from Kennedy Terry, 2017, p. 565

As explained by Young and Bayley (1996), language variation is likely to be constrained by a combination of linguistic and extralinguistic factors rather than a single factor, and different linguistic variables are often constrained, or influenced, differently by the same set of factors. For example, the results of Kennedy Terry (2022a, 2022b) for the schwa deletion variable for the same group of 17 L2 French learners corroborate the significant role that social networks play in the L2 acquisition of variation; however, for this variable, both the SNSS score and time spent in the TL community were significant extralinguistic predictors of variation.

The results of the Rbrul analysis for the extralinguistic influences on schwa deletion (/ə/ realized as [œ] or null, as in *tu me dis* [ty mœ di] ~ [tym di] 'you tell me') from Kennedy Terry (2022b) are shown in Table 8.6. The extralinguistic factor groups included in the Rbrul analysis are the same as those used in Kennedy Terry (2017) for the /l/ deletion variable: SNSS score, period of SA/interview number (i.e., time in the TL community), languages spoken at home, previous experience with French (i.e., contact with French NSs), prior coursework in French, and study center in France.

A number of important comparisons can be made between the Rbrul results in Table 8.5 for /l/ deletion (Kennedy Terry, 2017) and the results in Table 8.6 for schwa deletion (Kennedy Terry, 2022b). First, although certain factors within each factor group are favorable to deletion and others are unfavorable, the *range*, or the difference between the most and least favorable factors within a factor group, is much smaller for schwa deletion than it is for /l/ deletion. For example, a score of 5–9 points on the SNSS for SA is shown to be favorable to schwa deletion with a factor weight of 0.65 and a score of 0 points is shown to be unfavorable to deletion with a factor weight of 0.29. The difference between these two factor weights, the range, is 0.36. Conversely, Table 8.5 shows that the most favorable factor weight for /l/ deletion was 0.79 for a score of 5–6 points on the SNSS and the least favorable was a score of 0 points with a factor weight of 0.11. The range in the factor weights for /l/ deletion is 0.68 demonstrating that the SNSS score is a stronger individual predictor for /l/ deletion than it is for schwa deletion.

Additionally, Table 8.6 for the schwa deletion variable from Kennedy Terry (2022b) shows that the most favorable SNSS score (5–9 points) and the most favorable amount of time in the TL community (interview #3 for the year-long participants) have positive factor weights of 0.65 and 0.62, respectively, but neither factor is extremely favorable to deletion as compared to a score of 5–6 points on the SNSS for /l/ deletion with a factor weight of 0.79 (Table 8.5, Kennedy Terry, 2017). These results reflect the fact that for schwa deletion, unlike /l/ deletion, social network strength and time in the TL environment work together to predict acquisition and neither factor

TABLE 8.6 Rbrul analysis for schwa deletion by extralinguistic factor group

Extralinguistic factor groups [a]	N	Log-odds	Deletion %	Weight	p
SNSS score [b]					5.33e-12
5–9 (50–99 points)	1731	0.634	14.0	.65	
1–4 (10–49 points)	3291	0.280	8.1	.57	
0 (0–9 points)[c]	499	−0.914	2.0	.29	
Period of SA / interview #					0.00112
Interview #3 (year-long)	1365	0.474	14.1	.62	
Interview #2 (year-long)	1324	0.309	10.0	.58	
Interview #1 (year-long)	1095	−0.275	7.0	.43	
Interview #2 (semester)	870	−0.131	6.9	.47	
Interview #1 (semester)	867	−0.376	6.8	.41	
Total/Input (corrected mean)	5521		9.4	.02	

Notes: Log likelihood = −1298.358; df 18; intercept = −3.696.

[a] All factor groups significant at p < .05. Factor groups not selected as significant are not shown in the table. These include languages spoken at home; previous experience with French; prior coursework in French; study center.

[b] SNSS results include both mid-year scores (year-long students only) and final scores (year-long and semester students).

[c] SNSS scores of "0" include interview #1 results for learners who did not demonstrate any instance of schwa elision at the first interview and results for one semester learner who had no regular contact with NSs at the final interview (Jade). Tokens from the initial interviews were assigned SNSS scores based on the group averages for interviews #2 and #3. For example, if a learner was already eliding schwa at 1–9% during interview #1, these tokens were assigned a SNSS score of 2. If a learner was eliding at 10–19% during interview #1, these tokens were assigned a SNSS score of 4, and 20–25%, a score of 5.

Source: Reprinted with permission from Kennedy Terry, 2022b, p. 293

group is a predominant influence. Finally, the overall rates of schwa deletion are much lower than they are for /l/ deletion, even at the final interview and in the most favorable contexts, and this reflects a much slower and gradual process of acquisition.

Pozzi (2021, Model Study 7) also used a mixed-effects model (Rbrul, Johnson, 2009) to examine the L2 acquisition of *vos*, the informal second-person singular form commonly used in place of *tú* 'you' in some Latin American countries, by 23 L1 English speakers during a semester of SA in Buenos Aires, Argentina. In this study, Pozzi used a modified version of the SNSS for SA (Kennedy, 2012) to examine not only the impact of social networks on L2 acquisition but also the role of certain extralinguistic factors known to influence L2 acquisition and use during SA: time in the TL community, proficiency level, task type, and explicit instruction on the use of *vos* in Argentine Spanish. Pozzi also incorporated the linguistic factor of mood (indicative or imperative). In Pozzi (2021), speech data were collected three times during the semester (beginning, middle, end) via Skype interviews with the researcher and each interview consisted of 20 minutes of informal conversation, as well as an oral discourse completion task (DCT) and two role plays, all of which were designed to elicit the use of *vos* by the learners. Linguistic and sociolinguistic data for the Rbrul analysis in Pozzi (2021) included over 1200 tokens of *vos* and *tú*, the SNSS for SA completed at the second and third interviews, and a background questionnaire completed before the SA period.

Table 8.7 displays the results of the Rbrul analysis in Pozzi (2021). Of the six linguistic and extralinguistic factors considered in this study, the Rbrul analysis identified four factors that were statistically significant predictors of the use of *vos* by the L2 learners: task type, mood, proficiency level, and the score on the SNSS. The results in Table 8.7 demonstrate that the DCT task slightly favored the use of *vos* over *tú* with learners using *vos* 65.8 percent of the time in the DCT versus 65.1 percent of the time in the role plays. These usage rates are predicted by a slightly favorable Rbrul factor weight of 0.545 for the DCT versus a slightly unfavorable factor weight of 0.427 for the role plays. The results for mood were more varied with learners using *vos* 68.9 percent of the time in the present indicative (factor weight = 0.563) versus 53.1 percent in the imperative (factor weight = 0.284). Proficiency level also influenced the use of *vos* with learners at the beginning level using *vos* 46.9 percent of the time (factor weight = 0.394), intermediate learners using *vos* 50.3 percent of the time (factor weight = 0.321), and advanced learners using *vos* a full 77.2 percent of the time (factor weight = 0.606).

TABLE 8.7 Rbrul analysis comparing *Vos* and *Tú* verb forms

Factor group	Factor	Logodds	N	% Vos	Weight
Task	Oral DCT	0.236	514	65.8	.545
	Role plays	−0.236	315	65.1	.427
Tense	Present	0.589	652	68.9	.563
	Imperative	−0.589	177	53.1	.284
SNSS	High	1.154	158	99.1	.793
	Mid	−0.210	403	70.2	.494
	Low	−0.944	268	43.3	.319
Proficiency	Advanced	0.681	487	77.2	.606
	Beginning	−0.180	143	46.9	.394
	Intermediate	−0.500	199	50.3	.321
Total	Input		829	65.5	.713

Source: Reprinted with permission from Pozzi, 2021, p. 11

Finally, the Rbrul analysis identified social networks with TL speakers (as measured by the SNSS for SA) as the strongest predictor of the use of *vos* of all six factors considered in the analysis. This is demonstrated by the very favorable factor weight of 0.793 associated with a 'High' score on the SNSS and a 99.1 percent usage rate of *vos*. A 'Mid' SNSS score was associated with a usage rate of 70.2 percent and a slightly unfavorable factor weight of 0.494. A 'Low' SNSS score was associated with a usage rate of 43.3 percent and an unfavorable factor weight of 0.319.

In Table 8.8, the results of Pozzi (2021) are shown by individual learner, including the learner's total use of *vos* (expressed as a percentage of time), initial proficiency level, and the SNSS score at the second and third interviews. These results demonstrate that higher scores on the SNSS for SA, as well as higher initial proficiency levels, are associated with higher levels of *vos* production by the learners in this study. Pozzi also noted the correlation between a 'High' score on the SNSS and advanced proficiency at the outset of SA: as shown in Table 8.8, only learners who began SA with an advanced level of Spanish were able to form the dense and multiplex social networks with TL speakers that allowed them to achieve a 'High' score on the SNSS. Moreover, although 14 learners began the SA period with advanced proficiency, only five of these 14 were able to create strong social networks with TL speakers. These results support previous research demonstrating that learners often struggle to initiate and maintain networks with TL speakers during SA (Hasegawa, 2019; McManus, 2019).

It is useful to contrast the results of Pozzi (2021) with those of Pozzi and Bayley (2021) who examined the L2 acquisition of a phonological, rather than morphological, feature of Buenos Aires Spanish (BAS) among the same group of 23 American learners studying in Argentina. In this study, Pozzi and Bayley focused on the acquisition of *sheísmo/zheísmo*, or the use of [ʃ] and [ʒ], respectively, for segments represented orthographically as "y" and "ll", such as in the pronunciation of the word llave [jaβe] 'key', pronounced as [ʃaβe] with *sheísmo* or [ʒaβe] with *zheísmo*. In the data analysis using Rbrul (Johnson, 2009), this study considered a range of potential linguistic factors, such as the phonological environment of the site for potential *sheísmo/zheísmo* and the morphological status of the word in which *sheísmo/zheísmo* would be used by BAS speakers.

The extralinguistic factors considered in the analysis included most of those in Pozzi (2021): proficiency level, time in the TL environment, task type/speech style, and the score on the SNSS for SA. Additionally, Pozzi and Bayley incorporated the age of the speaker with whom the learner had the most contact as an extralinguistic factor separate from the overall SNSS score. Data from Pozzi and Bayley (2021) included over 4,800 tokens representing sites for potential *sheísmo/zheísmo* gathered from

TABLE 8.8 *Vos* usage by speaker with proficiency level and SNSS score

Speaker	Total % vos production	Proficiency level	*SNSS
Brittany	95.5	Advanced	High
Ryan	95.8	Advanced	High
Kelly	93.6	Advanced	High
Mary	81.1	Advanced	High
Andrea	95.2	Advanced	High
Emily	96.4	Advanced	Mid
Kerry	89.2	Advanced	Mid
Jenny	75.7	Advanced	Mid
Amy	52.3	Advanced	Mid
Valerie	62.9	Advanced	Mid
Erin	85.0	Advanced	Mid
Tyler	53.2	Advanced	Low, Mid
Alicia	72.7	Advanced	Low, Mid
Alison	67.6	Advanced	Low
Kathryn	75.6	Beginning	Low, Mid
Chelsea	32.4	Beginning	Low
Kim	34.6	Beginning	Low
Julia	38.1	Beginning	Low
Mariah	84.4	Intermediate	Mid
Andrew	63.0	Intermediate	Mid
Eddie	40.5	Intermediate	Low, Mid
Melanie	35.3	Intermediate	Low, Mid
Camille	16.2	Intermediate	Low

*When two SNSS scores are displayed, the first is from Time 2 and the second is from Time 3. When only one SNSS score is displayed, the SNSS score at Time 2 and 3 was in the same range.

Source: Reprinted with permission from Pozzi, 2021, p. 12

20-minute sociolinguistic interviews, a reading passage from an Argentine comic strip, and a word list, all of which were completed by the learners on three occasions: at the beginning, in the middle, and at the end of the semester of SA.

The results from the Rbrul analysis in Pozzi and Bayley (2021) are shown in Table 8.9. The analysis identified two linguistic factors favoring the use of *sheísmo/zheísmo*, with learners producing more instances of *sheísmo/zheísmo* in word-initial placements ('Phonological environment-location') and in vowel-ll-vowel constructions ('Word type'), such as in the word *ella* 'she'. Additionally, among the extralinguistic factors, only time in the TL environment predicted significant and rapid gains in *sheísmo/zheísmo* over the semester of SA with learners increasing their use of *sheísmo/zheísmo*

TABLE 8.9 Rbrul analysis for *sheísmo/zheísmo* (BAS) usage

Factor group	Factor	Logodds	N	% BAS	Weight
Word type	Vowel-ll-vowel (*ella*, etc.)	0.899	1577	63.2	.702
	Other	−0.278	2392	53.3	.421
	yo	−0.621	890	57.9	.34
Phonological	Initial	0.421	2034	57.2	.62
environment—	Medial	−0.421	2825	57.4	.413
location					
Time	3	2.614	1570	89.0	.94
	2	1.898	1571	83.1	.884
	1	−4.512	1718	4.7	.012
Totals	Input		4859	57.3	.508

Source: Reprinted with permission from Pozzi & Bayley, 2021, p. 119

from 4.7 percent to 83.1 percent of the time by the second interview and then again to 89 percent of the time at the final interview.

It is important to note that the results of Pozzi and Bayley for *sheísmo/zheísmo* are unusual among studies investigating the L2 acquisition of phonological variables (either stylistic or regional) in which learners only begin to show sensitivity to TL norms (George, 2014; Kennedy Terry, 2017, 2022a, 2022b; Knouse, 2013; Regan et al., 2009) and rarely approximate TL usage rates after a single semester of SA. Moreover, unlike the majority of the studies reviewed in this chapter and elsewhere in this volume, social networks with TL speakers were not found to be a significant influence on the use of *sheísmo/zheísmo*, potentially because all learners in this study showed significant increases in the use of *sheísmo/zheísmo* over the course of the SA period. That is, unlike other phonological variables such as Castilian theta θ in L2 Spanish (George, 2014; Knouse, 2013) and /l/ deletion and schwa deletion in L2 French (Kennedy Terry, 2017, 2022a, 2022b; Regan et al., 2009), *sheísmo/zheísmo* appears to be a phonological variable that is easily acquired by learners during SA regardless of the strength of their social networks with TL speakers.

Pozzi and Bayley (2021) suggest that *sheísmo/zheísmo* may be relatively easy for learners to implement because it is used in all phonological contexts, is considered a prestige form, and it is highly salient. The results by individual learner support these conclusions as all 23 learners increased their use of *sheísmo/zheísmo* between the first and third interviews. At the same time, although social networks with TL speakers were not shown to be a significant predictor of *sheísmo/zheísmo* use at a group level, the authors point out that all five learners who achieved a 'High' score on the SNSS for

SA also used *sheísmo/zheísmo* categorically like the native BAS speakers in their social networks. That is, while only six of the 23 learners used *sheísmo/zheísmo* categorically at the final interview, five of these six learners achieved a 'High' score on the final SNSS.

Conclusion

The results of the studies described in this chapter highlight the importance of understanding the nature of the linguistic data that has been gathered during the course of a study, as well as the initial hypotheses and goals of the researcher, in order to explore the relationship between participation in social networks and specific linguistic outcomes. For example, it is critical to understand whether the linguistic data gathered from study participants is uniform, like that produced in a written cloze test, or not uniform, like speech data gathered during informal or semi-structured interviews. Additionally, given the diversity of research featured in this volume, in terms of participants, languages, linguistic outcomes, and learning contexts, it is essential for the researcher to identify, at the outset of the study, the dependent and independent variables, or predictive factors, that will be used to examine and draw conclusions from the data so as to select the most appropriate tools for inferential statistical analysis.

Discussion Questions

1. Compare and contrast two types of linguistic data (e.g., written versus spoken or structured elicitation tasks versus informal interviews). What are the advantages and limitations of each in terms of the data analysis that may be conducted? Based on the research that you have read about in this volume, what types of data would be more likely to reflect the influence of social networks with TL speakers and why?
2. Consider the goals and outcomes of the research presented in this chapter—what have you learned about the role of social networks in L2 acquisition and development? Write a summary of the most important findings.
3. Imagine a research study that you would like to conduct applying SNA to the L2 learning context. Once you have determined the participants and the focus of the study, consider what type of linguistic data you would need to gather and the methods you would use to gather this data. Once you have an idea of the data set, explain which tools you would you use for inferential statistical analysis and justify your choice based on the research described in this chapter.

9

USING SOCIAL NETWORK ANALYSIS TO EXAMINE LINGUISTIC OUTCOMES

Network Structure and Composition

Introduction

In addition to inferential statistics (Chapter 8), researchers using social network analysis (SNA) to examine linguistic and sociolinguistic outcomes have a variety of tools available to investigate the relationship between participation in social networks with target-language (TL) and co-national/first language (L1) speakers and second language (L2) development and use. In this second chapter on linguistic data analysis, we focus on research that explores correlations between network structure and network composition and specific linguistic and sociolinguistic outcomes among L2 learners.

Sociocentric (Macro-level) Network Analysis

Model Study 14 by Bernstein (2018) demonstrates the benefits of combining qualitative, ethnographic data about a learner's participation in the macro-level social network of a preschool classroom with quantitative data on L2 acquisition to question long-standing beliefs about the interconnectedness of social position, interaction, and language learning opportunities. In this study, Bernstein (2018) operationalized what King and Mackey (2016) refer to as a 'layering' of research perspectives to examine both the *process* of interaction and the linguistic *products*, or outcomes, of such interaction in a US Head Start preschool classroom with over 50 percent L2 English learners at the early stages of acquisition. For this study, Bernstein articulated and adopted an approach which the researcher calls Participation in Networks of Practice, or P-NoP, an approach that incorporates elements from both

DOI: 10.4324/9781003174448-9

the Network of Practice (NoP, Brown & Duguid, 2001) and the Individual Network of Practice (INoP, Zappa-Hollman & Duff, 2015) frameworks. Both frameworks draw on concepts related to communities of practice (Lave & Wenger, 1991) and SNA to explain the flow of information in the macro-level network (NoP) and the opportunities for individual participation in the macro-level network by means of an egocentric network (INoP). In Model Study 14, Bernstein relied on weekly classroom observations and interviews to reconstruct the egocentric and sociocentric (i.e., full or macro-level, see Chapter 7) networks within the preschool classroom and then correlated P-NoP with four indicators of L2 acquisition for each participant.

Over the course of an academic year, Bernstein (2018) acted as an adult volunteer in the preschool classroom in which the research was conducted (see Chapter 6 for a description of Bernstein's data collection techniques). To examine the macro-level network within the classroom, Bernstein analyzed field notes and video recordings and used labels that students assigned to each other throughout the course of their interactions (e.g., 'bad drawer', 'good student') in order to create a social-positioning map that reflected the types of roles that each participant fulfilled within the classroom network. This social-positioning map was then compared to a network diagram created using UCINET software (Borgatti et al., 2002) based on interviews in which students named their preferred classroom playmates. The resulting network diagram was then compared to a calculation of observed interactions over the last three months of school to ensure accuracy.

Bernstein's (2018) observations focused on four of the 11 female English language learners (ELLs) in the class: three L1 Nepali speakers and one L1 Turkish speaker, all aged 3;9–4;0 years old at the beginning of the year. To explore correlations between classroom social networks and L2 acquisition for these four focal participants, Bernstein created a video corpus from the classroom observations during the first and last three months of the school year and transcribed all segments featuring the four focal participants. Bernstein then compared each participant's language use at the beginning and the end of the year, analyzing the transcripts for four elements: (1) the number of English turns (i.e., utterances using consecutive English words) per hour; (2) the number of unique lexical items per hour; (3) mean-length-of-utterance (MLU); and (4) the number of utterances with verbs per hour.

Using the macro-level network diagram, or Classroom NoP (CNoP), Bernstein (2018) identified two 'cliques' within the network where a clique indicates that all members identified each other as 'preferred playmates'. From this CNoP, Bernstein identified two participants who provided representative cases of network centrality, Kritika, and network peripherality, Hande. Kritika was an L1 Nepali speaker who was named as a preferred playmate by six classmates, more often than any other student in the class, and who was positioned at both the center of the CNoP and one of the classroom cliques. Kritika's position at the center of the CNoP can be seen in Figure 9.1. Hande was the only L1 Turkish speaker in the class and, as shown in Figure 9.1, was connected to the CNoP by a single L1 English playmate that she named during the interview. Moreover, Hande was not named by any classmate as a preferred playmate. Additionally, Kritika was considered academically competent and viewed as an "authoritative knower of classroom practices" (p. 822) by both peers and teachers. In contrast, Hande joined the class late in September and, as the only Turkish speaker, spent most of the year quietly observing other students and engaging in solitary activities (and often monologuing), even when she played alongside other students. Bernstein noted that by the end of the year, Hande was using more English to interact with her peers; however, these interactions often took the form of teasing, interrupting, or shouting to the teachers, none of which were well received by her classmates.

While the existing research on social networks in L2 acquisition would predict that Kritika would make greater proficiency gains over the course of the year due to her greater access to L2 peer interactions, the results of Bernstein's (2018) linguistic data analysis demonstrate the opposite trend: Hande made greater gains than Kritika on all four proficiency measures and she also made the greatest gains of all four female students

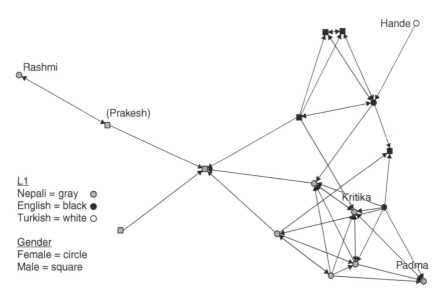

FIGURE 9.1 Head Start preschool classroom network of practice (NoP) (reprinted with permission from Bernstein, 2018, p. 821)

in the focal group. Not only did Hande achieve the greatest gains, but in some cases, the increases were three or four times those of her peers, such as in the number of English words used per hour and the number of unique lexical items per hour. Hande also more than doubled her MLU (from 2.07 to 4.54 words per analysis of speech unit; AS-unit, Foster et al., 2000) and increased the percentages of utterances with verbs from 25 percent to 84 percent over the course of the year.

In response to Hande's success, Bernstein (2018) called upon the work of Lave and Wenger (1991) who explained that peripherality within a CoP or social network may not necessarily place the participant in an inferior position for accessing the resources of the network and it may, in fact, be an 'empowering' position if it is a place from which "one moves toward more-intensive participation" (1991, p. 53). Bernstein thus hypothesized that Hande's position at the periphery of the CNoP allowed her to rotate around the classroom and listen to her classmates' conversations without feeling any pressure to participate, or to participate in specific ways. This freedom to listen and 'notice' the language around her, as well as the freedom to engage in high levels of self-talk in English, contributed to Hande's significant proficiency gains over the course of the year. In contrast, Bernstein concluded that Kritika's need to maintain her authority at the center of the CNoP may have resulted in missing out on language learning opportunities because she feared making a mistake or revealing her lack of comprehension. Based on these results, Bernstein urges researchers and practitioners to expand the accepted definitions of 'interaction' and 'participation' to include more than overt production and/or production that includes the negotiation of meaning with another interlocutor, in order to better understand how observation of interaction, and the silent but active listening or self-talk that accompanies this observation of interaction, may contribute to language acquisition.

Similar to Bernstein (2018), Paradowski et al. (2021a) also used sociocentric network analysis to examine the role of in-network TL interactions on L2 acquisition during short-term study abroad (SA) in Poland and in an at-home language learning context. The full project involved gathering egocentric social network data for 332 L2 Polish learners in the SA context and 40 L2 Japanese or L2 Swedish learners in the at-home context and then combining this egocentric network data into sociocentric network diagrams for groups of learners based on their assigned language classes. The egocentric network questionnaire asked students to list all of their contacts, the language/s used with each contact, the intensity of the relationship, and the 'direction' of the relationship (whether it was a one- or two-way relationship). Using a full network approach and computational SNA, Paradowski et al. created full network diagrams (sociograms) for each class of learners that included all contacts (*alters*) with whom the learner reported having a direct relationship, as well as the networks in which the contacts participated but in which the learner did not participate directly. Paradowski et al. explained that while the majority of the contacts within the sociogram were students, the full network approach allows for the incorporation of the extended social networks of teachers, family, and friends who interacted directly with the learner but who also maintained their own, separate ego-based networks. This quantitative survey data was supplemented by semi-structured interviews conducted with nine SA participants and seven at-home participants.

Similar to the sociocentric analysis in Hasegawa (2019, Model Study 11), the full network analysis used by Paradowski et al. incorporates all of the links within the egocentric network of the learner, as well as *alter-alter* links connecting the learner's contacts to the members of their own networks. In their study, Paradowski et al. focused on 'network centrality' by incorporating the direction of the links (*out-link* vs. *in-link*) between learners and the members of their networks. An *out-link* is established for individual A when individual A reports having a connection to individual B (whether or not individual B reports a similar connection) and an *in-link* is established for individual B when individual A reports this connection. Bidirectional links are established when both individual A and individual B report a mutual connection when depicting or describing their social networks.

Additionally, Paradowski et al. calculated 'weighted network centrality' by incorporating the intensity of the interactions between different individuals. An example of this is shown in Figure 9.2 where thicker lines represent a greater frequency of interaction and arrows indicate the direction of interactions (out-link vs. in-link). The results of Paradowski et al. (2021a) demonstrated that network structure has a significant impact on L2 acquisition during SA. For the SA learners in the study, higher levels of outgoing interactions (measured as 'weighted out-degree centrality') were associated with higher levels of progress in the TL and higher levels of incoming interactions ('weighted in-degree centrality') were negatively associated with progress in the TL.

More detailed results from Paradowski et al. (2021b) for the same group of SA learners demonstrated that while a high level of *total* incoming interactions (including TL, L1, and other language interactions) was negatively correlated with measures of subjective improvement in the TL (e.g., pronunciation, vocabulary, cultural knowledge), a high level of incoming interactions *in the TL* was positively correlated with measures of objective improvement (e.g., performance on pre- and post- placement tests). Additionally, high levels of outgoing interactions in the TL were positively correlated with

Interactions in TL only*, **, ***	Interactions in any language*, **, ***

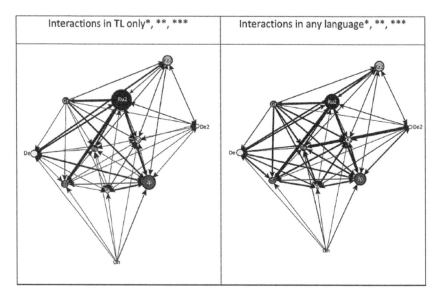

FIGURE 9.2 Sociocentric network diagrams of L2 Polish learners (reprinted with permission from Paradowski et al., 2021a, p. 101)

both subjective and objective improvement measures. In light of these results, the authors refer to Swain's (1985, 1998) Output Hypothesis, which supports the idea that learners who reported having relationships with specific individuals (e.g., out-links) maintained higher levels of output in the TL than learners who did not report as many out-links, or whose out-links were of lower intensity. Finally, Paradowski et al. (2021b) identified two additional factors that were negatively correlated with improvement in the L2: weighted incoming communications with teachers in a non-TL language and proficiency in English as a lingua franca. Both of these resulted in lower levels of performance in the L2 at the end of the SA period.

Interaction Patterns within Social Networks

In an analysis of learner interactions within social networks, Model Study 16 by Palfreyman (2021) examined longitudinal changes (from 2003 to 2018) to the English language learning opportunities available to 41 Emirati females studying at a government university in Dubai. Both the original study by Palfreyman (2006) and the follow-up analysis (Palfreyman, 2021) focused specifically on participants' interactions in informal language learning networks (ILLNs) and included interactions both inside and outside of the family home. The results of Palfreyman (2021) demonstrated that the use of English outside of the home in all four skills (e.g., speaking, listening, reading, writing) had increased over time, with the most significant increase in listening. The opposite trend was shown for English use inside of the home: English use decreased in all four skills with speaking showing the most significant decrease.

Additionally, results from Palfreyman (2021) showed a reduced reliance on assistance in English at home and a change in the source of the assistance (shown in Table 9.1). Results also showed a significant drop in assistance from brothers in favor of sisters, as well as a significant increase in assistance from online sources, with websites and internet chatting being the most frequent. While participants listed friends, followed closely by sisters, as the first source of help in English in both 2006 and 2021, the 2021 results showed that online sources had moved into the third position, eclipsing assistance from fathers, teachers, and brothers.

From these results, Palfreyman (2021) concluded that looser social networks contributed to the increased use of English outside of the home and

TABLE 9.1 Source of assistance with English ranked by results of Mann-Whitney U-test for 2018 results

	2003	*2018*
Friend	0.94	0.80
Sister	0.85	0.68
Web	0.04	0.63***
Older sister	0.13	0.33
Father	0.14	0.17
Teacher	0.18	0.17
Brother	0.62	0.16*
Younger sister	0.00	0.14
Mother	0.05	0.11
Nobody	0.12	0.07
Cousin	0.04	0.07
Older brother	0.23	0.05
Younger brother	0.03	0.00
Laptop	0.04	0.00
Husband	1.00	0.00
Dictionary	0.12	0.00
Myself	0.06	0.00

Note: Results of Mann-Whitney U-test presented on a scale of 0 (not mentioned) to 2 (First Resort).
*$p < .05$, ***$p < .001$

Source: Adapted from Palfreyman, 2021, p. 128

that inside of the home, the increased education level of female household members led to a decreased reliance on brothers and teachers for assistance. At the same time, results also demonstrated that the female participants themselves were assisting other household members with English language learning at higher rates, reflecting the overall increased education level of young females in Dubai.

With a similar focus on network interaction patterns, Mougeon and Rehner (2015) used qualitative data gathered through surveys and interviews to create engagement 'profile portraits' for 61 L2 French university learners in Ontario, Canada based on their active commitments to learning and using the TL. Measures of engagement included activities such as having regular contact with Francophones through extracurricular activities or employment and having studied, or having plans to study, in a Francophone environment. From this survey and interview data, the researchers divided the participants into six profile portraits, including 'engaged', 'moderately engaged', and 'minimally engaged' learners, and then further differentiated the profiles based on whether the participant was bilingual or multilingual.

Linguistic analysis from Mougeon and Rehner (2015) showed that the 'engaged multilinguals' used the highest average number of words in their interviews (4,257) in French, followed closely by 'engaged bilinguals' (3,728), and that both groups used a number of idiomatic expressions in French. These results contrast sharply with the average number of words per interview for the 'minimally engaged bilinguals" (2,846) and the 'minimally engaged multilinguals' (2,644). The minimally engaged learners also used many more requests for clarification or repetition in the interviews and nearly 50 percent had difficulty maintaining a conversation with a native speaker outside of the classroom setting.

Mougeon and Rehner (2015) also analyzed the linguistic data from the sociolinguistic interviews for the use of certain formal and informal variants in French. The researchers expected the 'engaged multilinguals and bilinguals' to use the informal variants at the highest levels and the 'minimally engaged' learners to use them at the lowest levels and the data analysis confirmed this expectation. These results are shown in Table 9.2. Moreover, the researchers expected the use of two highly frequent sociolinguistic variables, the use of *on* 'one' in place of *nous* 'we' and the deletion of the negative particle *ne*, to follow the engagement portraits closely and the data demonstrated this trend as well. In fact, the data demonstrated that the 'engaged multilingual learners' approached TL speaker rates for these two sociolinguistic variables, with learners using *on* in place of *nous* 95 percent of the time and deleting *ne* 83 percent of the time (see Table 9.2).

In order to examine change in engagement level over time, Mougeon and Rehner (2015) interviewed 14 of the 19 students after a three-year

Linguistic Outcomes: Network Structure and Composition **163**

TABLE 9.2 Rates of use of linguistic variants by profile portrait

Informal (formal) variants	Engaged multilinguals	Engaged bilinguals	Moderately engaged bilinguals	Moderately engaged multilinguals	Minimally engaged bilinguals	Minimally engaged multilinguals	Total informal (formal) variant use
On (nous)	314 (17) [95%]	134 (27) [83%]	313(106) [75%]	82 (40) [67%]	248(129) [66%]	26 (60) [30%]	1,117 (379)
Ø (ne)	327 (67) [83%]	156 (137) [53%]	271 (507) [35%]	144 (159) [48%]	265 (515) [34%]	32 (162) [16%]	1,195 (1,547)
Tu (vous)	12 (18) [40%]	6 (5) [55%]	24 (20) [55%]	15 (2) [88%]	12 (14) [46%]	1 (3) [25%]	70 (62)
Falloir (devoir/besoin/nécessaire)	17 (72) [19%]	26 (16) [62%]	26 (132) [17%]	17 (61) [22%]	10 (131) [7%]	1 (28) [3%]	97 (440)
Job (emploi/travail)	6 (21) [22%]	2 (13) [13%]	2 (46) [4%]	0 (14) [0%]	4 (30) [12%]	3 (18) [14%]	43 (350)
Rester (habiter/vivre)	3 (50) [6%]	3 (19) [14%]	1 (58) [2%]	0 (18) [0%]	5 (57) [8%]	7 (26) [21%]	19 (228)
Total informal (formal) [%]	679 (245) [73%]	327 (217) [60%]	637 (869) [42%]	258 (294) [47%]	544 (876) [38%]	70 (297) [19%]	2,515 (2,798)
TOTAL	924	544	1,506	552	1,420	367	5,313

Note: The percentages represent the percentage of informal variant use to formal variant use within each cell.

Source: Reprinted with permission from Mougeon & Rehner, 2015, p. 444

interval and found that these learners had increased their engagement level and overall commitment to learning L2 French. Additionally, results from these 19 students demonstrated that students at all engagement levels had increased their use of the informal sociolinguistic variants over time. One anomaly did appear in the longitudinal data: after a three-year interval, the 'minimally engaged bilinguals' demonstrated a higher use of the informal variants than the 'moderately engaged bilinguals and multilinguals', due in large part to their high use of *on* in place of *nous*. The researchers hypothesized that the high rate of *on* usage among 'minimally engaged bilinguals' may be the result of a developmental stage or may be the result of the near-categorical use of *on* in both Canadian and European French, as well as by French instructors. Finally, the researchers pointed out that many of the learners in the 'minimally engaged' category continued to have social contact with native Francophones despite having decided not to pursue higher-level coursework in French which may have contributed to their continued use of the informal variant.

Like Palfreyman (2021, Model Study 16) and Mougeon and Rehner (2015) who examined network interaction patterns of L2 learners in their home countries, both Van Mol and Michielsen (2015) and Bracke and Aguerre (2015) examined network interaction patterns to understand how program design and accommodations during SA impact network formation and TL acquisition. In their study, Van Mol and Michielsen (2015) used an online survey which asked Erasmus SA exchange participants to rate their level of interaction with local, co-national, and international students on a scale of 1–5 with 1 being the lowest level of interaction ("not at all") and 5 the highest level of interaction ("very much"). Results included responses from over 700 students from six different countries and showed that for all of the student groups, except students from the UK, the highest levels of interaction during the Erasmus exchange occurred with other international students. Students from the UK reported their highest levels of interaction with co-nationals.

Van Mol and Michielsen (2015) supplemented the quantitative survey results with qualitative data gathered through interviews and focus groups involving 71 university students who had either participated in an Erasmus exchange program (49 students) or had decided not to participate in an exchange program (22 students). The qualitative data confirmed that students who studied abroad in larger co-national or international cohorts tended to rely on these social networks upon arrival in the host country, that many social networks (with incoming and outgoing Erasmus students) were formed online prior to SA, and that relationships with fellow Erasmus students in the host country were encouraged through orientation programs and events that bring students together on a consistent basis. Additionally, a number of local, nonexchange participants who participated in the focus groups indicated that because they already had established family and friend networks with associated time commitments, they simply did not have the time or the desire to add international students to their networks. By including both exchange and nonexchange students in their interviews and focus groups, the research of Van Mol and Michielsen (2015) provides an alternate perspective that contributes important insights about the combination of forces that can make it extremely difficult for SA participants to create and maintain the type of social networks that will allow them to become active participants in the TL community.

Similarly, Bracke and Aguerre (2015) examined the communities of practice (CoP) in which Erasmus SA participants interacted and the discursive strategies employed by these students during a semester or year in Bordeaux, France. The 52 student participants for this study came from 19 different countries and the self-reported French proficiency levels of the participants at the beginning of the SA period included 60 percent intermediate and 40 percent advanced learners. The authors created and distributed an online questionnaire focused on the students' social activities in three specific areas (e.g., personal, educational, and public) and their attitudes toward language learning and use. The results reported in this study related to the survey questions targeting 12 specific discursive strategies used by learners to maintain involvement in conversations and that incorporate both linguistic and sociocultural knowledge.

The results of Bracke and Aguirre (2015) indicated that Erasmus participants living in a shared accommodation (e.g., a flat or house) interacted with more diverse groups of people than students living in university residence halls. Their results also showed that students living in the university residence halls interacted primarily with other students. For example, approximately 20 percent of students living in university residence halls reported interacting with French nonstudents while over 50 percent of the students living in shared accommodations reported interacting with French nonstudents. In the educational domain, over 40 percent of students in shared accommodations reported having 'information interactions' with French students as compared to 20 percent of participants living in university residence halls. Participants living in shared accommodation also participated more regularly in organizing events related to their home culture (75 percent of participants), but these events incorporated French speakers or other foreign nationals at a much higher rate (approximately 80 percent) than events organized by the participants living in university residence halls (less than 40 percent). Overall, the authors concluded that living situation had a clear impact on the CoPs that Erasmus students joined in the public domain during their stay in France. The authors argued that students in shared accommodation "have more diverse practices, these practices are more informal, and they involve more diverse people, at a higher level of engagement" (Bracke & Aguirre, 2015, p. 152).

Social Network Composition

The Impact of Network Composition on Group Results

Similar to Palfreyman (2021, Model Study 16) and Mougeon and Rehner (2015), an early study by Ferenz (2005) examined the impact of at-home social networks on L2 English development. In this study of six Israeli graduate students, Ferenz used sociolinguistic interviews and a background questionnaire to examine the influence of social network composition, specifically academic and nonacademic social contacts, on access to advanced academic literacy practices in L2 English. The sociolinguistic interviews consisted of two parts, with the first part focusing on the participant's language background, attitude, and identity, as well as their membership in an academic network, and the second part focusing specifically on advanced academic literacy practices. The interview data were then categorized according to four themes: (1) academic environment, (2) social environment, (3) identity and goals, and (4) L2 advanced academic literacy practices.

Like Carhill-Poza (2015, Model Study 12), Ferenz separated the network members listed in the 'social environment' category into academic and nonacademic contacts in order to identify social relationships that would be expected to promote advanced academic literacy. In addition to the qualitative data gathered in the interviews, participants completed a questionnaire which focused specifically on the number of social network contacts in three different environments (at home, work, the university), the languages used with each contact (English or Hebrew), and activities conducted within the university environment. Table 9.3 shows the participants' social networks including those members "with whom they discuss their disciplinary writing tasks", categorized by the environment in which interactions occur.

The results from Ferenz (2005) demonstrated that some participants had greater access to academic literacy practices through a network of professors and advisors at the university, with advisors playing a key role in the acquisition of advanced L2 English literacy practices for four of the six participants. As shown in Table 9.3, within the social environment, two of the participants reported collaborating with academic peers in the writing and review process (e.g., Sara and Rachel) and two reported speaking with work colleagues outside of the university environment on topics related to

TABLE 9.3 Social networks by participant and environment

	Sara	Rachel	Miriam	David	Leah	Judith
Academic	Advisor, Professors, Students	Advisor, Professors, Students	Advisor	Advisor	–	–
Nonacademic	Spouse	–	Spouse	Co-workers, Spouse	Co-workers, Friend	Neighbor

Source: Reprinted with permission from Ferenz, 2005, p. 345

TABLE 9.4 Desired social identity by participant

	Sara	Rachel	Miriam	David	Leah	Judith
Identity	Academic	Academic	Academic	Professional	Professional	Professional

Source: Reprinted with permission from Ferenz, 2005, p. 348

their research or their academic writing (e.g., David and Leah). Interview data also revealed that the self-categorized social identity of the participants (as primarily academic or professional) and their future career goals also impacted the social networks that participants created. As shown in Table 9.4, students planning academic careers (e.g., Sara and Rachel) had broader networks within the academic institution than those whose goals focused on careers outside of academia (e.g., Leah and Judith). Finally, the participants were divided in their approach to academic literacy practices with three preferring to use English throughout the writing process, from idea formation to the writing phase, and three using Hebrew for pre-writing activities and then translating their ideas into English. Interestingly, the three participants who used English throughout the writing process all had an academic, rather than professional, orientation toward L2 English and had also included their academic advisors as important members of their social networks (e.g., Sarah, Rachel, Miriam). From these results, Ferenz concluded that social identity and career goals motivated the participants to create social networks that were either academically or professionally oriented and, in turn, those with academically oriented social networks were assisted and supported in their development of advanced academic literacy practices in L2 English.

In another small-scale study of seven SA learners who spent an academic year studying at a French university and living with a French host family, Gautier and Chevrot (2015) evaluated learners' social networks using data gathered through contact diaries and questionnaires. From these diaries and questionnaires, Gautier and Chevrot used NetDraw (Borgatti, 2002) and UCINET software (Borgatti et al., 1999) to create detailed models of the learners' social networks and to calculate network density (Borgatti et al., 2013) based on the total number of possible ties within the network. For example, if a network consists of ten members, and the number of possible ties between various members is 45, a network with only 25 effective (actual) ties is said to have a density of .55 or 55 percent, where higher density scores indicate more closely-knit speech communities. Using this density calculation, Gautier and Chevrot followed Bidart et al. (2011) in labeling the learners' networks as 'dense' (if the density score was 30 percent or above) or 'composite' if the density score was below 30 percent. Learner networks were further differentiated based on the L1 of the network members (English or French) and the amount of time spent speaking English and French as recorded in the contact diary. Using these two criteria related to network density and composition, Gautier and Chevrot identified two learners with dense Anglophone networks, three learners with composite (i.e., loose) Anglophone networks, and two learners with composite Anglophone and Francophone networks. The models of each type of network are shown in Figure 9.3 where black squares represent L1 English speakers and white circles represent L1 French speakers.

In their study, Gautier and Chevrot (2015) focused on the acquisition of two well-studied stylistic variables in L1 French: variable liaison realization and the deletion/retention of the negative particle *ne* 'not', where the realization of variable liaison and the retention of *ne* are considered formal variants. As predicted by the researchers, the two learners with composite Anglophone and Francophone networks spoke more French, 27 hours per week on average, than the learners with dense or composite Anglophone networks. Moreover, both learners with composite Anglophone and Francophone networks also reduced their usage of the formal variants (variable liaison realization and *ne* retention) over the three-month period, showing alignment with TL speaker norms. In contrast, the learners with dense Anglophone networks reported speaking only about six hours of French per week with TL speakers and maintained their high usage rates of the formal variants over the three-month period.

While the three learners with composite Anglophone networks reported speaking French only one hour more per week with TL speakers (seven hours per week) than learners with dense Anglophone networks, the results from Gautier and Chevrot (2015) for these learners demonstrate a potentially beneficial effect of a looser L1 network during SA. For example, two of the three learners with composite Anglophone networks decreased their realization rates of variable liaison during the three-month period and two of the three learners decreased their rates of *ne* retention, with one learner decreasing her use of both of the formal variants over the three-month

Characteristics of networks	Types of social networks
	Dense Anglophone social networks [Neil and Cristina]
2 learners: - Density > 30 % - Mean amount of time spent speaking French: 347 min per week (6h)	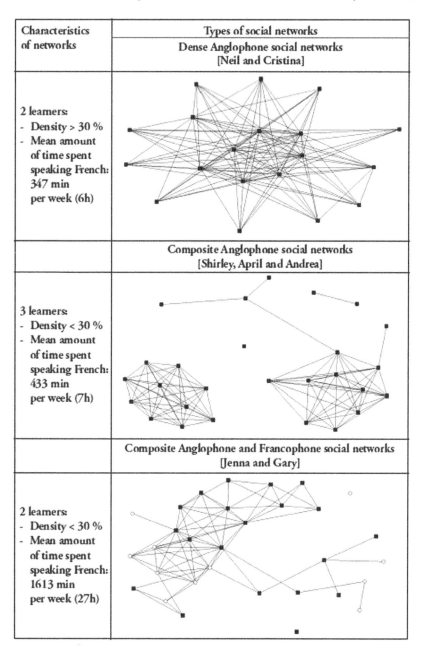
	Composite Anglophone social networks [Shirley, April and Andrea]
3 learners: - Density < 30 % - Mean amount of time spent speaking French: 433 min per week (7h)	
	Composite Anglophone and Francophone social networks [Jenna and Gary]
2 learners: - Density < 30 % - Mean amount of time spent speaking French: 1613 min per week (27h)	

FIGURE 9.3 Network graphs by composition and structure (reprinted with permission from Gautier & Chevrot, 2015, p. 178)

period. These results indicate that network density, in addition to the L1/L2 language use patterns within the learner's network, may contribute to a learner's ability to, and perhaps willingness to, access, notice, and acquire TL norms through their interactions with TL speakers during SA.

SNA has also been used to examine the attitudes and perceptions of language learners residing in the TL environment. For example, in their study of adult L2 French learners in Montreal, Lindberg and Trofimovich (2020) examined the role of social networks with speakers of Quebec French in learners' attitudes toward the Quebec variety of French. In this study, Lindberg and Trofimovich used recordings of two native French speakers from Metz, France, one of whom was introduced to the participants as being a Quebec French speaker. Following these introductions, 106 L2 French learners of varying proficiency levels and varied L1 backgrounds used quantitative scales to rate each native speaker according to perceived accentedness, comprehensibility, and status (i.e., perceived intelligence or competence as a French teacher). Participants were also asked to evaluate the two speakers using qualitative assessments such as "pure", "international", "unattractive", and "unsophisticated" and participants indicated whether they had feelings of solidarity with the speaker, such as a desire to have the speaker as a teacher or a desire to speak like the teacher.

After evaluating the speech samples, participants in Lindberg and Trofimovich (2020) completed a background questionnaire that included quantitative assessments of their own exposure to and familiarity with European and Quebec French, as well as questions regarding their attitudes toward the two French varieties. Finally, participants completed a social network questionnaire modeled on the work of Doucerain et al. (2015) which included four quantitative measures: the number of French speakers in the learner's network (L2 network size), an average closeness rating for all network members (L2 intimacy), a density measure incorporating the number of nonisolated members within the network (L2 inclusiveness), and an overall density measure based on the total number of links between network members (L2 density).

The quantitative results for this study demonstrated only one significant difference in their impressions of the two speakers: the speaker who was introduced as a Quebec French speaker received slightly lower scores in response to the question about whether the participant would like to "sound like the Quebec speaker". Results from the qualitative assessment demonstrated that participants assigned positive and negative descriptors to the two speech samples at roughly equal percentages after listening to the recordings—with over 80 percent of the responses being positive for both European and Quebec French. The researchers did find that certain positive descriptors (e.g., "international, proper, sophisticated, elegant, pure") were associated with European French at much higher rates than with Quebec French. Various examples of the qualitative assessments of both speakers are shown in Table 9.5.

Additionally, Lindberg and Trofimovich (2020) noted that the qualitative responses were much more negative toward Quebec French on the background questionnaire than following the audio activity. That is, when participants were asked about their general attitude toward European and Quebec French on the background questionnaire, and were provided with a list of descriptors to choose from, they used negative descriptors to describe Quebec French three times more frequently than when they evaluated the guised speech sample (67.1 percent negative on the questionnaire versus 19 percent negative in the audio activity). More specifically, 76 out of 106 participants reported that Quebec French was "accented", 47 reported that it was "difficult", and 41 said that it was "unclear". The researchers interpreted these results to indicate that although the participants evaluated the two speech samples as comparable,

TABLE 9.5 Qualitative assessments of European and Quebec French guise speech samples

Sample reasons for participants' preferred speaker:

Preference for European French guise	*Preference for Quebec French guise*
"[She] speak as native France French. She didn't use the accent, her voice was pure and international."	"I'm more used to her pronunciation and the rest of the people at Quebec pronounces like her."
"Preferred that accent and more universal (standard)."	"If you are living in Quebec, you should get in use to this accent."
"I felt that it's more useful to learn standard French as it is better understood worldwide."	"Since I live in Quebec, I would choose this teacher at the moment."
"Because French originated in France and I prefer French teachers."	"Since I personally need to get more used to a Quebecois accent."
"More sophisticated."	"Easier to understand, more accented speaking."
"More elegant and was easy to understand and clear, which is required."	"Because she has the accent Quebecois and I want to learn like that."
"More used to France French accent, so find it easier to follow."	"I liked the more accented voice."

Source: Reprinted with permission from Lindberg and Trofimovich, 2020, p. 833

the participants held negative attitudes and biases against Quebec French that were revealed in the questionnaire.

In terms of social networks with Quebec French speakers, Lindberg and Trofimovich (2020) found no significant correlation between social network density and the participant's rating of the "comprehensibility" of the speech samples, but there was a significant negative correlation between network density and the participant's desire to "sound like the speaker". The researchers found that participants with density scores in the top 25 percent assigned lower scores (62 out of 100 points) to the Quebec guise speech sample than did participants with social network density scores in the lowest 25 percent, whose ratings averaged 77 out of 100 points. From these results, Lindberg and Trofimovich concluded that familiarity with the Quebec variety of French through their dense social networks had exposed these participants to some widely held beliefs about the superiority of European French over Quebec French. Because these negative attitudes are shared and expressed by many Quebec French speakers themselves, the researchers concluded that the L2 French learners with greater access to Quebec French speakers had adopted the same negative attitudes toward Quebec French as the members of their TL-speaking networks. Similar results are reflected in those of Diao (2017, Model Study 10) which is discussed in the next section.

The Impact of Network Composition on Individual Results

Model Study 15 by Kurata (2010) provides an example of how a close examination of the composition of an L2 learner's social network, as well as the interactions within that network, may yield important insights about how social networks with TL speakers contribute to L2 acquisition. In this study, Kurata (2010) focused on the network composition of a single L1 German/L2 Japanese university student residing in Australia and used a conversation analytic (CA) approach to examine alternations between English and Japanese in the learner's interactions with L1 Japanese speakers in his social network.

In Kurata's (2010) study, an examination of two recorded conversations with two L1 Japanese friends revealed that although it can be difficult for L2 learners to gain access to L2 learning opportunities when the dominant language is English, interactions with TL speakers can facilitate L2 acquisition in a number of ways. First, the CA approach used by Kurata demonstrated that participating in interactions with TL speakers, even interactions equally split between the target L2 and English, provided opportunities for listening and 'noticing' practice for the L2 Japanese learner. Second, the range of conversation topics discussed by the two

TL speakers in the learner's network and shared with the learner, such as Japanese cultural practices regarding marriage and family, contributed to the development of the learner's sociocultural awareness in L2 Japanese. Third, the TL interactions within his social network provided the learner with opportunities to receive corrective feedback and to accept or reject the language choice decisions (e.g., English or Japanese) of his interlocutors. Finally, Kurata concluded that by observing and participating in interactions with multiple TL speakers at the same time, the learner had acquired skills such as suggesting appropriate subtopics and 'adjusting his footing' with his interlocutors. That is, by participating in a social network with multiple TL speakers, the learner acquired a level of interactional competence in L2 Japanese that might not have been acquired without access to this network.

In another study using SNA with a specific focus on network composition, Model Study 10 by Diao (2017) demonstrates that to better understand L2 development, especially in the area of sociolinguistic variation, researchers must consider not only the quantity and quality of TL interactions within social networks, but also the social, political, and ideological norms reflected in the linguistic behavior of the TL speakers. In this study, Diao (2017) analyzed the homestay environments of three American speakers of 'transnational Mandarin', a variety of Mandarin used by Chinese diaspora communities, during SA in Shanghai. Specifically, Diao examined the production (or avoidance) by three American students of a dental/retroflex merger that is considered a nonstandard phonological variable in transnational Mandarin. Importantly, Diao noted that all three students were familiar with a transnational variety of Mandarin before participating in SA. Using a case study approach to SNA, Diao considered how the stance of the participant, as well as the identity of the host family or roommate, contributed to the co-construction of L2 identity, including both an awareness of the nonstandard feature of transnational Mandarin and a willingness, or nonwillingness, to use it.

The first learner in Diao's (2017) study, Yun, lived in Shanghai with a host mother and grandmother, both of whom could speak standard Mandarin, but who often chose not to do so claiming that the standard pronunciation was too difficult. In Diao's analysis of the host mother's speech, results demonstrated that she used the nonstandard dental/retroflex merger about 30 percent of the time (see Table 9.6). Diao's analysis also showed that Yun used the nonstandard feature nearly 60 percent of the time in her TL interactions (see Table 9.7), presumably to align with the host mother and grandmother and with the Shanghai identity and culture. In the interviews, Yun also demonstrated integrative motivation (Gardner, 1985; Gardner & Lambert, 1959) to align with the TL culture by expressing that she liked the people from Shanghai.

TABLE 9.6 Tokens and frequency of the retroflex/dental merger by Chinese hosts

	Yun's host mother	Jin (Melissa's roommate	Hui (Hasan's roommate)
Merger token	536	0	26
Merger frequency	29.31%	0%	4.41%
Standard frequency	70.69%	100%	95.59%

Source: Reprinted with permission from Diao, 2017, p. 92

TABLE 9.7 Tokens and frequency of the retroflex/dental merger by focal participants

	Yun	Melissa	Hasan
Total retroflex syllables	562	1450	2481
Merger (dental)	325	290	2401
Standard (retroflex)	237	1160	80
Merger frequency[a]	57.83%	20%	96.78%
Standard frequency[a]	42.17%	80%	3.22%

[a] *Merger frequency was calculated as the percentage of retroflex syllables produced as dental. Standard frequency was calculated as the percentage of retroflex syllables produced as retroflex.*

Source: Reprinted with permission from Diao, 2017, p. 92

A second learner, Jin, lived with a Chinese roommate in Shanghai who was studying to be a teacher. Unlike Yun's host mother and grandmother, Jin's roommate used the standard pronunciation 100 percent of the time (Table 9.6) and corrected Jin when she used the local variant (see Table 9.7). Jin also indicated that she received a lot of negative feedback on her pronunciation from her teachers, so she was very aware of the difference between the standard and nonstandard forms and what these meant in terms of sociolinguistic capital. Diao's (2017) analysis demonstrated that Jin used the nonstandard pronunciation only 20 percent of the time which was the lowest in the group of learners.

A third learner in Diao's study, Hasan, had been raised with a nonstandard speaking nanny from Sichuan. Interviews with Hasan demonstrated that he was clearly very attached to his nanny and to her way of speaking. For example, Hasan recorded conversations so that he would not forget how she spoke and Hasan told his roommate that he wanted to learn Mandarin in order to speak with his nanny. Although Hasan received negative corrective feedback from his teachers and from his roommate (who used the standard variant 95 percent of the time, see Table 9.6), Hasan also received positive feedback on his accent in social settings. Diao (2017) reported that Hasan seemed to be very attached to the nanny's way of speaking and that he associated this way of speaking with positive reactions from Chinese people in general. Hasan also believed that having a nonstandard Chinese accent made him even more Chinese. Diao concluded that for Hasan, his accent was his culture, and this accent reflected the language of personal relationships as well as his identity as a transnational Chinese speaker from North America (see Table 9.7).

Conclusion

The research described in this chapter provides a number of useful examples of how the structure of the learner's network and the nature of the interactions within the network can be used to examine potential correlations with linguistic outcomes. For example, by focusing on the structure of the full social network within which the learner operates (i.e., sociocentric network analysis), and within which the learner's egocentric network is situated, researchers like Bernstein (2018, Model Study 12) and Paradowski et al. (2021a, 2021b) have been able to predict patterns of L2 development and use. Additional research, such as Model Study 16 by Palfreyman (2021) and Mougeon and Rehner (2015), has examined interactions within learners' at-home networks to understand how networks with co-nationals support language learning (Palfreyman, 2021), as well as how networks with TL speakers and engagement with the TL culture impact the use of informal linguistic variants (Mougeon & Rehner, 2015). A number of studies, such as Van Mol and Michielsen (2015) and Bracke and Aguerre (2015), have also used SNA to explore correlations between SA program design and student accommodations and opportunities for TL interactions. Finally, a number of studies have used SNA to examine learner attitudes toward the TL and perceptions about TL speakers (Lindberg & Trofimovich, 2020) and to correlate these attitudes and perceptions with linguistic performance (Diao, 2017, Model Study 10). All of these studies, and those discussed in the previous chapter on inferential statistical analysis, represent the myriad ways that SNA can be applied to linguistic data to examine, understand, and predict L2 acquisition and development.

Discussion Questions

1. Review the different methods of analysis described in this chapter and in the previous chapter on inferential statistics. Can you identify additional aspects of social network participation with TL speakers, aspects that have not been considered in the research described in this chapter, that might influence L2 development and use? How might you incorporate these elements into a study applying SNA to L2 acquisition?
2. The results of Bernstein (2018) seem to contradict much of the research on the role of interaction and participation in social networks, by

highlighting the rapid progress made by Hande, a long-term observer of, but infrequent participant in, her classmates' interactions. Discuss whether the results of this study could be generalized to adult learners—what differences exist between child and adult learners that might impact the role of social networks and, consequently, the trajectory of language acquisition for each?

3. Palfreyman (2021) uses comparative data from two cohorts separated by 15 years to highlight the influence of social and political change on the role of social networks in L2 English acquisition in the UAE. What other changes have occurred since a number of these studies were conducted that might impact the structure or role of social networks available to language learners today?

4. A number of studies (Carhill-Poza, 2015; Wiklund, 2002) have shown that young people, like adult immigrants, have trouble developing friendships with TL-speaking peers and that this influences their language acquisition and use. In future studies, what type of questions should SNA researchers ask to better understand this phenomenon?

10

SOCIAL NETWORK ANALYSIS

New Tools, Communities, and Learning Contexts

Introduction

The tools available for researchers to examine the social networks of second language (L2) learners have changed markedly in the last 20 years, as have the methods for analyzing the composition of these networks, and continuing advances in technology will facilitate social network analysis (SNA) research in both physical and online contexts. For example, software programs such as UCINET (Borgatti et al., 2002), igraph (Csárdi & Nepusz, 2006), and Gephi (Bastian et al., 2009) have made it possible to depict social networks with hundreds, if not thousands, of network ties and multiple network zones, facilitating the potential application of SNA to large-scale studies such as geographic vowel shifts. These automated network tools are also highly useful for small-scale research projects common in second language acquisition (SLA) as they facilitate the transformation of information gathered online into quantitative network strength measurements and diagrams that can be easily shared and manipulated. Additionally, these powerful network mapping tools allow researchers to pursue new lines of inquiry in L2 acquisition, such as the impact of relationships with co-nationals and other international students, as well as with target-language (TL) speakers, both inside and outside of the TL community or the language classroom using either an egocentric or sociocentric network approach. Finally, the use of computer-assisted network diagramming techniques has also facilitated the analysis of previously unexplored elements of the relationships within learners' social networks, such as the 'direction' of interaction and the 'centrality' of a network member (Paradowski et al., 2021a, 2021b), and for

DOI: 10.4324/9781003174448-10

much larger communities of language learners. While certainly not unique to the field of linguistics, sophisticated network diagramming tools have given SLA researchers access to previously unreachable and undiscovered aspects of L2 interaction and development.

Using Advanced Networking Tools to Analyze L2 Development Patterns

The research on sociocentric, or full, networks described in the previous chapters (e.g., Bernstein, 2018, Model Study 14; Hasegawa, 2019, Model Study 11) highlights the integral role that advanced network mapping tools play in this relatively new line of inquiry in L2 acquisition. Sociocentric network mapping for large groups of language learners, during study abroad (SA) or otherwise, would simply not be possible without the assistance of computer-generated social network diagrams. For example, Hasegawa (2019, Model Study 11) used Gephi (Bastian et al., 2009) to conduct a macro-level analysis of the social networks of three different groups of L2 Japanese learners enrolled in three different short-term SA programs in Japan. Using the technology afforded by the Gephi networking program, Hasegawa was able to incorporate the survey results of over 90 SA participants into macro-level network diagrams of the three different SA programs in order to identify the defining characteristics of each network and program. It is difficult to imagine how this research could have been carried out using only manual diagramming techniques. Similarly, Paradowski et al. (2021a, 2021b) used igraph (Csárdi & Nepusz, 2006) to depict both the ego-networks and the full networks of over 300 L2 Polish learners during an intensive summer language program in Poland—an analysis that would have been impossible, because of the broad scope, if not for the availability of sophisticated networking tools. Additionally, Paradowski et al. (2021a, 2021b) examined 'weighted degree centrality' (i.e., the intensity and frequency of each relationship) and 'directionality' (i.e., who provides output and who receives input) within the macro-level networks of these 300 learners, which represents a level of complexity unattainable through manual SNA techniques alone.

Even small-scale studies such as Gautier and Chevrot (2015), who examined the acquisition of sociolinguistic competence in L2 French of seven L1 English learners during SA in France, can leverage the benefits of software such as NetDraw (Borgatti, 2002) to create detailed models of the learners' social networks and UCINET (Borgatti et al., 1999) to calculate network density by comparing existing network ties to possible network ties within a complete network. Similarly, C. Li et al. (2021, Model Study 8) examined the influence of social networks on the pragmatic choices made by eight L2 Chinese learners during SA and used E-Net (Borgatti, 2006) to draw the complete network of each learner and to calculate network heterogeneity, network density, and to identify 'structural holes' (Burt, 1992, 2000), or isolated network members who were connected to ego only. Clearly, studies focused on the macro-level social networks of language learners and the varied interlocutors with whom they interact on a daily basis, including co- and other-nationals, TL speakers, and even contacts at home and abroad, have benefitted from the availability of sophisticated network diagramming and modeling techniques that provide a high level of precision on a scale that was simply not feasible using manual methods of SNA.

Computer-generated network models have also made possible the examination of previously understudied aspects of L2 interaction and acquisition. For example, Gallagher (2019) used a statistical modeling tool created for SNA to examine 'willingness to communicate' (WTC) in classroom L2 English learners. This study aimed to test two hypotheses related to the influence of social networks on L2 interpersonal communication: (1) learners with access to multiple groups of speakers will show higher levels of innovation and motivation for communicating in the L2 because individual groups tend to be homogenous in their thoughts and actions, and (2) communication between L2 learners will be facilitated by reciprocal relationships where both speakers acknowledge and benefit from an existing relationship. Instead of focusing on the individual characteristics that might influence WTC in the L2, such as having an extroverted personality or a positive attitude toward the L2, Gallagher's study examines how situational factors and social interdependence within the classroom contribute to a language learner's readiness to speak up and speak out in the L2.

Gallagher (2019) employed SNA to conduct a sociocentric analysis focused on two specific aspects of network ties: reciprocity and brokerage. Gallagher explained that reciprocity refers to the exchange of mutual benefits between network members, where both parties give and receive benefits, and that reciprocity may be direct or indirect. In direct reciprocity, two network members provide and receive benefits to and from each other within a dyad (one-to-one relationship). In indirect reciprocity, a third network member is involved in the giving and receiving of benefits forming a cyclic triad where everyone gives and receives benefits but not necessarily to and from the same person. Gallagher further explains that reciprocity within social structures is important because it has been shown to reduce anxiety and increase confidence, trust, and predictability in interpersonal exchanges (Gudykunst & Nishida, 2001; Molm, Collett, et al., 2007; Molm, Schaefer, et al., 2007). Additionally,

Gallagher explains that research on reciprocity demonstrates that indirect exchanges, such as in cyclic triads, reinforce norms and foster solidarity among members to a higher degree than direct dyadic exchanges (Molm, Collett, et al., 2007).

Gallagher (2019) also incorporated the role of 'brokerage' into the analysis where a brokerage position (Freeman, 1979) is occupied by a network member who serves as the singular connection between two otherwise unconnected network members, that is, where a structural hole in the network would otherwise exist. Holding a brokerage position is thought to confer a high level of control on the broker who may use this position to foster connections and cohesiveness among network members. Brokers themselves are also considered to have certain advantages within the network because they interact with multiple clusters, or groups, and are thus able to make interesting and varied contributions to conversations within the network. At a macro level, brokerage is thought to render network exchanges less uncertain, while at the same time more diverse, because the brokers keep information flowing from group to group. From this previous research on social network structures, Gallagher hypothesized that reciprocity through dyadic and triadic exchanges, as well as macro-level and local brokerage activity, would lead to higher levels of security, self-confidence, and therefore increased WTC, in the L2 classroom.

The 75 adult L2 English learners in Gallagher's (2019) study included 51 females and 24 males, with an average age of 24 years, who were enrolled in a month-long course on English for Academic Purposes (EAP). Of the 75 learners who agreed to participate in the study, 46 learners came from the People's Republic of China, with the remaining 29 participants coming from 15 different countries around the world. Participants completed a questionnaire at the end of the course from which WTC in L2 English was calculated. Questions focused on how often each participant would initiate conversation in English in a variety of social situations and with three types of 'receivers': friends, acquaintances, and strangers. Participants also provided a self-evaluation of their English skills in four areas (e.g., speaking, understanding, reading, writing) using a Likert scale from 1–7 points. Finally, Gallagher asked participants to list up to ten people with whom they had discussed important topics over the previous two weeks thereby indicating an 'outgoing' network tie. While participants were permitted to name persons outside of the EAP cohort, very few did so and these names were excluded from the sociocentric network diagram created from the name-generator activity.

Using an *autologistic actor attribute model* (ALAAM, Daraganova & Robins, 2013), a statistical modeling tool for SNA, Gallagher incorporated individual characteristics as independent variables, similar to logistic regression, as well as the influence of network ties and the individual characteristics of other network members into a sociocentric network model. According to Gallagher, ALAAMs can incorporate the effects of incoming and outgoing network ties (i.e., network position) and shared outcomes within network clusters (e.g., network contagion). Gallagher further explained that while many models of network ties view the resulting network structure as a dependent variable, ALAAMs assume that the network structure is an independent variable that influences the behavior of the members within the network, including their WTC. In this study, Gallagher used MPNet to estimate the ALAAMs (Wang et al., 2009) and UCINET (Borgatti et al., 2002) to measure 'flow betweenness', or how often a node acts as a broker within the network, in order to understand the influence of dyadic and triadic communication (through brokerage) on WTC among L2 English learners.

Using the ALAAM, Gallagher created an initial model that incorporated outgoing, incoming, and reciprocal network ties, as well as shared effects within a network cluster and two types of triadic relationships (cyclic and transitive). The final model also incorporated the effects of cross-cultural and out-of-class reciprocal relationships and met the author's criteria for Goodness of Fit (Gallagher & Robins, 2015). The positive and negative effects on WTC based on the ALAAM network model are displayed in Figure 10.1 (diagrams a–g).

As shown in Figure 10.1 (a), learners who reported more outgoing ties in the name-generator activity, either among co- or other-nationals, had higher levels of WTC. This was also true for learners who assigned themselves higher L2 proficiency ratings. Additionally, Figure 10.1 (b) shows that learners who reported more direct reciprocal network ties with someone from another country or culture had higher levels of WTC, as did learners who were involved in triadic (indirect) reciprocal relationships (shown in Figure 10.1(f)). Both of these results support the researcher's hypotheses pertaining to reciprocity—Gallagher attributed the positive effects of reciprocal intercultural ties to feelings of security among participants who have both acknowledged the importance of the ongoing relationship during the name-generator activity.

Gallagher also noted that because WTC can be seen as both contributing to social structures and benefitting from them, the higher levels of WTC among participants who forge intercultural connections may lead to higher levels of participation among more reticent participants. That is, the high WTC of some learners may positively influence the WTC of other learners by motivating them to engage more fully in L2 interactions. A final positive effect on WTC was found for network members who served as brokers between large network clusters (i.e., flow betweenness) and this was

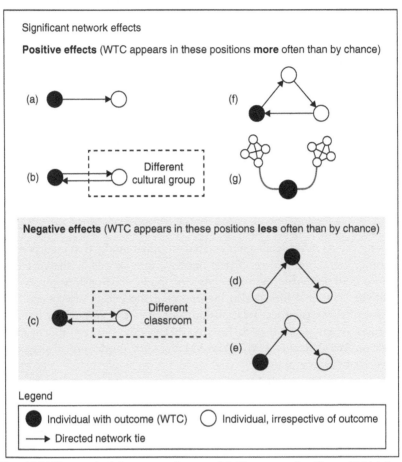

Significant network effects

Positive effects (WTC appears in these positions **more** often than by chance)

(a)

(b) Different cultural group

(f)

(g)

Negative effects (WTC appears in these positions **less** often than by chance)

(c) Different classroom

(d)

(e)

Legend

● Individual with outcome (WTC)   ○ Individual, irrespective of outcome

⟶ Directed network tie

Note: ALAAM = autologistic actor attribute model. Please note that Figure 10.1(g) is an abstract representation of flow betweenness.

FIGURE 10.1   Significant network patterns based on ALAAM (reprinted with permission from Gallagher, 2019, p. 207)

attributed to the brokers' access to high levels of novel information coming from multiple groups and the brokers' privileged position as the source of this novel information (shown in Figure 10.1(g)).

In contrast, Gallagher (2019) found WTC to be lower for learners who acted as brokers or sources of information in two-path (noncyclic) triads— where the circle remained open and each learner interacted with only one other member of the triad (as shown in Figure 10.1(d) and 10.1(e)). Gallagher hypothesized that brokers with higher levels of WTC to start may have been more successful in fostering interactions between the members of the triad, ultimately allowing the triad to close and become a cyclic triad which supports WTC among all members (shown in Figure 10.1(f)). Brokers who were unsuccessful in closing the circle and fostering interactions between the members of the triad (leaving the triad open) may have lost confidence in their abilities to forge network connections which may have negatively influenced their own levels of WTC. Finally, learners who reported relationships involving out-of-class participants had lower levels of WTC (shown in Figure 10.1(c)), indicating that the classroom cohort itself exerted a positive influence on WTC.

Gallagher's (2019) study is important to the current discussion for two reasons. First, this study is representative of the broad reach of SNA within linguistics, but also within related disciplines focused on human behavior (e.g., psychology, sociology, anthropology, etc.). Second, Gallagher's study demonstrates the power of computer-assisted networking tools and computer-generated models of social network activity—technology that allows researchers to conduct fine-grained examinations of novel aspects of human behavior, linguistic or otherwise, that were previously unreachable using manual approaches to SNA.

Applying SNA to Virtual Networks and Online Communities

The research in this section examines online exchanges involving TL, L2, and multilingual speakers on social networking sites in order to better understand the role that virtual communities and networks play in language acquisition and use.

Tracking L2 Development through Online Social Network Participation

In addition to facilitating a closer and more varied examination of how the structure and composition of a learner's egocentric or sociocentric network influences L2 acquisition, technology has fundamentally altered the way that learners interact with the TL both inside and outside of the classroom. Outside of the classroom, new forms of virtual interaction and social networking (e.g., Discord, Facebook, Instagram, Snapchat, TikTok, WeChat, WhatsApp, and X (formerly Twitter)) offer potentially rich sources of linguistic data to complement the live interviews, questionnaires, and written and oral elicitation tasks that currently form the core of SLA research. These virtual communities also provide alternate ways for L2 learners to connect with TL speakers, and with other L2 learners, and new opportunities to benefit from the social networks available in the virtual world.

Studies such as Back (2013) have used learner interactions on social networking sites to supplement data gathered through questionnaires and participant interviews in an effort to reduce the inherent biases in participant self-reporting. That is, because many social networking sites retain a record of the participants' interactions, participants do not have to rely on memory to determine how often they used the TL and with whom. Moreover, data gleaned from social networking sites reduces the impact of the observer's paradox (Labov, 1972b) because participants are not specifically communicating with the researcher, but instead with their friends and connections on social media. In Back's (2013) study of L2 development in online interactions, three female L2 Portuguese learners agreed to allow the researcher to become a 'friend' on the social networking site Facebook allowing the researcher to view and analyze the participants' postings during a semester of SA in Brazil. Two learners were L1 Spanish/fluent English speakers and one was an L1 English speaker who had learned Spanish as an L2. All three had completed one year of university Portuguese (tailored for Spanish speakers) before beginning the SA program and all three were active Facebook users with 200–300 Facebook friends. While the L1 Spanish speakers divided their Facebook posts equally between English and Spanish, the L2 English speaker posted primarily in English.

Back's (2013) research questions focused on the participants' use of the TL in Facebook posts and how this usage compared with their self-reported language use on the Language Contact Profile (LCP, Freed et al., 2004). Back was also interested in characterizing the participants' interactions on Facebook and in analyzing these interactions for vocabulary acquisition. With these goals in mind, Back analyzed ten months of Facebook posts (pre-departure, SA period, post-SA), conducted pre- and post-SA interviews with the participants, and had the participants complete a modified LCP upon their return from SA. With regards to the participants' interactions on Facebook, the researcher focused on two specific types of postings in the TL: (1) status updates, or single communications sent by the participant to all of their Facebook friends simultaneously, and (2) Facebook wall postings, or communications from the participant to a specific friend which the participant posts on the friend's Facebook page or 'wall'. Quantitative data analysis focused on the frequency and content of the participants' postings in the TL: the total number of posts and the frequency and onset of use of specific lexical items. The quantitative data was supplemented by a discourse analysis of the qualitative pre- and post-SA interview data and an examination of the participants' responses from the LCP. The researcher also examined the participants' use of computer-mediated, extralinguistic features on Facebook such as emoticons and abbreviations.

For each of the three learners, Back examined both the frequency of Facebook postings in Portuguese, both in terms of the total number of words and the total number of postings, as well as the average length of

TABLE 10.1 Total words posted on Facebook January–September 2011

Participant name	Total words posted, all languages	Words posted in Portuguese	Percentage of words posted in Portuguese
Luisa	4,955	2,505	50.6%
Mariana	6,859	1,065	15.5%
Donna	4,867	85	1.8%

Source: Reprinted with permission from Back, 2013, p. 382

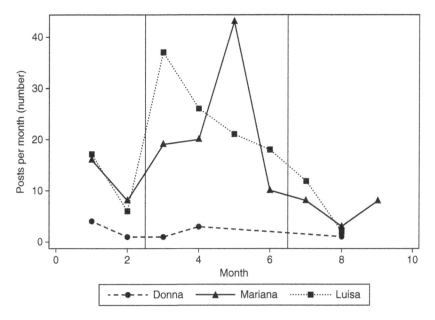

FIGURE 10.2 Number of posts per month in Portuguese by learner (reprinted with permission from Back, 2013, p. 383)

each posting during the ten-month period. The analysis of the number of Portuguese words posted on Facebook (Table 10.1) demonstrates that only one learner, Luisa, used Portuguese words at least half of the time in her Facebook postings (50.6 percent) with the other two learners showing a low level of use of Portuguese during the ten months: Mariana used Portuguese 15.5 percent of the time and Donna used Portuguese only 1.8 percent of the time. Additionally, both Luisa and Mariana showed an increase in the total number of postings in Portuguese (Figure 10.2) during the SA period, increasing from less than 20 per month before SA to approximately 35 postings (Luisa) and 45 postings (Mariana) per month while in Brazil.

As shown in Figure 10.3, Back also examined the length of the Facebook postings and demonstrated that Luisa's postings in Portuguese doubled in length (from approximately 13 to 26 words per posting) over the ten-month period while the other two participants ended the observation period lower than where they started (10–11 words per posting). The self-reported use of Portuguese on the LCP supports these results: while both Luisa and Mariana reported using Portuguese with TL speakers outside of class approximately five hours per day, Luisa also reported engaging in extended conversations with her host family in Portuguese for twice as long each day (two hours) than did Mariana and Donna (one hour per day).

The qualitative analysis of the participants' Facebook postings yielded compelling results that provide a fuller picture of the participants linguistic development during SA. Luisa, who used Portuguese over 50 percent of the time on Facebook, also used Portuguese in her status updates which included both Portuguese and non-Portuguese speakers. Back explained that Luisa was enthusiastic about sharing her knowledge of Portuguese, and even used the postings as teaching opportunities, while the responses from Luisa's friends demonstrated that they were generally enthusiastic about trying to understand her postings in Portuguese. Back also reported that Luisa often used Facebook to communicate with Brazilian friends

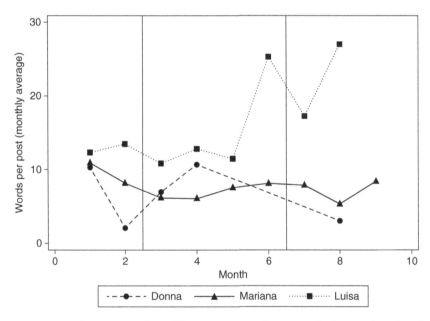

FIGURE 10.3 Average number of Portuguese words per post by learner (reprinted with permission from Back, 2013, p. 384)

and that these exchanges demonstrated Luisa's pragmatic competence through the use of informal language, humor, and paralinguistic features (such as *rsrs*, the Portuguese equivalent of *lol*). Like Luisa, Mariana used Facebook to communicate with Brazilian friends and she demonstrated her developing grammatical and sociolinguistic competence in these exchanges; however, unlike Luisa, Mariana limited her use of Portuguese to wall postings to specific Portuguese-speaking friends. Donna's use of Portuguese was infrequent and generally limited to contacts within the SA group.

A third analysis of the Facebook data focused on the use of each participant's most frequent TL words, the use of TL words that are not Spanish cognates, and the use of computer-mediated communication (CMC) tools, such as abbreviations. Beginning with the least prolific Facebook user of Portuguese, Donna's most frequently used words on Facebook were shown to be primarily Spanish cognates. In contrast, the Wordle (i.e., word cloud) analysis of Luisa's most frequently used words included a number of noncognate words with Spanish and popular CMC abbreviations, such as *vc* for *você* 'you' and *né* for *não é* 'isn't that so?'. Similarly, Mariana's Wordle analysis showed a number of noncognates with Spanish, as well the frequent use of two abbreviations: *vc* and *rsrs*. A further analysis of Mariana's use of *vc* demonstrated that prior to the SA period, Mariana only used the full noun *você*, but by the third month of SA, she was using *você* and the abbreviated form *vc* at nearly the same frequency.

Back's (2013) results are a prime example of the power of online social networks and the technology behind them: using data gathered from Facebook interactions alone, Back was able to trace the acquisition and the onset of use of a sociolinguistic variant by a language learner (e.g., Mariana's use of *vc* for *você* 'you')—a goal shared by many SLA researchers. Moreover, the data gathered from Facebook were reflected in the results of the post-SA interviews: both Luisa and Mariana were able to easily conduct their interviews in Portuguese, but Donna had difficulty using the TL in the post-SA interview. Although Back hypothesized that their background as heritage speakers of Spanish may have positively influenced both Luisa and Mariana's ability to engage in the TL and with TL speakers, Back argued that SLA researchers and language instructors should leverage the opportunities provided by social media for all L2 learners. These opportunities and advantages include the availability of accurate, real-time data on specific elements of L2 development, as well as the ability to connect learners with TL speakers through online networks with the goal of developing grammatical, lexical, and socio-pragmatic competence in the L2.

The Influence of Online Social Network Structure on Language Use

Social networking sites, and the virtual communities created on these sites, have also been shown to impact patterns of language use among the members of online social networks. In one example, Eleta and Golbeck (2014) demonstrated that the composition of online social networks, specifically the multilingual speakers who occupy roles as 'gatekeepers' and 'language bridges' between different linguistic groups, directly influenced the language choice of multilingual users of Twitter (now X).

As explained by Eleta and Golbeck (2014), Twitter is an online social network that is most frequently used for the rapid dissemination of information in short posts (less than 140 characters). Within the Twitter platform, messages can be shared with 'followers' either in the form of original, user-generated posts (i.e., a public post called a 'tweet'), responses to other users' posts, or the 'retweeting' of previous posts written by a different user. In Eleta and Golbeck's (2014) study, the authors identified 92 Twitter users who regularly posted in both English and in another language and examined each user's last 50 Twitter posts. The authors also used SNA to depict each user's egocentric network, including both first-order ties linked directly to ego and second-order ties linking the members of ego's network to each other (see Chapter 2). The egocentric network analysis resulted in the identification of over 25,000 network members who were categorized into an adjacency list to track the relationships between network members and were then assigned a language label (including English and 18 other languages) based on the language choice in their past 30 posts.

Eleta and Golbeck used Gephi (Bastian et al., 2009) to depict the social networks of all 92 Twitter users and from this analysis, identified 25 users with monolingual (or very small) networks, 62 users with bilingual networks, and 5 users with trilingual networks. The authors focused on three specific properties associated with the 62 bilingual networks: (1) the degree of connection between the language groups in the network (i.e., few vs. many connections), (2) the degree of integration of one group within another (i.e., zero, partial, or complete integration), and (3) the size of the language groups (i.e., similar or different in size). From this analysis, the authors identified and created graphic representations of five primary types of bilingual social networks which are shown in Figure 10.4 (readers are referred to the web version of Eleta & Golbeck, 2014 for full-color network diagrams with interpretations).

For example, as shown in Figure 10.4 (1), one type of network identified by Eleta and Golbeck (2014) is a 'gatekeeper' network which refers to a network that includes two groups of speakers that are similar in size (shown as small clusters on each end of the network diagram), but separated by language and connected by only a few bilingual network members or

(1)   (2)

(3)   (4)   (5)

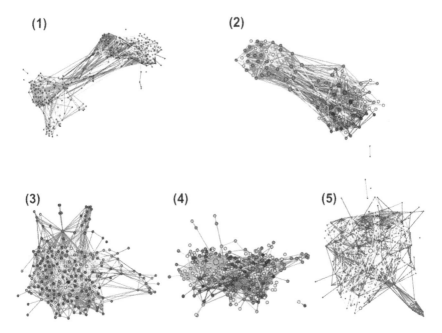

FIGURE 10.4   Representations of bilingual social networks on Twitter (reprinted
with permission from Eleta & Golbeck, 2014, p. 428)

nodes. Figure 10.4 (2) shows a 'language bridge' network that is similar to
a 'gatekeeper network', but is characterized by a larger number of speakers
connecting the two groups. In this diagram, the clusters on each end appear
less pronounced because of the larger number of 'bridge' speakers in the
middle. Three other types of networks involve groups that are very different
in size and include a network with one dominant and one 'peripheral
language group' shown in Figure 10.4 (3). In Figure 10.4 (3), the large
center cluster represents the dominant group of English speakers and the
small network of Portuguese speakers appears slightly separated and to the
right of the main cluster. In Figure 10.4 (4), there is a partial integration
('union') of two language groups where the Greek speakers (left cluster
shaded in light gray) have merged and mixed with the English speakers
(right cluster shaded in darker gray). Finally, Figure 10.4 (5) shows a
network where a small group of English speakers (dark gray shading at the
top of the larger cluster) has been fully subsumed within the larger, more
dominant group of Arabic speakers ('integration').

These qualitative groupings were supported by quantitative analysis
demonstrating that both gatekeeper and language bridge networks
(Figures 10.4 (1) and 10.4 (2)) have more intra-language group
connections than inter-language group connections and are therefore

considered 'separated' networks. In contrast, the union and integration networks (Figures 10.4 (4) and 10.4 (5)) demonstrate high levels of inter-language connections (the *cross-language edge ratio*) and a high incidence of bilingualism and are considered 'integrated'. Finally, because the 'peripheral' networks include a very small number of L2 speakers, they could not be analyzed using the same criteria. A comparison between the qualitative network visualization using Gephi and the quantitative classification based on network statistics (e.g., *cross-language edge ratio, L2 inner/crossing edge ratio, bilingual ratio*) confirmed that the network statistics correctly predicted the qualitative network classifications shown in Figure 10.4 for 51 of the 62 bilingual networks; the integrated networks were predicted with the highest level of accuracy (100%) and the peripheral networks were predicted at the lowest level of accuracy (less than 50%).

A final factor analysis was conducted by Eleta and Golbeck (2014) to determine the influence that the language preferences of network members and the level of multilingualism among network members have on the language choice of the 62 bilingual users selected for study. Recall that the language label assigned to each network member, as well to each ego, was based on language use in their previous Twitter posts (e.g., English, a majority L2, or a combination of English and the L2). The authors hypothesized that both a larger proportion of English speakers in the network, and/or a higher level of multilingualism within the network, would predict higher levels of English use by each individual user. As predicted by the authors, the results of the regression analysis demonstrated that the proportion of English-labelled network members was a statistically significant predictor of English use by each user. Similarly, the proportion of L2 network members was negatively correlated with the use of English by the focal users but positively correlated with the use of the L2 by these same users. A third predictor, the level of multilingualism within the network, was operationalized as 'entropy', or the level of unpredictability of language use within the network, and was positively correlated with both the use of English and the L2 by each user. Because entropy predicted both English and L2 use, the authors concluded that the hypothesis correlating increased multilingualism with increased use of English was not confirmed.

Additional research such as Paul and Friginal (2019) demonstrates that structural differences in online social networks may influence users' linguistic production in various ways. In their study, Paul and Friginal examined how network 'symmetry' or 'asymmetry' in online social networking platforms, such as those created on Facebook and Twitter (now X), impact the quality of L2 written production. According to the authors, a symmetric network, such as Facebook, refers to a network where relationship connections must be mutually acknowledged through a 'friend' request and acceptance. In an asymmetric network, such as Twitter, there is no requirement for connections to be mutually acknowledged—user A may 'follow' user B without having an established relationship with user B. The authors hypothesized that these different network structures would lead to different linguistic outcomes for a group of L2 Chinese learners at the beginning and intermediate levels.

An initial short-term study of ten days included 27 L1 English/L2 Chinese learners divided equally across two social networking platforms, Facebook and Twitter. During the data collection periods, the participants were required to post on Facebook or Twitter five times per week on five different days; however, they were allowed to choose the other participants from their group with whom they interacted, thus simulating a more natural social network formation. Moreover, the participants were required to write posts that reflected their developing abilities in L2 Chinese in order to eliminate the possibility that participants would post the same sentence each day. Posts were coded for the number of Chinese characters used (in Pinyin), the number of sentences, and the number of grammatical errors in each post. Only grammatical errors associated with the learner's level of L2 Chinese were counted as errors. Posts were also coded as 'interactive' if they were part of a conversation involving at least one other person or 'not interactive' if the post was isolated and/or did not receive a reply.

In order to facilitate data collection, participants were asked to 'friend' or 'follow' a teaching assistant who was both a research assistant on the project and an L1 Chinese speaker. The research assistant monitored the participants' daily posts and compared these to the daily reports that participants submitted which included: (1) their most complex sentence of the day, (2) their total number of sentences, and (3) a screenshot of the sentence (with surrounding context). Data analysis included the participants' Facebook and Twitter posts as well as an examination of pre- and post-questionnaire responses.

The results of the short-term study indicated that the participants in the Facebook group increased their affinity for the Facebook platform over the course of the project. At the same time, there were more 'follows' initiated on Twitter (13.6) than friend requests on Facebook (5.5), indicating that participants were more reluctant to initiate social connections on Facebook than they were on Twitter. Additionally, there were nearly twice as many Twitter users who did not communicate with anyone at all during the observation period (7.67 Twitter users versus 4 Facebook users). In terms of the quantitative results, the Facebook users posted both significantly more sentences and more interactive posts than the Twitter users (shown in Figure 10.5); however, the Facebook users made significantly more grammatical errors than the Twitter users in posts of a similar number of characters. Additionally, the qualitative results from the post-questionnaires

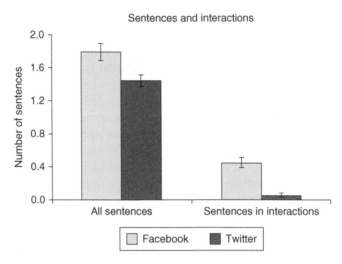

FIGURE 10.5 Comparison of sentences and interactions by Facebook and Twitter users, short-term study (reprinted with permission from Paul & Friginal, 2019, p. 603)

revealed that there were significant differences in the participants' belief that using the platform had improved their reading skills in L2 Chinese and in their motivation to create "interesting/meaningful" posts on the platform: in both cases, the Facebook users indicated a more positive response than the Twitter users. Finally, users in both groups preferred to communicate with participants who had the same level of proficiency, or a higher level of proficiency, in L2 Chinese.

In addition to the 10-day study, Paul and Friginal (2019) conducted an additional study of 50 days which included data from a small number of intermediate learners only (Facebook = 3; Twitter = 5). Despite the smaller number of participants, the results were similar to those of the short-term study: Facebook users posted more sentences and more interactive posts than Twitter users and they also made more grammatical errors for posts of a similar number of characters.

Of the three studies described in detail in this section, only Eleta and Golbeck (2014) explicitly applied SNA to the analysis of online L2 interactions. At the same time, both Back (2013) and Paul and Friginal (2019) focused on groups of L2 learners that were organized into social networks by means of an online networking platform and the results of these studies contribute valuable insights into the broader applications of SNA in L2 research. Additionally, the research of Eleta and Golbeck (2014), which explicitly applied SNA to online language use, makes important contributions in terms of understanding the role of social network composition in language choice among multilingual speakers. Moreover, this research provides a view into how online communities of users self-organize into language groups which, depending on their network structure, may or may not promote the sharing of information across linguistic boundaries and the raising of intercultural awareness.

Applying SNA to the Classroom Language Learning Context

Supplementing In-Person Learning with Online Social Networking Tools

A number of studies have explored the role of online social networking in conjunction with, or in place of, traditional classroom language learning. For example, Akbari et al. (2016) compared two groups of 20 adult Iranian graduate students, one in a face-to-face L2 English learning environment and the other in an online course organized through a Facebook group utilizing Skype video technology for synchronous interactions. In this study, Akbari et al. sought to understand the role of online social networks in the enhancement of student engagement (Astin, 1984) where higher levels of engagement are believed to contribute to increased learning.

Akbari et al. (2016) reported that, at the start of the course, both the Facebook and the in-person groups were comparable in terms of their intermediate L2 English proficiency based on a pre-test using the Test of English as a Foreign Language (TOEFL, Educational Testing Service, 2011). Additionally, groups were similar in terms of the ratio of male to female participants and age, as well as in their results on the competence questionnaire designed to assess the participants' confidence in their language learning abilities. Although small differences in these measures were revealed at the pre-test, the differences were not significant. Pre- and post-test measures also included the Intrinsic Motivation Inventory (IMI) developed by Ryan and Deci (2000), a social network questionnaire focused on how "easy" and "useful" participants found online social networks to be for their language learning, and a structured interview. Finally, engagement in the language learning process was measured by tracking the Facebook and in-person activity levels of each group of learners where activity included interactions such as feedback statements, homework submissions, and questions to the instructor and others.

Over the month-long English course, both groups met every weekday for synchronous language classes (20 hours total) that consisted of informal conversation, grammatical presentations and practice, and reading and writing activities. Students were encouraged and required to interact orally with each other during the class sessions, but Facebook students interacted with each other in writing outside of the one-hour class sessions while the in-person group met for 40 additional minutes each day in order to complete a peer review of writing activities.

Results from the analysis of variance indicated a significant main effect for the experimental Facebook group. While both groups improved their TOEFL scores between the pre- and post-test, the post-test scores for the Facebook group were significantly higher than those for the in-person learning group. Moreover, the post-test interviews corroborated the results of the post-test TOEFL scores—all of the participants in the Facebook group believed that they had experienced a high degree of learning during the month-long course (indicated by a response of "much" or "very much") while only 25 percent of the participants in the in-person class indicated a similar belief. Additionally, whereas 80 percent of the Facebook learners believed that they had made significant progress in both their speaking or reading skills, none of the in-person class participants believed that they had made significant improvements in both areas and only 40 percent of the in-person participants believed that they had significantly improved their speaking skills during the month. Results for engagement (based on participant activity levels) and intrinsic motivation (measured using the IMI) also indicated significantly higher scores for the Facebook group over the in-person group. Finally, correlation coefficients demonstrated a significant positive effect for engagement on the TOEFL post-test results for the Facebook group but not for the in-person group. For the in-person group, a significant positive correlation was found between motivation and the TOEFL pre- and post-tests.

The results of the study by Akbari et al. (2016) confirm the hypothesis that interactions among language learners in online social networks, such as those created on Facebook, have a positive impact on linguistic outcomes. Moreover, these results indicate that the improvements in linguistic performance are a direct result of the higher levels of engagement in (i.e., quality and quantity of participation) and motivation for the language learning process through the medium of an online social network. Finally, in addition to the quantitative data supporting the use of Facebook groups in L2 teaching, an important contribution of this study is the qualitative interview data that clearly indicates that the participants themselves believed that their language learning benefitted from participating in an online social network. The results of Akbari et al. (2016) are supported by those of Akoto (2021) who demonstrated the self-perceived benefits of collaborative multimodal writing using Google Docs among elementary L2 French learners. This finding alone is crucial for L2 instructors and SLA researchers alike: when students believe that their language learning efforts will produce desired linguistic outcomes, students can be expected to engage regularly in these efforts.

Using Virtual Exchanges to Create Social Networks with TL Speakers

Virtual social networks, created and maintained through sustained interactions with TL speakers on live video-chat platforms, also have the potential to offer language learners many of the benefits associated with in-person, physical social networks. For example, Warner-Ault (2020) demonstrated that virtual conversation exchanges between a group of intermediate L2 Spanish learners and TL speakers through the TalkAbroad platform resulted in both oral proficiency gains and increased cultural awareness among learners. In this study, two groups of intermediate Spanish learners (n = 39) engaged in five 30-minute conversation exchanges with TL Spanish speakers during a semester-long L2 Spanish course using TalkAbroad—an online video platform which facilitates interactions between TL speakers, who are trained and paid for their work, and language learners, who pay a fee for the use of the platform.

Prior to the video conversation exchanges, student participants were prepped for cultural discussions by engaging in class discussions focused on cultural self-awareness, including how Americans are perceived by people from other cultures. Students also conducted an in-depth analysis of the "three Ps" (products, practices, perspectives) of American culture which form the basis of the American Council on the Teaching of Foreign Languages (ACTFL) cultural framework developed from Byram's (1997) concept of 'critical cultural awareness'. Through class discussions, participants in this study analyzed American cultural perspectives such as freedom, consumerism, and competition and were able to identify and understand the relationship between these perspectives and their own behavior, attitudes, and values. Specifically, class discussions focused on comparisons between US holidays and those in the TL culture which prepared students to discuss these topics with their TalkAbroad conversation partners. At the end of the semester, students engaged in a critical comparison of the concept of 'happiness' in their own culture and in that of their conversation partner, and they also used their TalkAbroad conversations to prepare and present an analysis of cultural products and practices in the target culture to their classmates.

Post-test results from Warner-Ault (2020) revealed that both groups of learners made significant gains in their Oral Proficiency Interview (OPI; ACTFL) scores: 72 percent increased their OPI scores by one level, 5 percent increased by two levels, and the remaining 23 percent stayed at the same level. In addition to reporting pre- and post-test OPI scores, Warner-Ault (2020) included the quantitative results of a survey aimed at understanding how students perceived the TalkAbroad conversation exchanges with TL speakers. Specifically, Warner-Ault used a survey created by Litzler et al. (2018) to evaluate the benefits of a virtual exchange program (using Skype and Facebook) between L2 English learners at a Spanish university and L2 Spanish students at an American university between 2015 and 2016. As shown in Table 10.2, the results of Warner-Ault's (2020) survey on the benefits of TalkAbroad were similar to those reported by Litzler et al. (2018) for Skype and Facebook. On a Likert scale of 1–5 (where 5 = strongly agree), average responses from both groups exceeded 4 points for statements related to the TalkAbroad and Skype/Facebook activities, such as "I liked the conversations/activities", "My partner helped me when I was having difficulties with the language", "My level of the foreign language increased", and "I have a better understanding of the other country's culture and lifestyle". Additionally, although the participants in Warner-Ault's (2020) study rated the TalkAbroad conversations as slightly more difficult that the students using Skype and Facebook in Litzler et al. (2018), 2.62 versus 2.5, respectively, these same students expressed a higher level of satisfaction with the TalkAbroad activities (4.57) than did the students using Skype and Facebook (4.11) and they also believed that their level of foreign language had improved to a greater degree: TalkAbroad (4.37) versus Skype/Facebook (4.13).

Warner-Ault (2020) also added questions pertaining to the students' critical cultural awareness of cultural products, practices, and perspectives in both their home culture and the TL culture, as well as questions pertaining to the participants' desire to study in or travel to Spain or Latin America, and students' responses exceeded 4.4 (strongly agree) for all four supplemental questions. The quantitative survey results from Warner-Ault (2020) were supported by qualitative responses to open-ended questions about the perceived benefits of the TalkAbroad experience.

In a subsequent study by Warner-Ault (2022), 20 students enrolled in a synchronous online intermediate/advanced Spanish course at a North American university completed five 15-minute video-chat conversations with TL speakers using the platform Conversifi to supplement class discussions and projects in a course entitled "Technology, Culture and Social Change". Similar to the participants in Warner-Ault (2020), the participants in this study were prepared to engage in critical cultural comparisons with their conversation partners through a course focus on cultural awareness and intercultural communicative competence—course sub-themes were developed and examined using authentic materials (e.g., articles, films, television shows) from Spain and Latin America and these sub-themes served as the basis for the live interactions on Conversifi. To determine the self-perceived benefits of the Conversifi exchanges, Warner-Ault (2022)

TABLE 10.2 Comparison of survey results from Warner-Ault (2020) and Litzler et al. (2018)

Survey question	TalkAbroad (N = 35)	Litzler et al. (2018)	
"I liked the TalkAbroad conversations."	4.57	"I liked the Skype and Facebook activity."	4.11 (N=66)
"The TalkAbroad conversations were difficult for me."	2.62	"The activities on Facebook and Skype were difficult for me to do."	2.5 (N=65)
"I didn't know what to talk about with my TalkAbroad partner."	2.0	"I didn't know what to talk about with my partner on Skype."	2.44 (N=63)
"My TalkAbroad partner helped me when I was having difficulty with the language	4.11	"My partner on Skype helped me when I was having difficulties with his/her native language."	4.15 (N=65)
"More guidance from the teacher at the start would have made the TalkAbroad conversations easier."	2.5	"More guidance from the teacher at the start would have made the Skype activity easier to do."	2.58 (N=68)
"My level of the foreign language increased thanks to the TalkAbroad conversations this semester."	4.37	"My level of the foreign language increased thanks to the Skype activity this semester."	4.13 (N=68)
"I have a better understanding of the other countries' culture and lifestyle thanks to the TalkAbroad conversations."	4.48	"I have a better understanding of the other country's culture and lifestyle thanks to these activities."	4.48 (N=68)

Source: Reprinted with permission from Warner-Ault, 2020, p. 7

used a similar survey instrument to Warner-Ault (2020) and found that overall satisfaction with the Conversifi exchanges was lower than with TalkAbroad in Warner-Ault (2020). For example, student responses to statements such as "I liked the Conversifi conversations" and "My level of foreign language increased thanks to the Conversifi conversations this semester", ranged between 3.5 and 3.95 (out of 5 points) whereas the responses from the students using TalkAbroad exceeded 4.0 for the same questions.

Warner-Ault (2022) pointed out that a number of important differences exist between the two studies and these likely impacted the survey results. First, conversation partners on TalkAbroad are paid for their interactions with language learners, and they are also trained to be sympathetic listeners and to adjust their speech to the needs of learners. In contrast, the Conversifi platform pairs college students with different native languages with each other so that each student is both the language coach and the language learner. Additionally, the students using Conversifi are required to complete a certain number of conversations for their own language class, and they may either pay for the conversations in which they are the learner or they may earn credits toward future conversations by playing the role of language expert. Warner-Ault (2022) pointed out that this platform design, along with the higher proficiency level of the participants, may have led to lower overall perceived benefits from the Conversifi exchange. Moreover, all of the participants in the 2022 study had participated in an online exchange in at least one previous course (either using TalkAbroad or Conversifi), and this previous experience with the TL culture, and with the act of explicitly engaging in cultural comparison, may have led to the perception that the second (or third) exchange was not as beneficial as the first. One final consideration is that the data for the 2022 study were gathered during the Spring semester of 2021 when students had been living through the global COVID-19 pandemic for over a year. Warner-Ault reported that this may have contributed to their overall fatigue with online interactions despite the potential benefits of the intercultural exchange.

Despite the overall lower quantitative results for the Conversifi platform in Warner-Ault's (2022) study, 75 percent of the participants mentioned improved language skills in the open-ended survey question about the benefits of the Conversifi conversations. Additionally, the survey results for the supplemental statements related to awareness of cultural products, practices, and perspectives, and student interest in travelling to or studying in Spain or Latin America, ranged between 3.85 and 4.15 (shown in Table 10.3) indicating that most participants agreed with these statements. Moreover, open-ended questions specific to the global pandemic revealed that the pandemic was a cultural "rich point" (Agar, 2006) in the Conversifi conversations which allowed students, along with their partners, to explore similarities and differences in their experiences, both at an individual and national level.

Conclusion

The research highlighted in this chapter examines how social networks may be leveraged inside and outside of the classroom language learning

TABLE 10.3 Comparison of survey results from Warner-Ault (2020) and Warner-Ault (2022)

Statement	Average Score Spring, 2018 TalkAbroad (N=35)	Average Score Spring, 2021 Conversifi (N=20)
"The TalkAbroad/Conversifi activities helped teach me about cultural products, practices and perspectives in Spain and/or Latin America."	4.46	4.15
"The TalkAbroad/Conversifi activities helped me become aware of cultural products, practices and perspectives in my own culture(s)."	4.62	3.9
"My interest in studying in Spain or Latin America has increased thanks to the TalkAbroad/Conversifi conversations."	4.51	3.85
"My interest in traveling to Spain or Latin America has increased thanks to the TalkAbroad/Conversifi conversations."	4.48	4.1

Source: Reprinted with permission from Warner-Ault, 2022, p. 99

context to encourage potentially beneficial interactions between groups of L2 learners, and between L2 learners and TL speakers, using virtual social networking sites, online collaborative tools, and virtual exchange platforms.

The results of studies such as Warner-Ault (2020) using the TalkAbroad platform and Warner-Ault (2022) using the Conversifi platform provide empirical evidence for the benefits of virtual social networks through the medium of virtual conversation exchanges in the simultaneous acquisition of both language and critical cultural awareness. These virtual opportunities for TL interactions have the potential to offer a supplement to traditional, on-site, in-person interactional opportunities through which language learners build and maintain social networks with TL speakers and acquire the L2 as a result of participating in these networks. Additionally, the results of Akbari et al. (2016) demonstrate that interactions among L2 learners in online social networks have a positive impact on linguistic outcomes, potentially because the learners themselves believe that interacting online will lead to linguistic gains and this belief contributes to higher levels of engagement and motivation to learn the TL.

Moreover, as the recent pandemic has demonstrated, L2 learners may not always have the ability to travel to the TL environment in order to reap the potential benefits of in-person social networks with TL speakers.

Even before the global COVID-19 pandemic curtailed the in-country study or volunteer abroad opportunities available to L2 learners, many learners faced financial and familial barriers that precluded them from spending a semester or year in the TL community and virtual exchanges offer a viable alternative for these students. Additionally, even when learners cannot participate directly in virtual networks through conversation exchanges, research indicates that observation and analysis of TL speaker interactions within online social networks (e.g., Blattner et al., 2016; Blattner & Fiori, 2011), or participation in interactive virtual programming (Shiri, 2023) can be leveraged to raise at-home learners' socio-pragmatic and sociocultural awareness in the TL. As the research in this chapter clearly demonstrates, it is critical for SLA researchers working within the SNA framework to acknowledge that advances in technology, and their ability to connect language learners with each other and with TL speakers, even indirectly, will continue to be increasingly relevant in the coming years.

Discussion Questions

1. Think about the online social networks that you participate in regularly and consider how these networks might be leveraged to improve L2 acquisition. What types of benefits, in addition to those described in this chapter, are available to the L2 learner in online networks?

2. If you had the opportunity to design an online networking tool for L2 learners, what characteristics would it have? Think about some of the challenges inherent in online networking mentioned in this chapter and consider how your design would mitigate these challenges.

3. Based on your own L2 learning experience, or your familiarity with research in SLA, why do learners believe that online networking is beneficial to their learning and why do learners express a preference for online interactions versus in-person interactions?

4. Design a research study applying SNA to an online or virtual learning context. What group of learners would you analyze, what linguistic elements would you examine, and how would you conduct your study? What hypotheses would you make at the outset of the study?

REFERENCES

Adamson, H. D., & Regan, V. (1991). The acquisition of community speech norms by Asian immigrants learning English as a second language. *Studies in Second Language Acquisition, 13*, 1–22.

Agar, M. (2006). *Language shock: Understanding the culture of conversation.* William Morrow.

Akbari, E., Naderi, A., Simons, R.-J., & Pilot, A. (2016). Student engagement and foreign language learning through online social networks. *Asian-Pacific Journal of Second and Foreign Language Education, 1*(4), 1–22. https://doi.org/10.1186/s40862-016-0006-7

Akoto, M. (2021). Collaborative multimodal writing via Google Docs: Perceptions of French FL learners. *Languages, 6*, 140. https://doi.org/10.3390/languages6030140

Armstrong, N. (1996). Variable deletion of French /l/: Linguistic, social and stylistic factors. *Journal of French Language Studies, 6*, 1–21.

Arnett, C. (2013). Syntactic gains in short-term study abroad. *Foreign Language Annals, 46*, 705–712.

Ashby, W. (1984). The elision of /l/ in French clitic pronouns and article. In E. Pulgram (Ed.) *Romanitas: Studies in Romance Linguistics* (pp. 1–16). University of Michigan Press.

Astin, A (1984). Student involvement: A developmental theory for higher education. *Journal of College Student Personnel, 25*(4), 297–308.

Back, M. (2013). Using Facebook data to analyze learner interaction during study abroad. *Foreign Language Annals, 46*(3), 377–401.

Baker-Smemoe, W., Dewey, D. P., Bown, J., & Martinsen, R. A. (2014). Variables affecting L2 gains during study abroad. *Foreign Language Annals, 47*, 464–486.

Ballard & Tighe. (2006). *IDEA proficiency tests technical manual: Grades 9–12.* Author.

Bastian, M., Heymann, S., & Jacomy, M. (2009). Gephi: An open source software for exploring and manipulating networks. *Proceedings of the Third International*

Conference on Weblogs and Social Media, 3(1), 361–362. https://ojs.aaai.org/index.php/ICWSM/article/view/13937/13786

Bataller, R. (2010). Making a request for a service in Spanish: Pragmatic development in the study abroad setting. *Foreign Language Annals, 43,* 160–175.

Bayley, R. (1994). Consonant cluster reduction in Tejano English. *Language Variation and Change 6,* 303–326.

Bayley, R. (1996). Competing constraints on variation in the speech of adult Chinese learners of English. In R. Bayley & D. R. Preston (Eds), *Second language acquisition and linguistic variation* (pp. 98–120). John Benjamins.

Bayley, R. (1997). Variation in Tejano English: Evidence for variable lexical phonology. In C. Bernstein, T. Nunnally, & R. Sabino (Eds), *Language variety in the South revisited* (pp. 197–209). University of Alabama Press.

Bayley, R. (2013). The quantitative paradigm. In J. K. Chambers & N. Schilling (Eds), *The handbook of language variation and change* (2nd ed.) (pp. 85–107). Wiley–Blackwell.

Bayley, R., Cárdenas, N. L., Treviño-Schouten, B., & Vélez-Salas, C. M. (2012). Spanish dialect contact in San Antonio, Texas: An exploratory study. In K. Geeslin & M. Díaz-Campos (Eds), *Selected proceedings of the 14th Hispanic Linguistics Symposium* (pp. 48–60). Cascadilla Proceedings Project.

Bayley, R., & Escalante, C. (2022). Variationist approaches to second language acquisition. In K. L. Geeslin (Ed.), *The Routledge handbook of second language acquisition and sociolinguistics* (pp. 3–16.). Routledge.

Bayley, R., & Holland, C. L. (2014). Variation in Chicano English: The case of final (z) devoicing. *American Speech, 89,* 385–407.

Bayley, R., & Pease-Alvarez, L. (1996). Null pronoun variation in Mexican-descent children's Spanish. In J. Arnold et al. (Eds), *Sociolinguistic variation: Data, theory, and analysis* (pp. 85–99). Center for the Study of Language and Information, Stanford University.

Bayley, R., & Pease-Alvarez, L. (1997). Null pronoun variation in Mexican-descent children's narrative discourse. *Language Variation and Change, 9,* 349–371.

Bayley, R., & Regan, V. (2004). Introduction: The acquisition of sociolinguistic competence. *Journal of Sociolinguistics, 8,* 323–338.

Bayley, R., & Schecter, S. R. (Eds). (2003). *Language socialization in bilingual and multilingual societies.* Multilingual Matters.

Bernstein, K. A. (2018). The perks of being peripheral: English learning and participation in a preschool classroom network of practice. *TESOL Quarterly, 52,* 798–844.

Bidart, C., Degenne, A., & Grossetti, M. (2011). *La vie en réseau: Dynamique des relations sociales.* Presses Universitaires de France.

Blattner, G., Dalola, A., & Lomicka, L. (2016). Twitter in foreign language classes: Initiating learners into contemporary language variation. In V. Wang (Ed.), *Handbook of research on learning outcomes and opportunities in the digital age* (pp. 769–797). IGI Global.

Blattner, G. & Fiori, M. (2011). Virtual social network communities: An investigation of language learners' development of sociopragmatic awareness and multiliteracy skills. *CALICO Journal, 29*(1), 24–43.

Blondel, V. D., Guillaume, J. L., Lambiotte, R., & Lefebvre, E. (2008). Fast unfolding of communities in large networks. *Journal of statistical mechanics: Theory and experiment, 2008*(10), 10008.

Bloomfield, L. (1933). *Language*. Henry Holt.

Borgatti, S. P. (2002). *NetDraw software for network visualization*. Analytic Technologies.

Borgatti, S. P. (2006). *E-Network Software for Ego-Network Analysis* (Version 0.5) [Software]. Available from https://sites.google.com/site/enetsoftware1/Home

Borgatti, S., Everett, M. & Freeman, L. (1999). *UCINET 6.0: Version 1.00*. Analytic Technologies.

Borgatti, S., Everett, M., & Freeman, L. (2002). *UCINET for Windows*. Analytic Technologies. Available at https://sites.google.com/site/ucinetsoftware/home

Borgatti, S. P., Everett, M. G., & Johnson, J. C. (2013). *Analyzing social networks*. Sage.

Bortoni-Ricardo, S. M. (1985). *The urbanisation of rural dialect speakers: A sociolinguistic study*. Cambridge University Press.

Bourdieu, P. (1977). The economics of linguistic exchanges. *Social Science Information, 16*, 645–668.

Bracke, A. & Aguerre, S. (2015). Erasmus students: Joining communities of practice to learn French? In R. Mitchell, N. Tracy-Ventura, & K. McManus (Eds), *Social interaction, identity and language learning during residence abroad* (pp. 139–168). EUROSLA Monographs Series. The European Second Language Association.

Braun, V., & Clarke, V. (2006). Using thematic analysis in psychology. *Qualitative Research in Psychology, 3*, 77–71.

Brecht, R., Davidson, D., & Ginsberg, R. (1995). Predicting and measuring language gains in study abroad settings. In B. F. Freed (Ed.), *Second language acquisition in a study abroad context* (pp. 37–66). John Benjamins.

Brown, J. S., & Duguid, P. (2001). Knowledge and organization: A social-practice perspective. *Organization Science, 12*(2), 198–213.

Burt, R. S. (1985). General social survey network items. *Connections, 8*, 119–123.

Burt, R. S. (1992). *Structural holes: The social structure of competition*. Harvard University Press.

Burt, R. S. (2000). The network structure of social capital. *Research in Organizational Behavior, 22*, 345–423. https://doi.org/10.1016/S0191-3085(00)22009-1

Byram, M. (1997). *Teaching and assessing intercultural communicative competence*. Multilingual Matters.

Cameron, R. (1992). Pronominal and null subject variation in Spanish: Constraints, dialects, and functional compensation (Unpublished doctoral dissertation). University of Pennsylvania.

Canale, M., & Swain, M. (1980). Theoretical bases of communicative approaches to second language teaching and testing. *Applied Linguistics, 1*, 1–47.

Carhill-Poza, A. (2015). Opportunities and outcomes: The role of peers in developing the oral academic English proficiency of adolescent English. *Modern Language Journal, 99*(4), 678–695. https://doi.org/10.llll/modl.12271

Chamot, M., Racine, I., Regan, V., & Detey, S. (2021). Une ou des immersion(s)? Regard sur l'acquisition de la compétence sociolinguistique par des apprenants anglophones irlandais de FLE. In E. Pustka (Ed.), *La pronunciation du français langue étrangère: perspectives linguistiques et didactiques* (pp. 133–162). Narr Verlag.

Chappell, W., & Kanwit, M. (2022). Do learners connect sociophonetic variation with regional and social characteristics? The case of L2 perception of Spanish aspiration. *Studies in Second Language Acquisition, 44,* 185–209.

Cheshire, J. (1982). *Variation in an English dialect: A sociolinguistic study.* Cambridge University Press.

Cheshire, J., Fox, S., Kerswill, P., & Torgersen, E. (2008). Ethnicity, friendship network and social practices as the motor of dialect change: Linguistic innovation in London. *Sociolinguistica—International Yearbook of European Sociolinguistics/Internationales Jahrbuch für europäische Soziolinguistik, 22*(1), 1–23.

Chomsky, N. (1965). *Aspects of the theory of syntax.* MIT Press.

Chomsky, N. (1981). *Lectures on government and binding.* Foris.

Coleman, J. A. (2013). Researching whole people and whole lives. In C. Kinginger (Ed.), *Social and cultural aspects of language learning in study abroad* (pp. 17–46). John Benjamins.

Coleman, J. A. (2015). Social circles during residence abroad: What students do, and who with. In R. Mitchell, N. Tracy-Ventura, & K. McManus (Eds), *Social interaction, identity and language learning during residence abroad* (pp. 33–52). EUROSLA Monographs Series. The European Second Language Association.

Collentine, J. (2004). The effects of learning contexts on morphosyntactic and lexical development. *Studies in Second Language Acquisition, 26,* 229–250.

Csárdi, G., & Nepusz, T. (2006). The igraph package for complex network research. *InterJournal 2006, Complex Systems,* 1696. https://igraph.org/

Daraganova, G., & Robins, G. (2013). Autologistic actor attribute models. In D. Lusher, J. Koskinen & G. Robins (Eds), *Exponential random graph models for social networks: Theory, methods and applications* (pp. 102–114). New York, NY: Cambridge University Press.

DeKeyser, R. (2010). Monitoring progress in Spanish as a second language during a study abroad program. *Foreign Language Annals, 43*(1), 80–92.

DeKeyser, R. (2014). Research on language development during study abroad: Methodological considerations and future perspectives. In C. Pérez-Vidal (Ed.), *Language acquisition in study abroad and formal acquisition contexts* (pp. 313–326). John Benjamins.

Dewey, D. P., Belnap, R. K., & Hillstrom, R. (2013). Social network development, language use, and language acquisition during study abroad: Arabic language learners' perspectives. *Frontiers: The Interdisciplinary Journal of Study Abroad, 22,* 84–110.

Dewey, D. P., Bown, J., & Eggett, D. (2012). Japanese language proficiency, social networking, and language use during study abroad: Learners' perspectives. *Canadian Modern Language Review, 68,* 111–137.

Dewey, D. P., Ring, S., Gardner, D., & Belnap, R. K. (2013). Social network formation and development during study abroad in the Middle East. *System, 41,* 269–282.

Diao, W. (2017). Between the standard and non-standard: Accent and identity among transnational Mandarin speakers studying abroad in China. *System, 71,* 87–101.

Dodsworth, R. (2019). Bipartite network structures and individual differences in sound change. *Glossa, 4*(1), 1–29.

Dodsworth, R., & Benton, R. (2017). Social network cohesion and the retreat from Southern vowels in Raleigh, North Carolina. *Language in Society, 46,* 371–405.

Dodsworth, R., & Benton, R. (2020). *Language variation and change in social networks.* Routledge.

Dörnyei, Z. (2001). *Motivational strategies in the language classroom.* Cambridge University Press.

Doucerain, M., Varnaamkhaasti, R., Segalowitz, N. & Ryder, A. (2015). Second language social networks and communication-related acculturative stress: The role of interconnectedness. *Frontiers in Psychology, 6,* 1–12.

Eckert, P. (1988). Adolescent social structure and the spread of linguistic change. *Language in Society, 17,* 183–207.

Eckert, P. (2000). *Linguistic variation as social practice: The linguistic construction of identity in Belten High.* Blackwell.

Eckert, P. (2005). Variation, convention and social meaning. Paper presented at the Annual Meeting of the Linguistic Society of America, January 7.

Eckert, P. (2008). Where do ethnolects stop? *International Journal of Bilingualism, 12,* 25–42.

Eckert, P., & McConnell-Ginet, S. (1992). Think practically and look locally: Language and gender as community-based practice. *Annual Review of Anthropology, 21,* 461–488.

Eckert, P., & Wenger, E. (2005). Communities of practice in sociolinguistics: What is the role of power in sociolinguistic variations. *Journal of Sociolinguistics, 9,* 582–589.

Educational Testing Service. (2011). *TOEFL: test of English as a foreign language, test of written English. For comparing TOEFL scores.* Accessed on November 6, 2011 from www.ets.org/toefl/institutions/scores/compare/

Edwards, W. (1992). Sociolinguistic behavior in a Detroit inner-city black neighborhood. *Language in Society, 21,* 93–115.

Eleta, I., & Golbeck, J. (2014). Multilingual use of Twitter: Social networks at the language frontier. *Computers in Human Behavior, 41,* 424–432.

Emmel, N., & Clark, A. (2009). The methods used in connected lives: Investigating networks, neighbourhoods and communities. National Centre for Research Methods Review.

Ferenz, O. (2005). EFL writers' social networks: Impact on advanced academic literacy development. *Journal of English for Academic Purposes, 4,* 339–351.

Firth, A., & Wagner, J. (1997). On discourse, communication, and (some) fundamental concepts in SLA research. *Modern Language Journal, 81,* 285–300.

Firth, A., & Wagner, J. (2007). Second/foreign language learning as a social accomplishment: Elaborations on a reconceptualized SLA. *Modern Language Journal, 91*(s1), 800–819.

Fishman, J. A. (1991). *Reversing language shift.* Multilingual Matters.

Fleming, L., Colfer, L. J., Marin, A., & McPhie, J. (2011). Why the Valley went first: Aggregation and emergence in regional collaboration networks. In J. Padgett & W. Powell (Eds), *Market emergence and transformation* (pp. 520–544). Princeton University Press.

Flores-Ferrán, N. (2004). Spanish subject personal pronoun use in New York City Puerto Ricans: Can we rest the case of English contact? *Language Variation and Change, 16,* 49–73.

Foster, P., Tonkyn, A., & Wigglesworth, G. (2000). Measuring spoken language: A unit for all reasons. *Applied Linguistics, 21*(3), 354–375.

Freed, B. F. (1995). What makes us think that students who study abroad become fluent? In B. F. Freed (Ed.), *Second language acquisition in a study abroad context* (pp. 123–148). John Benjamins.

Freed, B. F., Dewey, D. P., Segalowitz, N., & Halter, R. (2004). The language contact profile. *Studies in Second Language Acquisition, 26*, 348–359.

Freeman, L. C. (1979). Centrality in social networks conceptual clarification. *Social Networks, 1*, 215–239.

Freeman, L. C. (2004). *The development of social network analysis: A study in the sociology of science.* Empirical Press.

Freeman, L. C. (2011/2016). The development of social network analysis—with an emphasis on recent events. In J. Scott & P. J. Carrington (Eds), *The Sage handbook of social network analysis* (pp. 26–39). Sage. https://doi.org/10.4135/978144 6294413

Freeman, L. C., Borgatti, S. P., & White, D. R. (1991). Centrality in valued graphs: A measure of betweenness based on network flow. *Social Networks, 13*, 141–154.

Furht, B. (Ed.). (2010). *Handbook of social network technologies and applications.* Springer.

Gal, S. (1978). Peasant men can't get wives: Language change and sex roles in a bilingual community. *Language in Society, 7*, 1–16.

Gal, S. (1979). *Language shift: Social determinants of linguistic change in bilingual Austria.* Academic.

Gallagher, H. C. (2019). Social networks and the willingness to communicate: Reciprocity and brokerage. *Journal of Language and Social Psychology, 38*(2), 194–214.

Gallagher, H. C., & Robins, G. (2015). Network statistical models for language learning contexts: Exponential random graph models and willingness to communicate. *Language Learning, 65*, 929–962.

Gardner, R. C. (1985). *Social psychology and second language learning: The role of attitudes and motivation.* Edward Arnold.

Gardner, R. C., & Lambert, W. E. (1959). Motivational variables in second-language acquisition. *Canadian Journal of Psychology/Revue canadienne de psychologie, 13*(4), 266–272. https://doi.org/10.1037/h0083787

Gardner, R. C., & MacIntyre, P. D. (1991). An instrumental motivation in language study: Who says it isn't effective? *Studies in Second Language Acquisition, 13*, 57–72.

Gass, S. M. (1997). *Input, interaction, and the second language learner.* Lawrence Erlbaum.

Gass, S. M. (2003) Input and interaction. In C. J. Doughty & M. H. Long (Eds), *The handbook of second language acquisition* (pp. 224–255). Blackwell.

Gautier, R., & Chevrot, J. P. (2015). Social networks and acquisition of sociolinguistic variation in a study abroad context: A preliminary study. In R. Mitchell, N. Tracy-Ventura, & K. McManus (Eds), *Social interaction, identity and language learning during residence abroad* (pp. 169–184). EUROSLA Monographs Series. The European Second Language Association.

Geeslin, K L., Fafulas, S., & Kanwit, M. (2013). Acquiring geographical norms of use: The case of the present perfect in Mexico and Spain. In C. Howe, M.

Lubbers, & S. Blackwell (Eds), *Selected proceedings of the 15th Hispanic Linguistics Symposium* (pp. 246–259). Cascadilla Proceedings Project.

Geeslin, K. L., & Gudmestad, A. (2008). The acquisition of variation in second-language Spanish: An agenda for integrating studies of the L2 sound system. *Journal of Applied Linguistics, 5*(2), 137–157. https://doi.org/10.1558/japl.v5i2.137

Geeslin, K. L., Gudmestad, A., Kanwit, M., Linford, B., Long, A. Y., Schmidt, L., & Solon, M. (2018). Sociolinguistic competence and the acquisition of speaking. In M. R. Alonso Alonso (Ed.), *Speaking in a second language* (pp. 1–25). John Benjamins.

Geeslin, K. L., with Long, A. Y. (2014). *Sociolinguistics and second language acquisition: Learning to use language in context.* Routledge.

George, A. (2013). *The acquisition of Castilian dialectal features during a semester abroad in Toledo, Spain* (Unpublished doctoral dissertation), University of Minnesota: Twin Cities.

George, A. (2014). Study abroad in central Spain: The development of regional phonological features. *Foreign Language Annals, 47,* 97–114.

Gorman, K., & Johnson, D. E. (2013). Quantitative analysis. In R. Bayley, R. Cameron, & C. Lucas (Eds), *The Oxford handbook of sociolinguistics* (pp. 214–240). Oxford University Press.

Gudykunst, W. B., & Nishida, T. (2001). Anxiety, uncertainty, and perceived effectiveness of communication across relationships and cultures. *International Journal of Intercultural Relations, 25,* 55–71.

Guiora, A. Z., Beit-Hallahmi, B., Brannon, R. C. L., & Dull, C. Y. (1972). The effects of experimentally induced changes in ego state on pronunciation ability in a second language: An exploratory study. *Comprehensive Psychiatry, 13*(5), 421–428.

Guiraud, P. (1954). *Les caractères statistiques du vocabulaire.* Presses universitaires de France.

Hasegawa, A. (2019). *The social lives of study abroad: Understanding second language learners' experiences through social network analysis and conversation analysis.* Routledge.

Heath, S. B. (1982). What no bedtime story means: Narrative skills at home and school *Language in Society, 11,* 49–76.

Heath, S. B. (1983). *Ways with words: Language, life and work in communities and classrooms.* Cambridge University Press.

Heller, M. (1987). The role of language in the formation of ethnic identity. In J. Phinney & M. Rotheram (Eds), *Children's ethnic socialization* (pp. 180–200). Sage.

Hérnandez, T. A. (2010). The relationship among motivation, interaction, and the development of second language oral proficiency in a study-abroad context. *Modern Language Journal, 94*(4), 600–617.

Holmes, J. (1996). Losing voice: Is final /z/ devoicing a feature of Maori English? *World Englishes, 15*(2), 193–205.

Howard, M. (2005). On the role of context in the development of learner language: In-sights from study abroad research. ITL *International Journal of Applied Linguistics, 148,* 1–20.

Howard, M. (2008). Morpho-syntactic development in the expression of modality: The subjunctive in French L2 acquisition. *Canadian Review of Applied Linguistics/Revue canadienne de linguistique appliquée, 11,* 171–191.

Højrup, T. (1983). The concept of life-mode. *Ethnological Scandinavica 1983*, 15–50.

Hualde, J. I. (2003). *The sounds of Spanish.* Cambridge University Press.

Huensch, A., & Tracy-Ventura, N. (2017). L2 utterance fluency development before, during, and after residence abroad: A multidimensional investigation. *Modern Language Journal, 101*, 275–293.

Hulsen, M., De Bot, K., & Zuyd, H. (2002). "Between two worlds"; Social networks, language shift, and language processing in three generations of Dutch migrants in New Zealand. *International Journal of the Sociology of Language, 153*, 27–52.

Hymes, D. (1972). On communicative competence. In J. Pride & J. Holmes (Eds), *Sociolinguistics* (pp. 269–285). Penguin Books.

Iino, M. (2006). Norms of interaction in a Japanese homestay setting: Toward a two way flow of linguistic and cultural resources. In M. A. DuFon & E. Churchill (Eds), *Language learners in study abroad contexts* (Vol. 15, pp. 151–176). Multilingual Matters.

Isabelli-García, C. (2006). Study abroad social networks, motivation, and attitudes: Implications for SLA. In M. Dufon & E. E. Churchill (Eds), *Language learners in study abroad contexts* (pp. 231–258). Multilingual Matters.

Isabelli- García, C. (2010). Acquisition of Spanish gender agreement in two learning contexts: Study abroad and at home. *Foreign Language Annals, 43*, 289–303.

Isabelli- García, C., Bown, J., Plews, J. L., & Dewey, D. P. (2018). Language learning and study abroad. *Language Teaching, 51*, 439–484.

Issa, B. I., Faretta-Stutenberg, M., & Bowden, H. W. (2020). Grammatical and lexical development during short-term study abroad: Exploring L2 Contact and initial proficiency. *The Modern Language Journal, 104*, 860–879.

Iwasaki, N. (2010). Style shifts among Japanese learners before and after study abroad in Japan: Becoming active social agents in Japanese. *Applied Linguistics, 31*, 45–71.

Jesus, L. M. T., & Shadle, C. H. (2002). A parametric study of the spectral characteristics of European Portuguese fricatives. *Journal of Phonetics 30*(3), 35–59.

Joan, A., & Ting, S.-H. (2017). Influence of social networks on language use of Kejaman speakers in Sarawak, Malaysia. *Oceanic Linguistics, 56*, 22–41.

Johnson, D. E. (2009). Getting off the Goldvarb standard: Introducing Rbrul for mixed-effects variable rule analysis. *Language and Linguistics Compass, 3*, 359–383.

José, B. (2010). The apparent time construct and stable variation: Final z devoicing in northwestern Indiana. *Journal of Sociolinguistics, 14*(1), 34–59.

Juan-Garau, M. (2018). Exploring oral L2 fluency development during a three-month stay abroad through a dialogic task. In C. Sanz & A. Morales-Front (Eds), *The Routledge handbook of study abroad research and practice* (pp. 193–207). Routledge.

Kanwit, M. (2022). Sociolinguistic competence: What we know so far and where we're heading. In K. Geeslin (Ed.), *The Routledge handbook of second language acquisition and sociolinguistics* (pp. 30–44). Routledge.

Kanwit, M., & Solon, M. (2023). Introduction: Historical overview, key constructs, and recent developments in the study of communicative competence. In M. Kanwit & M. Solon (Eds), *Communicative competence in a second language: Theory, method, and applications* (pp. 1–18). Routledge.

Kennedy, K. M. (2012). *What we don't learn in the classroom: The acquisition of sociolinguistic competence during study abroad* (Unpublished doctoral dissertation). University of California, Davis.

Kennedy Terry, K. M. (2017). Contact, context, collocation: The emergence of sociolinguistic competence during study abroad. *Studies in Second Language Acquisition, 39*, 553–578.

Kennedy Terry, K. M. (2022a). At the intersection of SLA and sociolinguistics: The predictive power of social networks during study abroad. *Modern Language Journal, 106*(1), 245–266.

Kennedy Terry, K. M. (2022b). Sociostylistic variation in L2 French: What schwa deletion patterns reveal about language acquisition during study abroad. In R. Bayley, D. R. Preston, & X. Li (Eds), *Variation in second and heritage languages: Crosslinguistic perspectives* (pp. 279–310). John Benjamins.

Kennedy Terry, K. M. (2023). Learning from locals: The impact of social networks with target-language speakers during study abroad. *L2 Journal, 15*(2), 92–109.

Kibler, A., Elreda, L. M., Hemmler, V., Rutt, A., Cadogan, S., & Fuentes, B. (2021). Social networks and patterns of participation in linguistically heterogeneous classrooms. In A. Carhill-Poza & N. Kurata (Eds), *Social networks in language learning and language teaching* (pp. 37–63). Bloomsbury. https://doi.org/10.5040/9781350114289.0008

King, K. A., & Mackey, A. (2016). Research methodology in second language studies: Trends, concerns, and new directions. *Modern Language Journal, S1*, 209–227.

Kinginger, C. (2008). Language learning in study abroad: Case studies of Americans in France. *Modern Language Journal, 92*, 1–124.

Kinginger, C. (2015). Language socialization in the homestay: American high school students in China. In R. Mitchell, N. Tracy-Ventura, & K. McManus (Eds), *Social interaction, identity and language learning during residence abroad* (pp. 53–74). EUROSLA Monographs Series. The European Second Language Association.

Kinginger, C. & Farrell, K. (2004). Assessing development of meta-pragmatic awareness in study abroad. *Frontiers: The Interdisciplinary Journal of Study Abroad, 10*, 19–42.

Kinginger, C., & Carnine, J. (2019). Language learning at the dinner table: Two case studies of French homestays. *Foreign Language Annals 52*(4), 850–872.

Knack, R. 1991. Ethnic boundaries in linguistic variation. In P. Eckert (Ed.), *New ways of analyzing sound change* (pp. 251–272). Academic Press.

Knight, S. M., & Schmidt-Rinehart, B. C. (2002). Enhancing the homestay: Study abroad from the host family's perspective. *Foreign Language Annals, 35*, 190–201.

Knouse, S. M. (2013). The acquisition of dialectal phonemes in a study abroad context: The case of the Castilian theta. *Foreign Language Annals, 45*, 512–542.

Köhler, R., & Galle, M. (1993). Dynamic aspects of text characteristics. *Quantitative Text Analysis, 62*, 46–53.

Krashen, S. (1985). *The input hypothesis: Issues and implications.* Longman.

Kurata, N. (2010). Opportunities for foreign language learning and use within a learner's informal social networks. *Mind, Culture, and Activity, 17*(4), 382–396.

Kurata, N. (2021). The effects of social networks on L2 experiences and motivation: A longitudinal case study of a university student of Japanese in Australia. In A. Carhill-Poza & N. Kurata (Eds), *Social networks in language learning and language teaching* (pp. 89–112). Bloomsbury.

Labov, W. (1966). *The social stratification of English in New York City.* Center for Applied Linguistics.

Labov, W. (1972a). *Language in the inner city: Studies in the Black English Vernacular.* University of Pennsylvania Press.

Labov, W. (1972b). *Sociolinguistic patterns.* University of Pennsylvania Press.

Labov, W. (1984). Field methods of the Project on Language Variation and Change. In J. Baugh & J. Sherzer (Eds.), *Language in use: Readings in sociolinguistics (pp. 28–53). Prentice-Hall.*

Labov, W. (2001). *Principles of linguistic change,* vol. 2: *Social factors.* Blackwell.

Labov, W., & Harris, W. A. (1986). De facto segregation of Black and White vernaculars. In D. Sankoff (Ed.), *Diversity and diachrony* (pp. 1–25). John Benjamins.

Lafford, B. A. (1995). Getting into, through, and out of a situation: A comparison of communicative strategies used by students studying Spanish abroad and "at home". In B. F. Freed (Ed.), *Second language acquisition in a study abroad context* (pp. 97–121). John Benjamins.

Lafford, B. A. (2004). The effect of the context of learning on the use of communication strategies by learners of Spanish as a second language. *Studies in Second Language Acquisition, 26,* 201–225.

Laks, B. (1980). *Différentiation linguistique et différentiation sociale: Quelques problèmes de linguistique française* (Unpublished doctoral dissertation). Université de Paris VIII-Vincennes, Paris.

Langman, J. (1998). "Aha" as a communication strategy: Chinese speakers of Hungarian. In V. Regan (Ed.), *Contemporary approaches to second language acquisition in social context: Crosslinguistic perspectives* (pp. 32–45). University College Dublin Press.

Langman, J., & Bayley, R. (2002). The acquisition of verbal morphology by Chinese learners of Hungarian. *Language Variation and Change, 14*(1), 55–77.

Lantolf, J. P. (2000). Second language learning as a mediated process. *Language Teaching, 33,* 79–96.

Lantolf, J. P., & Thorne, S. L. (2006). *Sociocultural theory and the genesis of second language development.* Oxford University Press.

Lanza, E., & Svendsen, B. A. (2007). Tell me who your friends are and I *might* be able to tell what language(s) you speak: Social network analysis, multilingualism & identity. *International Journal of Bilingualism, 11,* 275–300.

Lave, J., & Wenger, E. (1991). *Situated learning: Legitimate peripheral participation.* Cambridge University Press.

Lee, J., & Van Patten, B. (2003). *Making communicative language teaching happen* (2nd ed.). McGraw-Hill.

Leonard, K. R., & Shea, C. E. (2017). L2 Speaking development during study abroad: Fluency, accuracy, complexity, and underlying cognitive factors. *Modern Language Journal, 101*(1), 179–193.

LePage, R. & Tabouret-Keller, A. 1985. *Acts of identity: Creole-based approaches to language and ethnicity.* Cambridge University Press.

Lévi-Strauss, C. (1969). *The elementary structures of kinship*, rev. ed., trans. J. H. Bell, J. R. von Strumer, & R. Needham. Beacon Press.

Li, C., & Gao, X. (2017). Bridging 'what I said' and 'why I said it': The role of metapragmatic awareness in L2 request performance. *Language Awareness, 26,* 170–190.

Li, C., Li, W., & Ren, W. (2021). Tracking the trajectories of international students' pragmatic choices in studying abroad in China: A social network perspective. *Language, Culture and Curriculum, 34*(4), 398–416.

Li, W. (1994). *Three generations, two languages, one family: Language choice and language shift in a Chinese community in Britain.* Cambridge University Press.

Li, W., Milroy, L. & Pong, S. C. (1992). A two-step sociolinguistic analysis of codeswitching and language choice: The example of a bilingual Chinese community in Britain. In Li Wei (Ed.) (2000). *The bilingualism reader* (pp. 188–209). Routledge.

Li, X. (2010). Sociolinguistic variation in the speech of learners of Chinese as a second language. *Language Learning, 60,* 1–42.

Li, X. (2014). Variation of subject pronominal expression in L2 Chinese. *Studies in Second Language Acquisition, 36*(1), 39–68.

Li, X., Bayley, R., Zhang, X., & Cui, Q. (2022). An investigation of the use of the multifunctional particle *-le* by second language learners of Chinese. In R. Bayley, D. R. Preston, & X. Li (Eds), *Variation in second and heritage languages: Crosslinguistic perspectives* (pp. 15–40). John Benjamins.

Light, R., & Moody, J. (Eds) (2020). *The Oxford handbook of social network analysis.* Oxford University Press.

Lindberg, R., & Trofimovich, P. (2020). Second language learners' attitudes toward French varieties: The roles of learning experience and social networks. *The Modern Language Journal, 104*(4), 822–841.

Linford, B., Zahler, S., Whatley, M. (2018). Acquisition, study abroad and individual differences: The case of subject pronoun variation in L2 Spanish. *Study Abroad Research in Second Language Acquisition and International Education, 3*(2), 243–274.

Lippi-Green, R. L. (1989). Social network integration and language change in progress in a rural alpine village. *Language in Society, 18,* 213–234.

Litzler, M. F., Huguet-Jérez, M., & Bakleva, M. (2018). Prior experience and student satisfaction with E-Tandem language learning of Spanish and English. *International Journal of Interactive Mobile Technologies, 12*(4), 4–20.

Llanes, A. (2011). The many faces of study abroad: An update on the research on L2 gains emerged during a study abroad experience. *International Journal of Multilingualism, 8,* 189–215.

Llanes, A., & Muñoz, C. (2009). A short stay abroad: Does it make a difference? *System, 37*(3), 353–365.

Llanes, À., & Muñoz, C. (2013). Age effects in a study abroad context: Children and adults studying abroad and at home. *Language Learning, 63*(1), 63–90.

Long, M. H. (1980). *Input, interaction, and second language acquisition* (Unpublished doctoral dissertation). University of California, Los Angeles.

Long, M. H. (1983). Native-speaker/non-native speaker conversation and the negotiation of comprehensible input. *Applied Linguistics, 4,* 126–141.

Long, M. H. (1996). The role of the linguistic environment in second language acquisition. In W. C. Ritchie & T. K. Bhatia (Eds), *Handbook of second language acquisition* (pp. 413–468). Academic Press.

Lundell, F. F. & Arvidsson, K. (2021). Understanding high performance in late second language (L2) acquisition—What is the secret? A contrasting case study in L2 French. *Languages, 6*(1), 1–17. www.mdpi.com/2226-471X/6/1/32

Lybeck, K. (2002). Cultural identification and second language pronunciation of Americans in Norway. *Modern Language Journal, 86,* 174–191.

Lyster, R. (1998). Negotiation of form, recasts, and explicit correction in relation to error types and learner repair in immersion classrooms. *Language Learning, 48,* 183–218.

Lyster, R., & Ranta, L. (1997). Corrective feedback and learner uptake. *Studies in Second Language Acquisition, 19,* 37–66.

MacWhinney, B. (2000). *The CHILDES project: Tools for analyzing talk* (3rd ed.). Lawrence Erlbaum.

Magnan, S. S., & Back, M. (2007). Social inter action and linguistic gain during study abroad. *Foreign Language Annals, 40,* 43–61.

Malvern, D., & Richards, B. (2002). Investigating accommodation in language proficiency interviews using a new measure of lexical diversity. *Language Testing, 19*(1), 85–104.

Marin, A., & Wellman, B. (2011/2016). Social network analysis: An introduction. In J. Scott & P. J. Carrington (Eds), *The Sage handbook of social network analysis* (pp. 11–25). Sage.

Marriott, H. (1995). Acquisition of politeness patterns by exchange students in Japan. In B. F. Freed (Ed.), *Second language acquisition in a study abroad context* (pp. 197–224). John Benjamins.

Marshall, J. (2004). *Language change and sociolinguistics: Rethinking social networks.* Palgrave Macmillan.

Matsumoto, K., & Britain, D. (2009). The role of social networks in understanding language maintenance and shift in post-colonial multilingual communities—The case of the Republic of Palau in the western Pacific. *Essex Research Reports in Linguistics, 58,* 2.

McManus, K. (2019). Relationships between social networks and language development during study abroad. *Language, Culture and Curriculum, 32*(3), 270–284.

McManus, K., Mitchell, R., & Tracy-Ventura, N. (2014). Understanding insertion and integration in a study abroad context: The case of English-speaking sojourners in France. *Revue française de linguistique appliquée, 14*(2), 97–116.

Mendoza-Denton, N. (2002). Language and identity. In J. K. Chambers, P. Trudgill, & N. Schilling-Estes (Eds), *The handbook of language variation and change* (pp 475–499). Blackwell.

Mendoza-Denton, N. (2008). *Homegirls: Language and cultural practice among Latina youth gangs.* Blackwell.

Mercer, N., & Howe, C. (2012). Explaining the dialogic processes of teaching and learning: The value and potential of sociocultural theory. *Learning, Culture and Social Interaction, 1,* 12–21.

Meyerhoff, M., & Strycharz, A. (2013). Communities of practice. In J. K. Chambers & N. Schilling (Eds), *The handbook of language variation and change* (2nd ed.) (pp. 428–447). Wiley–Blackwell.

Milardo, R. M. (1988). Families and social networks: An overview of theory and methodology. In R. M. Milardo (Ed.), *Families and social networks* (pp. 13–47). Sage.

Milroy, L. (1980). *Language and social networks*. Blackwell.

Milroy, L. (1987). *Language and social networks* (2nd ed.). Blackwell.

Milroy, L. (2002). Social networks. In J. K. Chambers, P. Trudgill, & N. Schilling-Estes (Eds), *The handbook of language variation and change* (pp. 549–572). Blackwell.

Milroy, J., & Milroy, L. (1978). Belfast: Change and variation in an urban vernacular. In P. Trudgill (Ed.), *Sociolinguistic patterns in British English* (pp. 19–36). Arnold.

Milroy, J., & Milroy, L. (1992). Social network and social class: Toward an integrated sociolinguistic model. *Language in Society, 21,* 1–26.

Milroy, L., & Li, W. (1995). A social network approach to code-switching: The example of a bilingual community in Britain. In L. Milroy & P. Muysken (Eds), *One speaker, two languages. Cross-disciplinary perspectives on code-switching* (pp.136–157). Cambridge University Press.

Milroy, L., & Llamas, C. (2013). Social networks. In J. K. Chambers & N. Schilling (Eds), *The handbook of language variation and change* (2nd ed.) (pp. 409–427). Wiley-Blackwell.

Mitchell, J. C. (1986). Network procedures. In D. Frick, H. W. Hoefert, H. Legwie, R. Mackensen, & R. K. Silbereisen (Eds), *The quality of urban life* (pp. 73–92). de Gruyter.

Mitchell, R., McManus, K., & Tracy-Ventura, N. (2015). Placement type and language learning during residence abroad. In R. Mitchell, N. Tracy-Ventura, & K. McManus (Eds), *Social interaction, identity and language learning during residence abroad* (pp. 115–137). EUROSLA Monographs Series. The European Second Language Association.

Mitchell, R., Myles, F., & Marsden, E. (2019). *Second language learning theories* (4th ed.). Routledge.

Mitchell, R., Tracy-Ventura, N., & McManus, K. (2017). *Anglophone students abroad: Identity, social relationships, and language learning.* Routledge.

Molm, L. D., Collett, J. L., & Schaefer, D. R. (2007). Building solidarity through generalized exchange: A theory of reciprocity. *American Journal of Sociology, 113,* 205–242.

Molm, L. D., Schaefer, D. R., & Collett, J. L. (2007). The value of reciprocity. *Social Psychology Quarterly, 70,* 199–217.

Moreno, J. L. (1934). Who shall survive? A new approach to the problem of human interrelations. Nervous and Mental Disease Publishing Co.

Mougeon, F., & Rehner, K. (2015). Engagement portraits and (socio)linguistic performance: A transversal and longitudinal study of advanced L2 learners. *Studies in Second Language Acquisition, 37*(3), 425–456. https://doi.org/10.1017/S0272263114000369

Mougeon, R., Nadasdi, T., & Rehner, K. (2010). *The sociolinguistic competence of immersion students.* Multilingual Matters.

Nagy, N., Blondeau, H., & Auger, J. (2003). Second language acquisition and "real" French: An investigation of subject doubling in the French of Montreal Anglophones. *Language Variation and Change, 15*, 73–103.

Nooraie, R. Y., Sale, J. E. M., Marin, A., & Ross, L. E. (2020). Social network analysis: An example of fusion between quantitative and qualitative methods. *Journal of Mixed Methods Research, 14*(1), 110–124.

Norton Peirce, B. (1995). Social identity, investment, and language learning. *TESOL Quarterly, 29*(1), 9–31.

Ochs, E. (1988). *Culture and language development: Language acquisition and language socialization in a Samoan village*. Cambridge University Press.

Orozco, R., & Hurtado, L. M. 2021. A variationist study of subject pronoun expression in Medellin, Colombia. *Languages 6*.1, article 5.

Otheguy, R., & Zentella, A. C. (2012). *Spanish in New York: Language contact, dialectal leveling, and structural continuity*. Oxford University Press.

Otheguy, R., Zentella, A. C., & Livert, D. (2007). Language and dialect contact in Spanish in New York: Toward the formation of a speech community. *Language, 83*, 770–802.

Palfreyman, D. (2006). Social context and resources for language learning. *System, 34*(3), 352–70. https://doi.org/10.1016/j.system.2006.05.001

Palfreyman, D. M. (2021). Changing informal language learning networks in a Gulf Arab community. In A. Carhill–Poza & N. Kurata (Eds), *Social networks in language learning and language teaching* (pp. 113–137). Bloomsbury Academic.

Paradowski, M. B., Jarynowski, A. Czopek, K., & Jelinska, M. (2021a). Peer interactions and second language learning: The contributions of social network analysis in immersion/study abroad vs. stay-at-home environments. In R. Mitchell & H. Tyne (Eds), *Language and mobility: Study abroad in the contemporary European context* (pp. 100–116). Routledge.

Paradowski, M. B., Jarynowski, A., Jelinska, M., & Czopek, K. (2021b). Out-of-class peer interactions matter for second language acquisition during short-term overseas sojourns: The contributions of social network analysis. *Language Teaching, 54*, 139–143.

Paul, J. Z. & Friginal, E. (2019). The effects of symmetric and asymmetric social networks on second language communication. *Computer Assisted Language Learning, 32*(5-6), 587–618.

Pearson. (2009). *New York State testing program: English as a second language achievement test (NYSESLAT) 2008 administration. Technical Manual*. Author.

Pedersen, L. (1994). Linguistic variation and composite life modes. In B. Nordberg (Ed.), *The sociolinguistics of urbanization: The case of the Nordic countries* (pp. 87–115). de Gruyter.

Pérez Vidal, C., & Shively, R. L. (2019). L2 pragmatic development in study abroad settings. In N. Taguchi (Ed.), *The Routledge handbook of SLA and pragmatics* (pp. 355–371). Routledge.

Poplack, S., & Walker, D. C. (1986). Going through /l/ in Canadian French. In D. Sankoff (Ed.), Diversity and diachrony (pp. 173–198). Benjamins.

Pozzi, R. (2021). Learner development of a morphosyntactic feature in Argentina: The case of vos. *Languages, 6*, 1–18.

Pozzi, R. (2022). Acquiring sociolinguistic competence during study abroad: US students in Buenos Aires. In R. Bayley, D. R. Preston, & X. Li (Eds), *Variation in second and heritage languages: Crosslinguistic perspectives* (pp. 199–222). John Benjamins.

Pozzi, R., & Bayley, R. (2021). The development of a regional phonological feature during a semester abroad in Argentina. *Studies in Second Language Acquisition, 43*, 109–132.

Prell, C. (2012). *Social network analysis: History, theory, and methodology.* Sage.

Regan, V. (2010). Sociolinguistic competence, variation patterns and identity construction in L2 and multilingual speakers. *EuroSLA Yearbook, 10*, 21–37.

Regan, V., Howard, M., & Lemée, I. (2009). *The acquisition of sociolinguistic competence in a study abroad context.* Multilingual Matters.

Rehner, K. (2002). *The development of aspects of linguistic and discourse competence by advanced second language learners of French* (Unpublished doctoral dissertation). University of Toronto.

Rehner, K., Mougeon, R., & Nadasdi, T. (2003). The learning of sociolinguistic variation by advanced FSL learners: The case of *nous* versus *on* in immersion French. *Studies in Second Language Acquisition, 25*, 127–156.

Roy, J. (2011). *Sociolinguistic statistics: The intersection between statistical models, empirical data and sociolinguistic theory.* Paper presented at Methods in Dialectology XIV, London, Ontario.

Ryan, R. M., & Deci, E. L. (2000). Intrinsic and extrinsic motivations: Classic definitions and new directions. *Contemporary Educational Psychology, 25*, 54–67. http://dx.doi.org/10.1006/ceps.1999.1020.

Sankoff, D., & Cedergren, H. (1976). Les contraintes linguistiques et sociales de l'élision de /l/ chez les Montréalais [Linguistic and social constraints on /l/ elision in Montreal French]. In M. Boudreault & F. Mohren (Eds), *Actes du XIIIème congrès international de linguistique et philologie romanes* (pp. 1101–1117). Presses de l'Université Laval.

Sankoff, D., Tagliamonte, S. A., & Smith, E. (2005). *Goldvarb X: A variable rule application for Macintosh and Windows.* Department of Linguistics, University of Toronto.

Sanz, C., & Morales-Front, A. (2018). Introduction: Issues in study abroad research and practice. In C. Sanz & A. Morales-Frant (Eds), *The Routledge handbook of study abroad research and practice* (pp. 1–16). Routledge.

Sax, K. (2003). *Acquisition of stylistic variation by American learners of French* (Unpublished doctoral dissertation). Indiana University, Bloomington.

Schecter, S. R., & Bayley, R. (2002). *Language as cultural practice: Mexicanos en el norte.* Lawrence Erlbaum.

Schieffelin, B. B. (1990). *The give and take of everyday life: Language socialization of Kaluli children.* Cambridge University Press.

Schieffelin, B. B., & Ochs, E. (1986). Language socialization. *Annual Review of Anthropology, 15*, 163–191.

Schmidt, L. B. (2018). L2 development of perceptual categorization of dialectal sounds: A study in Spanish. *Studies in Second Language Acquisition, 40*, 857–882.

Schumann, J. (1978). *The pidginization hypothesis: A model for second language acquisition.* Newbury House.

Scott, J., & Carrington, P. J. (Eds). (2011/2016). *The Sage handbook of social network analysis.* Sage.

Segalowitz, N., & Freed, B. F. (2004). Context, contact and cognition in oral fluency acquisition: Learning Spanish in at home and study abroad contexts. *Studies in Second Language Acquisition, 26,* 173–199.

Segalowitz, N., & Ryder, A. (2006). Montreal Index of Linguistic Integration (MILI) (Unpublished questionnaire). Concordia University, Montreal, Quebec.

Serrano, R., Tragant, E., & Llanes, A. (2012). A longitudinal analysis of the effects of one year abroad. *Canadian Modern Language Review/Revue Canadienne des langues vivantes, 68*(2), 138–163.

Shin, N. L., & Otheguy, R. (2013). Social class and gender impacting change in a bilingual setting: Spanish subject pronoun use in New York. *Language in Society, 42,* 429–452.

Shiri, S. (2023). Interactive cultural activities in virtual study abroad during the pandemic and beyond. *L2 Journal, 15*(2), 54–70.

Silva-Corvalán, C. 1994. *Language contact and change: Spanish in Los Angeles.* Oxford University Press.

Slomanson, P., & Newman, M. (2004). Peer group identification and variation in New York Latino English laterals. *English World-Wide, 25,* 199–216.

Smemoe, W. B., Dewey, D. P., Bown, J., & Martinsen, R. A. (2014). Variables affecting L2 gains during study abroad. *Foreign Language Annals, 47*(3), 464–486.

Spolsky, B. (1989). Communicative competence, language proficiency, and beyond. *Applied Linguistics, 10,* 138–156.

SPSS. (2007). 16.0 for Windows [Computer software]. SPSS Inc.

Statology. www.statology.org/. Retrieved January 22, 2023.

Suárez–Orozco, C., Suárez–Orozco, M., & Todorova, I. (2008). Learning a new land: Educational pathways of immigrant youth. Harvard University Press.

Suárez–Orozco, C., Gaytan, F., Bang, H., Pakes, J., O'Connor, E., & Rhodes, J. (2010). Academic trajectories of newcomer immigrant youth. *Developmental Psychology, 46,* 602–618.

Swain, M. (1985). Communicative competence: Some roles of comprehensible input and comprehensible output in its development. In S. M. Gass & C. Madden (Eds), *Input in second language acquisition* (pp. 235–253). Newbury House.

Swain, M. (1995). The function of output in second language learning. In G. Cook & B. Seidlhoffer (Eds), *Principle and practice in second language acquisition studies: Studies in honour of H. G. Widdowson* (pp. 125–144). Oxford University Press.

Swain, M. (1998). The output hypothesis, second language learning and immersion education. In J. Arnau & J. M. Artigal (Eds), *Els Programes d'immersió: una perspectiva Europea/Immersion Programs: A European perspective* (pp. 127–140). Publicacions de la Universitat de Barcelona.

Swain, M. (2000). The Output Hypothesis and beyond: Mediating acquisition through collaborative dialogue. In J. P. Lantolf (Ed.), *Sociocultural theory and second language learning* (pp. 97–114). Oxford University Press.

Swain, M. (2005). The Output Hypothesis: Theory and research. In E. Hinkel (Ed.), *Handbook of research in second language acquisition and teaching* (pp. 471–484). Lawrence Erlbaum.

Swain, M., & Lapkin, S. (1995). Problems in output and the cognitive processes they generate: A step towards second language learning. *Applied Linguistics, 16*(3), 371–391.

Swain, M., & Lapkin, S. (1998). Interaction and second language learning: Two adolescent French immersion studies working together. *Modern Language Journal, 82*, 320–337.

Tarone, E., & Swain, M. (1995). A sociolinguistic perspective on second language use in immersion classrooms. *Modern Language Journal, 79*, 166–178.

Thompson, R. W. (1975). Mexican American English: Social correlates of regional pronunciation. *American Speech, 50*, 18–24.

Trentman, E. (2017). Oral fluency, sociolinguistic competence, and language contact: Arabic learners studying abroad in Egypt. *System, 69*, 54–64.

Van Mol, C., & Michielsen, J. (2015). The reconstruction of a social network abroad. An analysis of the interaction patterns of Erasmus students. *Mobilities, 10*(3), 423–444.

Vygotsky, L. (1978). *Mind in society: The development of higher psychological processes.* Harvard University Press.

Wang, P., Robins, G., & Pattison, P. (2009). *PNet: Program for the simulation and estimation of p* exponential random graph models.* Retrieved from www.melnet. org.au/pnet/

Warner-Ault, A. (2020). Promoting intercultural learning through synchronous video exchange: A TalkAbroad case study. *International Journal of Computer-Assisted Language Learning and Teaching, 10*(1), 1–14.

Warner-Ault, A. (2022). Global learning in a pandemic: Using synchronous video exchange to deepen intercultural understanding. In B. Zou, M. Thomas, D. Barr, & W. Jia (Eds), *Emerging concepts in technology-enhanced language teaching and learning* (pp. 89–110). IGI Global.

Watson-Gegeo, K. A., & Nielsen, S. (2003). Language socialization in SLA. In C. J. Doughty & M. H. Long (Eds). *The handbook of second language acquisition* (pp. 155–177). John Wiley & Sons.

Weedon, C. (1987). *Feminist practice and poststructuralist theory.* Blackwell.

Wenger, E. (1998). *Communities of practice: Learning, meaning, and identity.* Cambridge University Press.

Wetzels, W. L., & Mascaro, J. (2001). The typology of voicing and devoicing. *Language 77*(2): 207–244.

Wiklund, I. (2002). Social networks from a sociolinguistic perspective: The relationships between characteristics of the social networks of bilingual adolescents and their bilingual proficiency. *International Journal of the Sociology of Language, 153*, 53–92.

Wolfram, W., Moriello, B., & Carter, P. (2004). Emerging Hispanic English: New dialect formation in the American South. *Journal of Sociolinguistics, 8*, 339–358.

Wood, D., Bruner, J. S., & Ross, G. (1976). The role of tutoring in problem solving. *Journal of Child Psychology and Psychiatry, 17*(2), 89–100.

Wright, C. (2018). Effects of time and task on L2 Mandarin Chinese language development during study abroad. In C. Sanz & A. Morales-Front (Eds),

The Routledge handbook of study abroad research and practice (pp. 166–180). Routledge.

Young, R., & Bayley, R. (1996). VARBRUL analysis for second language acquisition research. In R. Bayley & D. R. Preston (Eds), *Second language acquisition and linguistic variation* (pp. 253–306). John Benjamins.

Zappa-Hollman, S., & Duff, P. (2015). Academic English socialization through individual networks of practice. *TESOL Quarterly, 49*, 333–368.

Zentella, A. C. (1997). *Growing up bilingual: Puerto Rican children in New York.* Blackwell.

Zentella, A. C. (2007). *Dime con quién hablas y te diré quién eres:* Linguistic (in) security and Latino/a unity. In J. Flores & R. Rosaldo (Eds), *A companion to Latina/o studies* (pp. 25–38). Blackwell.

Zhang, D. (2012). Co-ethnic network, social class, and heritage language maintenance among Chinese immigrant families. *Journal of Language, Identity and Education, 11*, 200–223.

Zhang, M. (2010). Social network analysis: History, concepts, and research. In B. Furht (Ed.), *Handbook of social network technologies and applications* (pp. 3–22). Springer.

INDEX

Note: References to figures appear in *italic* type; those in **bold** type refer to tables.

academic contacts 166–7, **167**
Academic English-Oriented social network types 143
academic English proficiency (AEP) 141–3
Academic Peers 141–2, **142**
Academic Spanish-Oriented social network types 143
acculturation model (Schumann) 40–3, 57
Aces group 11–12, *11*
acquisition period 41
active commitments to FSL learning 128–9
active contacts 109
activities 103–4, **104**
'acts of identity' framework 45
advanced network mapping tools 178–83
affective factors 42–3
African American and white speech 18–19
African American English (AAE) 4, 9–10, 14–15
African American Vernacular (AAVE) 25–6, 31
Aguerre, S. 65, 164–6
Akbari, E. 193–4
Akoto, M. 194–5
Alberto (Schumann) 39
alter-alter links 159

American Council on the Teaching of Foreign Languages (ACTFL) 57, 108–9, 133, 195
American culture 195
American students 4
Anglophone networks 168
Argentina 81–2
Arvidsson, K. 61, 77–8, **78**
at-home social networks 166
autologistic actor attribute model (ALAAM, Daraganova & Robins) 180–1, *182*
automated network tools 177

Back, M. 183–7, **185**, *185*, *186*, 192
Bastian, M. 121–2, 177, 178, 188
Bayley, R. 4–5, 33–7, 40, 55; acquisition of phonological feature of BAS 63–4, 151; influence of social networks with TL speakers 118–19; language variation 148; multivariate analysis using Varbrul programs 143–4; *sheísmo/zheísmo* 153–4, **153**; social network strength 47, 114; subject pronoun expression (SPP) studies 30, 33–5, **35**; /z/ devoicing studies 30, 35–7, **36**
Belfast studies (Milroy & Milroy) 4, 8
Benton, R. 8, 17–18
Bernstein, K. A. 50–1, 70–1, 97–9, *98*, 155–8, *157*

bilingual communities 23, 38
bilingual social networks 188, *189*
bilingual speakers 25–6
Black and white vernaculars 19
Bloomfield, L. 1, 5, 8, 9
el boque (East Harlem) 25–6, **25**, 37
Borgatti, S. P. 156, 167–8, 177, 178
Bortoni-Ricardo, S. M. 17
Bourdieu, P. 44
Bracke, A. 65, 164–6
Brazlândia, Brazil 17
Britain, D. 28–9
British-born Chinese children 24
'brokerage' 180
brother and sister speech patterns 30–1
"Buena Vista Courts" (Bayley and
    Holland) 36–7
Buenos Aires 149
Buenos Aires Spanish (BAS) 63–4, 127,
    151
burnouts social group (Detroit,
    Michigan) 20
Burt, R. S. 110
Byram, M. 195

California 30, 33
Carhill-Poza, A. 47, 69, 125–7, 141–3,
    142, 166
Caribbean Spanish speakers 34
Carnine, J. 49, 66, 67, 92–6, **93**, **94**
categories ('factor groups') 144
Chamot, M. 127
Cheshire, J. 14
Chevrot, J. P. 82, 110, 167–70, *169*,
    178
Chicanx English 33
Chinese in northern England study
    (Li Wei) 24–5
Chinese in Philadelphia study (Zhang)
    29–30
church membership 26–7
Classroom NoP (CNoP) 156–7, 158
classrooms 39–40, 193
classroom social networks 97–9, *98*
'cliques' 156
close-knit social networks 4
closeness networks (Model Study 11)
    122–5, *123*, *124*; *see also* network
    density
code-switching 36–7
cohesiveness of learner groups 42
Coleman, J. A. 121, *121*

communication density 9
communicative competence 54–5
communities of practice (CoP) 49–50,
    165
complexity measures 135, *136*
'comprehensible input' 51
computer-assisted network
    diagramming techniques 177–8
computer-generated network models
    179
computer-mediated communication
    (CMC) tools 187
concentric circles model (Coleman)
    121, *121*
congruence between groups 42
contact logs 81–3
Conversifi platform 196–9, **199**
COVID-19 pandemic 198, 200
'critical cultural awareness' (Byram)
    195
cross-racial interactions 19
Csárdi, G. 177, 178
cultural and situational influences 48
cultural distance (Schumann) 41
culture shock (Schumann) 43

Daraganova, G. 180–1, *182*
data analysis 191
data collection 75–81
D complexity measures 135, *136*
Deci, E. L. 193
dense social networks 87
dense ties 12–13, *13*
density 87, 101–6
density measures 16, 114–15
density scores 102
descriptive statistics 132–3, 138, **138**
Detroit study (Eckert) 5, 20
Detroit study (Edwards) 14–15
devoicing /z/ 35–6, **36**
Dewey, D. P. 47, 59–60, 86, 106–7,
    108, 109
dialect contact 34
dialect diffuseness 17
dialect maintenance and change study
    (Marshall) 8, 20–2
dialects 25
Diao, W. 49, 66–7, 92, 96–7, 173–5,
    174
diaries 81–3
diphthong reduction 17
'directionality' (Paradowski) 178

direct reciprocity 179
discourse and pragmatic competence
   64–5
discourse completion task (DCT)
   150–1
dispersion of networks 86
Dodsworth, R. 8, 17–18
dominant and migrant language choices
   see language choices
Doucerain, M. 170
Duff, P. 50
durability of relationships 87
Dutch migrants (Hulsen) 26
Dutch Reformed Church 26

East Harlem, New York City 25–6,
   25
Eckert, P. 5, 20, 49–50
'ecological perspectives' to L2
   development 47
Edwards, W. 8, 14–15
effect size 140
Egg, Austria 16
ego 12–14, 68, 76, 101, 110, 159,
   179, 188, 190
egocentric networks 12–13, 50, 68, 76,
   119–21
ego-permeability 43
Eleta, I. 188–90, *189*, 192–3
emergentist theories 51
E-Net (Borgatti) 179
engagement levels **128**, 129, 162, 164
English: Chinese migrants 24–5;
   devoicing of fricatives 36; dialects
   25; multilingual speakers Oslo 28;
   multiple dialects New York 25
English for Academic Purposes (EAP)
   180
English language learners (ELLs) 156
English learner (EL) proficiency
   classifications 71
English-Oriented Peers 141–2, **142**
entropy 190
Erasmus European Exchange program
   137
Erasmus SA participants 65, 68,
   164–6
ethnographic research 48
European French 170–2, **171**
exchange networks 13
external and internal modifiers 111
extralinguistic factors 146–8, 152

Facebook 184–7, **185**, *185*, 190–4,
   196
factor groups 144
'factor weight' (Rbrul program) 145–6
Ferenz, O. 73, 166–7, **167**
Filipino multilingualism 28
Filipinos in Oslo, Norway 27–8
first-and second-order network zones
   12–13, *13*, 119–20, *120*
first language (L1) speech communities
   5
first-order ties 12–13, *13*, 76
Fleming, L. 3
fluency 138–40, **138**, **139**
Francophone networks 168
Freed, B. F. 84, 184
Freeman, L. C. 2–3
French language: European and
   Quebec French 170–2, **171**; /l/
   deletion 127; *ne* deletion 127, 168;
   ne retention 168; *on* and *nous* 164;
   schwa deletion 127; *vous* and *tu* 92
French students 162–4
fricatives: /ð/ as (dh) 12; syllable and
   word final devoicing 36
'friend' requests 191
friendship multiplexity 103–4, *104*
friends (*kinship*) 103
Friginal, E. 190–2, *192*
Fujianese speakers 30

Gal, S. 23–4
Gallagher, H. C. 179–83, *182*
Gao, X. 64, 110
Gardner, R. C. 44
Gass, S. M. 52
'gatekeeper' networks 188–90, *189*
Gautier, R. 82, 110, 167–70, *169*,
   178
genetic method (Vygotsky) 66
Gephi (Bastian) 121–2, 177, 178, 188
German 24
global oral proficiency 57–60
Golbeck, J. 188–90, *189*, 192–3
Google Docs 194
grammatical accuracy 138–9, **138**
grammatical competence 60–1
graphic imagery 4
Grossdorf, Austria (Lippi-Green) 8, 16
group patterns of language use 16–17
Guiraud's Index 135, *136*, 138–9, **138**,
   139

hangout patterns (Thunderbirds, Labov) 10, *10*
Harlem study (Labov) 9–11, *10*, *11*
Harris, W. A. 15, 19
Hasegawa, A. 49, 50, 68, 121–5, *123*, *124*, 159, 178
Head Start preschool classrooms 71, 97, 155, *157*; *see also* Model Study 14 (Bernstein)
Heath, S. B. 48
hierarchical multiple regression analysis 141, **142**, 143
high density social networks 29–30
high-innovation regions 3
high performers 78–9, **78**
Holland, C. L. 35, 36–7, **36**
Howe, C. 46
Hulsen, M. 26, 28
Hungary 23–4
Huntly study (Marshall) 8, 20–2
Hymes, D. 54

identity 28, 44–5
igraph (Csárdi & Nepusz) 177, 178
immigrant and immersion student studies 69–71
indirect reciprocity 179
Individual Network of Practice (INoP) 50–1, 156
individual patterns of language use 16–17
individual variables ('factors') 144
inferential statistics 131–54; logistic regression 141–3; oral production task results **139**; statistical significance and correlations 132–41; *see also* Rbrul analysis
informal interactions 40
informal language learning networks (ILLNs) 50, 72–3, 160–1
in-link 159
Input Hypothesis (Krashen) 51–2
institutionalized language enforcement 29
instrumental motivation 43
integration and engagement 127–9
integration index (Bortoni-Ricardo) 17
'integration' networks 189, *189*, 190
integrative motivation (Gardner and Lambert) 43–4
intensity 87, 107
Interaction Hypothesis (Long) 53–4

interaction patterns 160–6
interactive ties 12–13
interconnectedness *see* density
inter-language group connections 189–90
internalization of learning 46
intra-language group connections 189–90
intrinsic motivation 43
Intrinsic Motivation Inventory (IMI) 193
'investment' (Norton Peirce) 44
Isabelli-García, C. 43–4, 58–9, 81–2, 119–20, *120*

Japanese 29
Jewish English, Michigan 36
jocks social group (Detroit, Michigan) 20
journals 81–3

Kanwit, M. 54
Kennedy, K. M. 4, 40, 63
Kennedy Terry, K. M. 55; acquisition of variable /l/ deletion 144–6; assessment of social network strength 114; /l/ deletion by linguistic factor group **145**, 146; measuring informal interactions 40; measuring social networks with TL speakers 47–8; Rbrul analysis for extralinguistic factor groups 146–7, **147**; Rbrul analysis for schwa deletion 148–9, **149**; SNSS for SA 88; social networks and L2 acquisition 63; sociolinguistic variation 132
Kibler, A. 71
King, K. A. 155
Kinginger, C. 49, 65–6, 67, 92–6, **93**, **94**
Krashen, S. 51–2
Kurata, N. 72, 83, 172–3

L1 and L2 grammar 52; *see also* second language (L2) learners
Labov, W. 5, 8–12, 18–20; Black and white vernaculars 15, 19; hangout patterns 10, *10*; observer's paradox 184; use of sociograms 1, 4, 9–10; use of variable (r) 11, *11*
Lambert, W. E. 44
Langman, J. 81

LANGSNAP project (Model Study 3, McManus; Mitchell) 59–60, 79, 84–5, 133–7
language and ethnicity 28
'language bridge' networks 188–90, *189*
language choices 24–5, 27–8, 38, 173, 188, 190
Language Contact Profile (LCP) 84, 184
Language Engagement Questionnaire (LEQ) 85–6, **85**, **86**
language learning at home 71–3
language maintenance 26
language shock (Schumann) 43
language socialization 48–51, 65–6
language variation 148
language variation and change (LVC) 3–4, 8, 40
Lantolf, J. P. 46
Lanza, E. 27–8
Lapkin, S. 52
Latina gangs (Mendoza-Denton) 30, 33, **33**
Latin America 63, 149–50
Latinos, North Carolina (Wolfram) 30–1, 37
Latinx, San Antonio (Bayley) 33–4, 35
Lave, J. 49, 158
/l/ deletion 127, 144–8, **145**, **147**
learner network composition 134, *134*
learners' networks 110
LePage, R. 19, 45
lexical complexity and social network formation 135, *136*
lexical richness 138–40, **138**, **139**
Li, C. 64–5, 110–14, 178–9
Likert scale 196
Lindberg, R. 170–2, **171**
linguistic and cultural knowledge 48–9
linguistic behavior 29
linguistic development 80–1
linguistic factor groups 144–6, **145**
linguistic performance 194
linguistic variants by profile portrait 162, **163**
Lippi-Green, R. L. 8, 15–16
Litzler, M. F. 196, **197**
live recordings 92–7
Li Wei 24–5, 26–7, 28

logistic regression 4; analysis 132; impact of social networks 141–3; and Rbrul 143–54
Longitudinal Immigrant Adaptation Study (Suárez-Orozco) 126
Long, M. H. 53–4
Lundell, F. F. 61, 77–8, **78**
Lybeck, K. 41–2, 57–8, 76–7, 77

Mackey, A. 155
Mann-Whitney U-test **161**
Maori English, New Zealand 35–6
Marin, A. 3
Marshall, J. 8, 20–2
mathematical and computational models 4
Matsumoto, K. 28–9
MATTR, complexity measures 135, *136*
McManus, K. 59–60, 79, 84–5, 133–7, *134*, *136*
men 16–17
Mendoza-Denton, N. 30, 33, 45
Mercer, N. 46
Mexican-American Spanish **35**, 36
Mexican-descent speakers 33–4
Mexican-origin speakers 34
Mexican Spanish-speaking social networks 34–5
Meyerhoff, M. 49
Michielsen, J. 68, 164
migrant and dominant language choices *see* language choices
migrants 17
Milroy, J. 1, 8, 14
Milroy, L. 1, 4, 8, 12, 14, 22
minority language maintenance 26–7
minority language social networks 26
Mitchell, J. C. 12
Mitchell, R. 51, 55, 79–80
Model Studies 42–3, 47
Model Study 1 (Lybeck) 41–2, 57–8, 76–7, 77
Model Study 2 (Isabelli-García) 43–4, 58–9, 81–2, 119–20
Model Study 3 (LANGSNAP project, McManus; Mitchell) 59–60, 79, 84–5, 133–7
Model Study 4 (Dewey) 47, 59–60, 86, 106–7
Model Study 5 (Serrano) 61, 137–41, *137*, **138**, **139**

Model Study 6 (Kennedy Terry) 47–8, 55, 63, 88, 114, 144–6
Model Study 7 (Pozzi and Bayley) 47, 55, 63–4, 114, 118–19, 144, 149–50
Model Study 8 (Li) 64–5, 110–14, *112*, *113*, 178–9
Model Study 9 (Kinginger and Carnine) 49, 66, 67, 92–6, **93**, **94**
Model Study 10 (Diao) 49, 66–7, 92, 96–7, 173–5
Model Study 11 (Hasegawa) 49, 50, 68, 122–5, *123*, *124*, 159, 178
Model Study 12 (Carhill-Poza) 47, 69, 125–7, 141–3, 166
Model Study 13 (Wiklund) 47, 70, 101–6, *102*, **104**, *104*, 109
Model Study 14 (Bernstein) 50–1, 70–1, 97–9, *98*, 155–8, *157*
Model Study 15 (Kurata) 72, 83, 172–3
Model Study 16 (Palfreyman) 50, 72–3, 90–1, 160–2, **161**, 166
Montreal Index of Linguistic Integration 86
Moreno, J. L. 1
morphosyntactic variables 17
motivation 43
Mougeon, F. 127–9, **128**, 162–4, **163**, 166
multilingual communities 27–30
multiple dialects 25
multiplexity 16, 21, 101–6, 109, 114, 133
multiplexity measures 16, *90*, 101–6, 115, 119
multiplex ties 12, 13, *13*
multivariate analyses 4, 21–2, 34, 143–4

Nagy, N. 71–2
native speakers (NSs) 110–11
naturalistic language learning 83
naturalistic speech data 63
ne (French) 127, 168
'neoVygotskian' perspectives 46
Nepusz, T. 177, 178
NetDraw (Borgatti) 167–8, 178
network density 87, 102, *102*, 168; *see also* closeness networks (Model Study 11)
network diagrams 111, *112*, *113*, 119–25, 156

network dispersion 109–14
network graphs *169*
network interaction patterns 162, 164
network mapping tools 177
network metrics: density and multiplexity 101–6; intensity, durability, and dispersion 106–9
network multiplexity 101, 103
Network of Practice (NoP) 50, 156
network patterns *182*
network strength 14, 17, 101
Network Strength Scale (NSS) 14
network ties 10, 12, 14, 38, 48, 51, 119–20, 122, 179, 181
Newman, M. 30, 31–2, **32**
New York African American English (Labov) 4
New York City Latino high school students (Slomanson and Newman) 31–2, **32**
New York European American Vernacular English (NYEAVE) 31
Nielsen, S. 48
non-academic contacts 166–7, **167**
Nonacademic English-Oriented social network types 143
Nonacademic Spanish-Oriented social network types 143
nonparametric statistical procedures 4
nonstandard phonological features 67, 96, 173
norm-enforcing social structures 4, 31
Norteñas (Latina gang, California) 33, **33**
Northern Cities Shift 20
Northern Ireland 1
Norton Peirce, B. 44
Norway 28, 76–7
NY State English as a Second Language Assessment Test (NYSESLAT) 126

Oberwart, Austria (Gal) 23–4
observer's paradox (Labov) 184
Ochs, E. 48
on and *nous* (French) 164
1390 Lames group 11–12, *11*
online social networks: classroom language learning 193; language use 188–93; and in-person learning 193–5; 'symmetry'/'asymmetry' 190–1; tracking L2 development 183–7; virtual exchanges 195–9

oral fluency 140
Oral Proficiency Interviews (OPI, ACTFL) 57, 108–9, 133, 195–6
out-links 159, 160
Output Hypothesis (Swain) 160
overt pronouns 34–5

Palau 29
Palfreyman, D. M. 50, 72–3, 90–1, 160–2, **161**, 166
Paradowski, M. B. 158–60, **160**, 178
participant interviews 75–81, 83
participant observations 97–9
Participation in Networks of Practice (P-NoP) 50, 155–6
passive ties 13
Paul, J. Z. 190–2, *192*
Pearson Correlation Coefficient 135
peasant status and language choice 24
peer cultural assignment **32**
peer social networks 126, 141
'peripheral language groups' 189, *189*
personal social networks *13*
Philadelphia speech communities 19
Philippines 27
phonological context 144–6, **145**
Phonological Environment-location **153**
phonological variables 17, 63–4, 116–18, 127, 151, 153–4
pidginization and pidgin languages 41
pleonastic /s/ in 2 sg. preterit 34
Portuguese Facebook postings 184–7, **185**, *185*, *186*
post-colonial communities 29
postvocalic /r/ 11
potential network effect scores 105, 109–10
Pozzi, R. 4, 40, 55; acquisition of phonological feature of BAS 63–4, 151; influence of social networks with TL speakers 118–19; Rbrul analysis of individual variables 144; Rbrul analysis *vos* and *Tú* verb forms 149–50, **150**; *sheísmo/zheísmo* 151–4, **153**; social network strength 47, 114; Spanish / s/ weakening 132; *vos* usage and SNSS score 151, **152**
'practice-based identity' (Mendoza-Denton) 45
pragmatic subjectivity (Li & Gao) 64, 110

pre-adolescent heterosexual marketplace 31
predicting speakers' language use 23–4
'preferred playmates' 156–7
Prell, C. 3
"principle of multiple causes" (Young & Bayley) 4–5
psychological distance (Schumann) 41, 43
Puerto Rican English (PRE) 25
Puerto Ricans 33–5; bilingual children 25–6; San Antonio, Texas 33–4, **35**
Puerto Rican Spanish 25, 35

qualitative data 164–5
qualitative interview data 77–8
qualitative network assessments 125–9
quantitative network metrics 100
quantitative network scales 114–19
quantitative social network analysis 100–6
Quebec French 170–2, **171**

Raleigh, North Carolina 17–18, 30
Rbrul analysis 143–54; comparing *vos* and *tú* verb forms 150–1, **150**; extralinguistic factor groups 146–9, **149**; factor weights 145–6; /l/ deletion **145**, 146–8, **147**; *sheísmo/zheísmo* (BAS) usage 153, **153**; significance testing 146; *step-up/step-down analysis* 146
Reading, England 14
reciprocity 179
regional variation 62
Rehner, K. 127–9, **128**, 162–4, **163**, 166
retroflex/dental merger **174**
Robins, G. 180–1, **182**
Ryan, R. M. 193

San Antonio Latinx study (Bayley) 33–4, 35
SASIQ responses **108**
/s/ aspiration and deletion 34
Schecter, S. R. 34
Schieffelin, B. B. 48
Schumann, J. 39, 40–4, 57
schwa deletion 127, 132, 148–9, **149**
second language acquisition (SLA) 1, 55, 132

second language (L2) learners 56;
immersion contexts 39; informal
interactions 40; L2 input and
output 51–3; L2 Japanese 83; L2
social identity 44–5; SNA research
framework 3–4; studies of language
variation 144; target-language social
networks 40–5
second-order ties 12–13, *13*, 76
Serrano, R. 61, 137–41, *137*, **138**, **139**
shared accommodation 165–6
sheísmo/zheísmo (BAS) 63–4, 127,
151–4, **153**
significance levels 132, 146
Siler City, North Carolina 30
Silicon Valley 3
Simulated OPI (SOPI) 57, 119–20
Skype 150, 196
Slomanson, P. 30, 31–2, **32**
Smemoe, W. B. 108–9
snowball sampling 90–1
social distance (Schumann) 41, 42
social dominance patterns 42
social interactions and shared processes,
Sociocultural theory (SCT) 46
social network analysis (SNA) 1–5;
bilingual communities 23; language
maintenance 23; limitations 18–22;
linking linguistic processing with
social context 55; regional linguistic
features 63; and SLA theories 40; TL
environment 56–7
social network data 109, 133–4
social network diagrams 12–13, *13*
social network framework 12–18
social networking 183; *see also* online
social networks
social network interaction data 137,
137
social network orientation 105
social network questionnaire (Marshall)
21
social networks: composition 166–72;
formation during study abroad 135;
important role 53–4; individual
aspirations 35–6; interaction
patterns 160–6; and language
choice 27; language maintenance
23–7; quantitative measurements
47; social environments 166–7,
167; sociolinguistic variation 30–7;
statistical analyses 140–1; studies 19

Social Networks Questionnaire (SNQ)
84–6, **85**, 133–4
social network strength indices 40
Social Network Strength Scale for SA
(SNSS for SA) 88–90, *89–90*,
114–19, **116**, **117–18**, 144
social network strength scale (SNSS)
63, 118–19, 146–52; Rbrul analysis
for /l/ deletion **147**, 148; Rbrul
analysis for schwa deletion 148–9,
149; Rbrul analysis of *vos* and *tú* verb
forms **150**; *vos* usage **152**
social orientation 36
social psychological perspectives 55
sociocentric network analysis 155–60
sociocentric network diagrams 121–5,
160
sociocentric networks 68
sociocultural theory (SCT) 46–8
socio-demographic categories 45
sociolinguistic interviews 20–2, 162,
166
sociolinguistics 1
sociolinguistic variation 1, 62–4, 72,
92, 132, 173
software programs 177
Solon, M. 54
Southern vernacular features 31
Southern Vowel Shift 17–18
Spanish dialects 25
Spanish-speaking communities 34
Spanish /s/ weakening 132
Spearman's rank order correlations 135
Standard Mandarin speakers 30
Stan (Model Study 2) 119–20, *120*
statistical modeling 179
Statistical Package for the Social
Sciences (SPSS) 139
statistical significance and correlations
132–41
step-up/step-down analyses 146
'structural holes' (Burt) 110
Strycharz, A. 49
Study Abroad Network Questionnaire
(SANQ) 110
study abroad (SA) students 4, 56–69,
149–54; American students 4;
Facebook 184–7; immersion contexts
39, 60–1; interaction patterns 164–5;
interviews **147**, **149**, 159–60;
language proficiency 131–2; learner
networks 135–6; oral production

140; Poland 158; social networks 43, 167–8; sociocentric network mapping 178–9; studies employing SNA 56–7; Type 2 variation 62; *see also* Model Study 10 (Diao); Model Study 11 (Hasegawa); Model Study 2 (Isabelli-García); Model Study 3 (LANGSNAP project, McManus; Mitchell); Model Study 4 (Dewey); Model Study 5 (Serrano); Model Study 6 (Kennedy Terry); Model Study 7 (Pozzi and Bayley); Model Study 9 (Kinginger and Carnine); Study Abroad Social Interaction Questionnaire (SASIQ) 86–7, **87**, 106
stylistic variation (Type 2 variation) 62
Suárez–Orozco, C. 126
subject-doubling 72
subject pronoun expression (SPP) 33–5, **35**
Sureñas (Latina gang, California) 33, **33**
Surveys and Questionnaires 84–92
Svendsen, B. A. 27–8
Swain, M. 52, 160
synchronous language classes 193–4
synchronous online courses 196
syntactic complexity 138–9, **138**, **139**

Tabouret-Keller, A. 19, 45
TalkAbroad 195–9, **197**, **199**
target culture acculturation 40–2
target language (TL) 39–40; data collection 75–6; environment 56–7, 170; interactions 82–3; motivation and investment 42–4; speakers 46–7, 62; virtual exchanges 195–9
"Technology, Culture and Social Change" course 196–8
Test of English as a Foreign Language (TOEFL) 193–4
then-now questionnaires 106
Th-pro variable (/I/ raising to /i/) 33
"three Ps" (products, practices, perspectives) 195
Thunderbirds youth group (Harlem) 10–12, *10*, *11*
ties (relationships) 12–13, *13*
traditional dialect features 17
'transnational Mandarin' 66–7, 173

Trentman, E. 120–1
Trofimovich, P. 170–2, **171**
"True Jesus Church" (Newcastle) 25, 27
tú 'you' *see vos* and *tú* (Latin America)
Twitter (X) 188–92, *189*
Type 2 variation (stylistic variation) 62

UCINET software (Borgatti) 156, 168, 177, 178
'union' networks 189, *189*, 190
uniplex relationships 12
urbanization index (Bortoni-Ricardo) 17
usted and *tú* (Spanish) 92

Vacation Day Camp (VDC) boys 11–12, *11*
Van Mol, C. 68, 164
Varbrul programs 143–4
variable final /z/ devoicing 35
variable liaison realization 168
variable (r) 11, *11*
variable /s/ aspiration and deletion 35
variants 4; formal 168; informal 12; lexical 30; linguistic 8; local 164; phonological 67; nonstandard 14; sociolinguistic 164; vernacular 15
variation: language 3; linguistic 49; patterns of 15; phonological 63; regional 62; sociolinguistic 1; stylistic 50; target-like 62; Type 2 62
variationist sociolinguistic studies 5
vernacular culture index (VCI) 14, 15
vernacular forms 39–40
virtual conversation exchanges 195
virtual networks 183–93, 195
vos and *tú* (Latin America) 63, 127, 149–50
vos usage and SNSS score 151, **152**
vous and *tu* (French) 92
vowel-ll-vowel constructions 152–3
vowel pronunciation 20
Vygotsky, L. 46, 66

Warner-Ault, A. 195–9, **197**, **199**
Watson-Gegeo, K. A. 48
weak ties 12–13, *13*
Weedon, C. 44
'weighted degree centrality' (Paradowski) 178

'weighted network centrality'
(Paradowski) 159
Wellman, B. 3
Wenger, E. 49, 158
White, Harrison 2–3
Wiklund, I. 47, 70, 101–6, *102*, **104**,
104, 109
Wilcoxon Signed Rank Tests (SPSS) 139
Wolfram, W. 30–1, 37
women 16–17, 24
word-initial placements 152
Word type 152, **153**
working-class neighborhoods 4

X (*Twitter*) 188–92, *189*

Young, R. 4–5, 148
Yun (Model Study 10) 173

Zappa-Hollman, S. 50
/z/ devoicing studies 30, 35–7,
36
Zentella, A. C. 25–6, **25**, 37
Zhang, D. 29–30
Zhang, M. 2
Zone of Proximal Development (ZPD)
46–8, 66